Doubled Plots

Doubled Plots

ROMANCE AND HISTORY

Edited by
Susan Strehle and
Mary Paniccia Carden

University Press of Mississippi / *Jackson*

www.upress.state.ms.us

The University Press of Mississippi is a member of the Association of American University Presses.

Copyright © 2003 by University Press of Mississippi
All rights reserved
Manufactured in the United States of America

Print-on-Demand Edition

Library of Congress Cataloging-in-Publication Data
Doubled plots : romance and history / edited by Susan Strehle and Mary Paniccia Carden.
    p. cm.
Includes bibliographical references and index.
978-1-60473-251-1 (cloth : alk. paper)
    1. Historical fiction, American–History and Criticism. 2. American fiction–Women authors–History and criticism. 3. English fiction–Women authors–History and criticism. 4. Historical fiction, English–History and criticism. 5. Love stories, American–History and criticism. 6. Love stories, English–History and criticism. 7. Literature and history–United States. 8. Literature and history–Great Britain. 9. Women and literature–United States. 10. Women and literature–Great Britain. 11. Plots (Drama, novel, etc.) I. Strehle, Susan. II. Carden, Mary Paniccia.
   PS374.H5 D68 2003
   813′.08109–dc21   20002156193

British Library Cataloging-in-Publication Data available

For our mothers,
all three teachers, readers, and models
of what wise women can make of
romanced history and historicized romance:

MARIE KELLY BELL (1923–2001)
SHIRLEY ECKERT STREHLE
SALLY DWYER PANICCIA

Contents

Acknowledgments ix

Introduction
Reading Romance, Reading History xi
Susan Strehle and Mary Paniccia Carden

Making Love, Making History
(Anti) Romance in Alice McDermott's *At Weddings and Wakes* and *Charming Billy* 3
Mary Paniccia Carden

History and the End of Romance
Danticat's *The Farming of Bones* 24
Susan Strehle

Stopping Traffic
Spectacles of Romance and Race in *The Last of the Mohicans* 45
Janet Dean

What "Race" Is the Sheik?
Rereading a Desert Romance 67
Susan L. Blake

Behind the Mask of Coquetry
The Trickster Narrative in *Miss Numè of Japan:
A Japanese-American Romance* 86
Huining Ouyang

Romancing the Borderlands
Josephina Niggli's *Mexican Village* 107
Rita Keresztesi

What's a Nice Girl like You Doing in a Book like This?
Homoerotic Reading and Popular Romance 127
Stephanie Burley

Desire and the Marketplace
A Reading of Kathleen Woodiwiss's
The Flame and the Flower 147
Charles H. Hinnant

A Story of Her Weaving
The Self-Authoring Heroines of Georgette Heyer's
Regency Romance 165
Karin E. Westman

The Race, Gender, Romance Connection
A Black Feminist Reading of African American
Women's Historical Romances 185
Rita B. Dandridge

Notes 203
Works Cited 213
About the Contributors 224
Index 227

Acknowledgments

We would like to thank the contributors to this volume, who impressed us with their professionalism at every step in the process. In this volume they share academic work we found excellent from the start. Each of them willingly condensed and revised for increasing unity in the collection, responding with thoughtfulness and speed to our requests. They made our editorial work a pleasure.

Catherine Dent, a graduate student at Binghamton University, compiled the works cited list with admirable patience and attention to detail. Ke Zheng, an undergraduate student at Binghamton, provided valuable computer assistance at all of the crisis points.

We are especially grateful to Suzette Henke, who as reader of our manuscript found much to admire in the book and who improved it with judicious suggestions. She provided detailed, rigorous, and thoughtful readings of each essay, supporting our collective revisions with keen insight and wisdom. Colleagues at both of our universities provided assistance and conversation that appear reflected in our work. We are grateful to David Bartine, Donette Francis, Michael Hames Garcia, Leslie Heywood, Richard McLain, William Spanos, Ruth Stanek, Albert Tricomi, Elizabeth Tucker, and Lisa Yun of Binghamton University and to Glenda Zumwalt, Lisa Coleman, and Randy Prus of Southeastern Oklahoma State University.

We thank Seetha Srinivasan of the University Press of Mississippi for her faith in the value of the project, as well for clear guidance and communication at each stage. We are also grateful to Walter Biggins and

Anne Stascavage of the editorial staff at the University Press of Mississippi for careful work on and attentive interest in the manuscript; working with this press has been very pleasant.

Our families, partners, and children have provided the support, encouragement, and inspiration that make romance possible, history matter. Andrew Milnor, good friend and partner, and Adam Spanos, best of sons, made contributions whose traces appear between the lines of this project. Kevin Carden's love, interest, and enthusiasm have been unflagging, while Patrick and Julia Carden have been an endless source of joy. These and other family members, including our mothers, have been reminders that love exceeds theoretical boundaries of all sorts.

Introduction

READING ROMANCE, READING HISTORY

—Susan Strehle and Mary Paniccia Carden

Signifying economies revolve around desire, and love, widely assumed to be a universal human experience, is both a language we all understand and a currency of indeterminate value. As the norm that directs communal comprehension, circumscription, and evaluation of human possibilities, the heterosexual romance plot frames a multitude of cultural, political, economic, and historical discourses. Few people's experience exactly fits the normative model of romance. But in the register of ideology, commonly held notions of civilization, humanity, and identity remain grounded in the structures of heterosexual union. In *Writing beyond the Ending*, Rachel Blau DuPlessis observes that "romance plots of various kinds, the iconography of love, the postures of yearning, pleasing, choosing, slipping, falling, and failing are, evidently, some of the deep, shared structures of our culture"(2). She argues that "these scripts of heterosexual romance, romantic thralldom, and a telos in marriage are also social forms expressed at once in individual desires and in a collective code of action including law: in sequences of action psychically imprinted and in behaviors socially upheld"(2). In other words, love not only makes the world go round, but the western world also makes certain forms and outcomes of love go round.

While the romance plot has seemed simple, common, even formulaic to some readers and critics, we argue for a more complex understanding of its relation to the cultures that shape it and therefore of its meaning. Each narrative of love expresses a compound and contradictory impulse: on the one hand, the narrative ventriloquizes cultural values, perpetuating and naturalizing patriarchal models of gender that project women's destined and desirable end in the family; on the other hand, the narrative talks back, revealing women's frustration, dissent, and potentially subversive responses to those patriarchal constructions. Love stories are cultural primers, instructing their primarily female readership how to behave, what to fantasize and wish for, and how to interpret the shapes their lives assume. In this sense, romance narratives reproduce and reaffirm the ideas about gender circulating in the culture where they are written and read. But in narrating a particular version of relationship between individualized protagonists, each love story also exceeds the bounds of the patriarchal given and reflects women's frustration with the limits inside which they struggle to create fulfilling roles and lives. Culture presses in on romance, dictating the forms love may take and its expression in language; romance exerts its own counterpressure, exceeding cultural prescriptions and erupting in unpredictable discursive moments. Romance has a "limit-breaking" quality, as Dana Heller observes: "romance has long been theorized by feminists and non-feminists alike as a limit-breaking genre, a genre of excess" (221).

The complex contradictions and duplicities of romance account for much of its interest and its hold on the reading public, we believe. Literary narratives of love may be specially attuned to the heteroglossia of cultural and countercultural voices inherent in romance, but these voices speak at cross-purposes in popular romance as well. The essays in this volume analyze romances of both kinds, finding dissenting perspectives flaring out in the midst of obedience and deeply held assent to cultural norms taking over and restricting impulses to more radical experiment. The widespread interest in romance, both popular and academic, and the rich and growing body of scholarship exploring its voices and values have made possible this new set of approaches, which collectively move the state of criticism of romance onward in diverse directions.

xiii ~ *Introduction*

HISTORICIZING ROMANCE

One of the oldest and most abiding literary forms, "romance" has served various overlapping and competing purposes in western texts. Romance in its earliest and most dignified sense was associated with a masculine heroic quest, defined by Northrop Frye in *Anatomy of Criticism*: "The essential element of plot in romance is adventure, which means that romance is naturally a sequential and processional form.... The complete form of the romance is clearly the successful quest....The central form of romance is dialectical: everything is focussed on a conflict between the hero and his enemy, and all the reader's values are bound up with the hero" (187). Romance-quests combined with the quest for a symbolic love occur in Greek pastorals such as *Daphnis and Chloe*, which follow the trials and ultimate triumph of young lovers, and in chivalric texts of the Middle Ages such as *Troilus and Criseyde*, *Tristan und Isolde*, and the Arthurian cycle, courtly tales which focus on a noble knight's quest to please an often distant lady (Abrams 35, 190–92). While courtly love framed these chivalric plots, it did not provide the subject, as Ian Watt observes: "In the romances ... while courtly love provided the conventional beginning and end, the main interest of the narrative lay in the adventures which the knight achieved for his lady, and not in the development of the love relationship itself" (136).

Because of its origins in mythic quests, romance is defined even today in standard literary reference books in ways that emphasize its unrealistic, fantastic, or supernatural qualities. The following excerpt from *A Handbook to Literature* places two kindred definitions of romance in a historical context:

In 1785 Clara Reeve in *The Progress of Romance* declared, "The Novel is a picture of real life and manners, and of the times in which it was written. The Romance in lofty and elevated language, describes what has never happened nor is likely to." This distinction has resulted in two distinct uses of *romance*. In common usage, it refers to works with extravagant characters, remote and exotic places, highly exciting and heroic events, passionate love, or mysterious or supernatural experiences. In another and more sophisticated sense, *romance* refers to works relatively free of the more restrictive aspects of realistic verisimilitude. (Holman and Harmon 413)

M. H. Abrams's popular *A Glossary of Literary Terms* makes similar observations: "the romance is said to present life as we would have it be—more picturesque, fantastic, adventurous, or heroic than actuality" (260). When Richard Chase argues that romance is uniquely prevalent in American fiction, he means that American novelists reject the limits of verisimilitude: "The greatest American fiction has tended toward the romance more often than the greatest European fiction" (14). He cites the famous descriptions of romance written by William Gilmore Simms—the romance "does not confine itself to what is known, or even what is probable. It grasps at the possible"—and by Nathaniel Hawthorne—the romance "has fairly a right to present that truth [of the human heart] under circumstances, to a great extent, of the writer's own choosing or creation" (Chase 17, 18). Romance of the mysterious, masculine quest-adventure type remains popular to this day, appearing in the Prince Valiant comic strip, the Star Trek television series and movies, and the Harry Potter books. But none of these forms, or any other man's adventure, are thought of now as "romance."

A second type of romance, the love story, has coexisted with the first from the beginning. Once the tale of "men entranced, enthralled, held in thrall by the eyes and mouths and hair of unobtainable mistresses," the romance as love story has gradually been feminized, rendered the affair of women: "men are now busy elsewhere, and they have left the field of love to women," writes Jan Cohn (5). While studies of medieval and Renaissance literature often continue to use the term romance for quest narratives, romance has taken on a different primary meaning for the reading culture at large. Romance now refers to the narrative of falling in love, with all of the obstacles, hesitations, failures, and delays that heighten tension and make the eventual consummation of the love relationship (whether physical or emotional) triumphant, or its absence cataclysmic. It is romance in this sense that the present volume explores.

While love is a perennial literary theme, narratives of the lover's quest took on special vitality only with the rise of the novel, in part because of the emphasis on individuated and plausible characters and realistic events that was typical of the novel genre and in part because of the increasing readership among middle-class women (Watt 32–34, 42–44). Yet, ironically, some early novelists and many critics and historians of the novel—including Watt himself—define the novel in opposition to the romance: novels were a boldly "new kind of writing," that constituted "a break with the old fashioned romances" (9–10). By the eighteenth century adventure-romance was already old, backward-looking, passé—in sum, conventional, while the novel aimed to be boldly new. At the same time, romance came to be associated with women, while the brave new world of novels belonged to men. So Richardson's Mr. B. imputes to Pamela an over-indulgence in fancies born of an over-indulgence in reading romance: "I never knew so much romantic invention as she is mistress of. In short, the girl's head's turned by romances, and such idle stuff, to which she's given herself up" (92). By 1739, writing what some consider the first novel, Richardson has already formed the dismissive connection between "girls," "romances," "idle stuff," and forms of behavior in which men—sensible, worldly men—believed they had no part. The impulse to distinguish novel (as realistic history) from romance (as sentimental fantasy) and then to attach the romance derisively to women—and women derisively to romance—has led critics to denigrate the genre of romance and to lose its intimate connection to the novel.

In the developing history of fiction, we would argue, romance and novel are effectively intertwined, reshaping each other in a continuing productive interchange. Indeed, most fiction includes romance elements, and many canonical novels *are* romances. Romance narratives—fiction focused on the ways identity expresses itself in the choice of a love partner, sometimes including the attempt to live with that choice in marriage—emerge in every century, written by men and women; they include *Pamela, Emma, Jane Eyre, Anna Karenina, Wuthering Heights, Great Expectations, Tess of the Durbervilles, The Golden Bowl, The Awakening, The Sun Also Rises, The Kiss of the Spider Woman,* and *The Remains of the Day.* The popularity of romance narratives derives from readers' fascination with the definition of self in the choice of a particular other to love, as well as the complex ways in which human love relations express and play out forms of desire, identity, and difference. These complexities often bubble just below the surface of a form that must negotiate the immense and multifaceted register of human desire within the limits of a few fairly rigid structures for its expression. Judging by the varieties of experience they foreground, romance narratives appeal to readers of every age, gender, race, class, and sexual preference.

A widespread popular interest in romance has led to the development of a romance mass-market industry over the past forty years. Specific lines of popular romance fiction have generated broad readership and good profits in the latter half of the twentieth century for publishing houses like Avon (which issued Woodiwiss's *The Flame and the Flower* in 1972), Harlequin (which claimed a readership of over 16 million women in North America by 1980), and more recently Dell, Fawcett, and Warner.[1] According to Eileen Fallon, about "one fourth of all books sold in the United States are romances" (xix).[2] Cathie Linz reports that "a staggering 35 to 40 percent of all mass market paperback sales" are romances, which appear in twenty languages in over one hundred international markets (11). Although some critics have been inclined to see popular romances as different altogether from literary romances, and like Richardson's Mr. B. to regard the popular variety as inferior, possibly damaging, and certainly frivolous, cultural studies has made visible the lines of connection between the two forms; more dramatically, it has made their joint affiliations to the culture that produces them both impossible to ignore.

ROMANCE IN CRITICAL CONTEXTS

The sophisticated academic reader, particularly the feminist critic interested in romance of either literary or popular variety, is most inclined to regard it as an oppressive tool of patriarchy and to object to its reliance on and perpetuation of damaging stereotypes. Readers may find the men in romance hyper-masculine, uncommunicative, and brutish, the women submissive and dull, intent only on winning and wedding a man. As Stevi Jackson explains, first wave feminists including de Beauvoir and second wave feminists including Firestone and Greer were

> unambiguously critical of romantic love. It was the bait in the marriage trap; it served to justify our subordination to men and rendered us complicit in that subordination; it involved an unequal emotional exchange in which women

gave more than they received; its exclusivity was taken as indicative of the emotional impoverishment of our lives; it diverted women's energies from more worthwhile pursuits. . . . romantic fiction . . . was represented simply as "dope for dupes." (50)

A kindred discussion of romance and/as oppression appears in Gilbert and Gubar's *The Madwoman in the Attic*. Exploring ways in which women artists negotiate a male-dominated literary tradition replete with debilitating and dangerous images of women, they characterize romance as "escapist literature" that creates "absurd misconceptions" (115). Castigating the "worn-out, hackneyed stories of romance" (158) and the "romantic coercions" that imprison and enslave women (605–06), they warn against "the glass coffin of romance" (68) in which illusions and lives might end. Gilbert and Gubar do not find any liberating potential, any hidden subversive impulses, in this genre which they understand as both product and unconscious reproducer of misogynist views of women, a genre which is the domain of women and yet out of women's control.

Jayne Ann Krentz, a successful author of popular romance fiction, gives clear voice to the opposite perspective. She argues that romance novels are about

female empowerment. Readers understand that the books celebrate female power. . . . the woman always wins. With courage, intelligence, and gentleness she brings the most dangerous creature on earth, the human male, to his knees. . . . Romance novels invert the power structure of a patriarchal society because they show women exerting enormous power over men. The books also defy the masculine conventions of other forms of literature because they portray women as heroes. . . . The subversive nature of the books is fundamental and inescapable. (5)

The perception of a counterpressure from patriarchal codes and values is missing here. The very notion that the heroine brings the human male to his knees to make a marriage proposal, and that the height of power she can expect is in accepting a posture of permanent subordination to this "dangerous creature," does not resonate with alarm or concern for the roles open to women heroes. Romance's subversion appears, quite simply, to work, as the power of patriarchal structures and values recedes into invisibility.[3]

We argue that romance reflects both the patriarchal oppression of women and women's strength in resisting, in forging appropriate forms of heroism. Depending on the writer, the text, and the reader, any given romance can take a position somewhere between critique of patriarchal oppression and affirmation of patriarchal codes and values—or, more interestingly, a position adopting elements of both simultaneously. The reader's desires and history also inflect the romance, and a narrative that strikes one critic as honoring women's empowerment may impress another as endorsing women's complicity with systemic limitations on their freedom. Telling women's stories, romances inevitably do both. The structural tension between a subservient approval of patriarchal codes and a subversive movement toward rebellion against cultural norms in favor of expanded options for women lends romance part of its interest and seductive power: it leans in both directions, expresses both potentials, and offers insights on both sides at the same time. As Stevi Jackson writes, "It is possible to recognise that love is a site of women's complicity in patriarchal relations while still noting that it can also be a site of resistance" (50).

Most critics of romance respond to its contradictory and conflicting nature, though they may emphasize one side over the other. The landmark study by Rachel Blau DuPlessis, *Writing beyond the Ending* (1985), emphasizes the extent to which, in nineteenth-century fiction, the success of the romance plot entailed the abandonment of the woman's quest-narrative. In other words, classic romance stifles women's spirit and self-development, and the marriage plot extinguishes the heroine's evolution as an individual in favor of her quiet integration into an acceptable social role: "at the resolution of the work, the energies of the *Bildung* were incompatible with the closure in successful courtship or marriage. Quest for women was thus finite; we learn that any plot of self-realization was at the service of the marriage plot and was subordinate to, or covered within, the magnetic power of that ending" (DuPlessis 6). DuPlessis defines the central project of twentieth-century women writers as "writing beyond" this ending, imagining alternate forms of integration and satisfaction, inventing "strategies that express critical dissent from dominant narrative" (5). She relies on a progressive model of history, in which the culture of the twentieth-century, including feminism, makes possible a different narrative of permissible roles for women. Her model conceals the extent to which some nineteenth-century romances include critique, dissent, and rebellion against culturally sanctioned endings and the extent to which some twentieth-century romances uphold and reaffirm them. Nonetheless, DuPlessis powerfully articulates the conflicts and ambiguities encoded in the romance plot.

Janice Radway's *Reading the Romance: Women, Patriarchy, and Popular Literature* (1984) is among the definitive studies of the popular romance genre. Radway studies a community of readers in a town she names "Smithton" and draws conclusions about the contradictory nature of successful romances and the covert rebellion attracting women to romance reading. Building on important earlier work by Snitow and Modleski, Radway's approach helped to introduce serious scholarship into the cultural forms, social contexts, and material conditions organizing women's domestic and reading lives.[4] Radway finds that "the romance originates in the female push toward individuation and actualization of the self," but "that drive is embodied within the language and forms created and prescribed by patriarchy"; therefore the romance leads to "a particular kind of female self, the self-in-relation demanded by patriarchal parenting arrangements" (147). In Radway's assessment, the romance speaks for patriarchy, instructing women readers "about . . . its meaning for them as women, that is, as individuals who do not possess power in a society dominated by men" (149). But while the romance legitimizes heterosexuality and marriage, it emerges from "the failure of patriarchal culture to satisfy its female members" and from the "relational poverty" readers experience in their lives (Radway 151). In Radway's understanding of the double-sided dynamic of love plots, the "ideal romance" reflects problems with/in patriarchy *as well as* women's longing for security and protection inside it, women's discontent and dissatisfaction with the limited possible outcomes of romance *together with* their concurrent desire for the fantasy partner who will nurture and value them.[5]

Other important critics have examined the double functions of romance in maintaining and interrogating social structures. Tania

Modleski's *Loving with a Vengeance* (1982) contends that "contemporary mass-produced narratives for women contain elements of protest and resistance underneath highly 'orthodox' plots" (25). In *Tradition/Counter Tradition: Love and the Form of Fiction* (1987), Joseph Allen Boone argues that romance speaks both for and against traditional constructions of gender and social values. He finds that "idealized love" has served a "public function as part of the ideological apparatus ensuring social stability" (7). However, literary love plots also convey "a simultaneous counter narrative: the persistent 'undoing' of the dominant tradition by the contradictions concealed within the specific forms that its representations of 'life' and 'love' have assumed" (Boone 2). Similarly, Jan Cohn's *Romance and the Erotics of Property: Mass-Market Fiction for Women* (1988) argues that popular romance is quietly subversive: "it answers desires that cannot be spoken, so powerfully would they subvert authority . . . what is desired is authority itself, the power and autonomy the social system denies women" (5). Cohn locates the subversive elements of romance at the subterranean level, while the surface reaffirms social structures: "Authority is challenged only at the deepest levels of romance; on the surface romance embraces and confirms conventional values [and] piously reaffirms the status of the patriarchal family" (5).[6] In Cohn's view, as in Modleski's and Boone's, conflicting impulses to critique and to affirm patriarchal traditions pull in opposite directions in the romance narrative.[7]

Two more recent books have special relevance to our project, the first for exploring connections between romance and history, the second for theorizing links between romance and postmodernism. Laurie Langbauer develops some implications of the exclusion of both women and romance from history in *Women and Romance: The Consolations of Gender in the English Novel* (1990). Langbauer considers "women and romance in terms of their utility within an imaginary dynamic, one that serves seemingly established positions—the male order and its literary tradition—enthroned within the system of power" (4–5). In the chapter "The Romance of History," she emphasizes history "*as* a category, a representation, a form" to which our relation "remains complicated and uncertain" (13). She argues that Ian Watt and Fredric Jameson both imagine a history "removed from gender" and thus "cover over and shore up strategies of dominance" (14, 13). Like the other critical approaches we have found most provocative, Langbauer's recognizes the discursive status of romance in ways that open up both its affiliation to patriarchal codes and its exposure of the power structures underlining and undermining those codes.

Diane Elam's *Romancing the Postmodern* (1992) argues that postmodernism and romance share a common concern with excess, located in the figure of woman. Romance, she says, "exists as a contradictory term from the start" and "remains an uncertainty: each text must in some way redefine what it means by 'romance'" (5, 7). Also uncertain, postmodernism "is a *way of thinking* about history and representation that claims there can be no final understanding"; postmodernism questions conventional historical narratives and abandons master narratives of history and politics (10–11). Romance and postmodernism are further linked "in forcing us to rethink the political" (19), for both have been read as progressive *and* reactionary:

> What is striking about these divergent positions [interpreting the politics of romance and postmodernism] is their ability to argue convincingly that the romance genre and postmodernism are used for political purposes—be it progressive or conservative, or a little of both at the same time. [They] are not seen as ideologically neutral. In fact, what seems to characterize them are their inevitably *political* contents and their necessary ideological reversibility. (21)

Elam understands a "necessary ideological reversibility" in romance's openness to carrying contradictory political freight, and sees in postmodernism the same "inexhaustible and disruptive" potential to occupy opposed spaces at the same time (24). Elam's startling connections not only turn romance from a frivolous backwater to a main current of postmodernism, but even more significantly they turn both romance and postmodernism from modes of Prufrockian indecision to sites of vital political struggle over how cultural meanings are constructed and valued. The contradictions and reversals that create gripping, unique, and unpredictable stories of love demand careful reading, for at stake even beyond the "happily ever after" ending are the ways power and value constitute and distribute themselves in the social world.

Despite the popularity of romance plots and their importance to our social and political environment, it remains true, as Jennie Wang argues, that love "has been only a marginal subject in the study of the English and the American novel.... Book-length publications on the subject of love are mostly studies in medieval and Renaissance literature, Victorian domestic novels, or popular romance. Relatively few have been written across literary periods from a contemporary postmodern perspective" (xv). One of the goals of this volume is to add to the study of romance in fiction from a postmodern perspective, which we see as crucially involving the decision to place romance, with all its shifting and multivalenced dynamics, erotics, and politics, in history, thus "historicizing romance." Romance narratives change their meaning in the context of feminism, poststructuralism, cultural studies, postcolonial theory, queer theory, and the development of increasingly sophisticated reading positions.[8] Romance narratives include film, popular fiction, literature both traditional and non-, narratives of ethnic groups whether canonical or not, and other formerly separated (and unprivileged) categories of fiction as well. History has changed romance; putting romance in the context of history makes visible new dimensions—contradictions, indeterminacies, and political ambivalences—of the perennial love theme and narrative genre.

ROMANCING HISTORY

At the same time, history itself has changed with its entry into the discursive arena that constitutes postmodernism. To "historicize" no longer means to hold up against an objective yardstick or to measure against the absolute ground of what "really" happened. The complex chain of linguistic and philosophical arguments (made by Saussure, Althusser, Barthes, Lacan, Foucault, and others) crystallized in Derrida's famous pronouncement, "there is nothing outside the text" (158), reshapes the practice of history: surrendering the illusion of an unmediated access to external fact, history has confronted the constructed, subjective, and linguistic nature of all textual accounts—narratives—of historical "truth." As early as the 1960s, Hayden White argued for the textual nature of history, which he defines in *Metahistory* as "a verbal structure in the form of a narrative prose discourse"; histories "contain a deep structural content which is generally poetic, and specifically linguistic, in nature" (ix). Following White's analysis of the figural origins of historical knowledge, Dominick LaCapra advances a vision of history as rhetoric, which can mean "seeing the phenomenon differently or transforming our understanding of it through reinterpretation" (18).

History lost its privileged status as a closed and final narrative outside the play of time or historicity, a narrative that could be constructed with authority and delivered with certainty. In their introduction to *Poststructuralism and the Question of History* (1987), Geoff Bennington and Robert Young argue that poststructuralism opened up historicity, while structuralism and Marxism had required closure (9). A refusal of "transcendental notion[s] of History as ultimate closure on relativising and perspectival analysis" leads toward the sense articulated by Lyotard, Derrida, and others of the historical as discursive (Bennington and Young 9). Bennington and Young conclude that poststructuralist approaches seek the historicity of history, its "difficult opening," and a "resistance to totalisation and synthesis is perhaps the major difficulty" posed by such approaches "to both traditional and dialectical accounts of history" (9).

History has become unstructured, linguistic, open, discursive, and in the process, ideological. Conjoining Althusser, Lacan, and Spinoza, Frederic Jameson proposes this formulation: "history is *not* a text, not a narrative, master or otherwise, but ... as an absent cause, it is inaccessible to us except in textual form, and ... our approach to it and to the Real itself necessarily passes through its prior textualization, its narrativization in the political unconscious" (35). We understand history only through its status as already-narrated account, and we approach reality through a set of (mis) representations which express the ideology implicit in their creation as text. History is not objective reality; "history and its writing," suggests Paul Hamilton, "appear to have become the same thing" (21). Seen in all its limits as the construction of a narrative hypothesis, or reinterpretation, historicism emphasizes the creativity available to the historian, whose work may expose and critique ideology as well as express it: "the historical character of interpretation allows us as critics continually to refocus a present that is always changing.... Historicism is the name given to this apparent relativizing of the past by getting to know the different interpretations to which it is open" (18, 19).

From the perspective of postmodernism, history has been "romanced"—turned from the public and civic realm of authoritative truth to the private realm of a text interpreted in the light of the reader's desire. History happens in the subjective, the preconscious, the textual, the linguistic—in the same arena as the romance. History, like romance, can be accessed only through the reading of signs, and signs are interpreted only through the lens of a previous narrative; no uninflected reading can exist. The narrative form that most pervasively structures our domestic lives is also at work on the available interpretations of history: the narrative of individual quest, progressive causal development, and intelligible social identifications through love, marriage, and the family. Indeed, Leslie Rabine argues in *Reading the Romantic Heroine: Text, History, Ideology* (1985) that "the traditional romantic quest narrative, which puts at its center the development of a single, individual hero, and which rests on strongly end-oriented, rationally ordered, monolinear chains of cause and effect, provides the conceptual form in which history is thought to happen" (3). When Gilbert and Gubar write that, at the end of Charlotte Brontë's *Shirley*, "history replaces mere romance in a world of stony facts" (398), they invoke a version of history as causal, progressive, and factual, while romance has implicitly opposite characteristics. Gilbert and Gubar overlook the extent to which one romance, involving freedom and authority for women, is replaced with another, involving marriage and mercantile triumph.

The consequences of the transformation of history and historiography for an understanding of texts that take as their subject various forms of history and romance include a strong emphasis on the process of interpretation, the importance of language and the plurality of signs, and the self-reflexive centrality of ideology and desire in narrative. Both history and romance organize human experience, but are subject to slippages, dissonances, and multiple interpretations. Both romance and history include fused contradictions, ideological reversibility, nostalgic longing for patriarchal authority, and an uneasy recognition of the ongoing shift toward forms of decentered pluralism. Where both romance and history could once be imagined straining to achieve "happily-ever-after" closure, critical readings are now skeptical of pat endings, open to ironic undercurrents, and attentive to the historicity of narratives. Such a critical climate tends to produce reading and writing against the grain.

The purpose of *Doubled Plots: Romance and History* is to read the relation of romance and history in this climate. The essays collected here do not simply compare romance and history or point out that romantic narratives are grounded in specific historical moments. Instead, they explore the ways in which all discourses of romance—the seemingly subjective, sentimental, and private—and history—the seemingly objective compendium of public fact—are implicated in and vitally necessary to each other. History and romance trope each other, exchanging expectations and purposes, sharing languages, creating the metaphors that hold cultures, institutions, families, and individuals together—or drive them apart. *Doubled Plots: Romance and History* represents the necessary next step in theorizing the functions, constructions, and interpenetrations of romantic and historical plotting. This collection of critical essays thinks about romance and history in multiple ways, finding new connections between their seemingly divergent narratives and exploring new implications in their internal contradictions. Reading the essays collected here, it becomes impossible to dismiss romance as a specifically female diversion or to endorse it as a vehicle for women's self-empowerment. Going beyond old assumptions that romance is either liberatory or oppressive, progressive or reactionary, these essays place romance in complex dynamics with history—the social, political, and economic web of various cultures and communities. Romance becomes critical in all the multiple senses of the word: a central or foundational notion, an analytical and even combative stance, a crisis point.

In developing this volume, we asked about possible intersections between romantic and historical desires. What happens, we wondered, when the discourse of romance is applied to history, and vice versa? Our collection includes essays that analyze the romance plot's construction and reconstruction with/in different political systems, racial structures, economic situations, gender and sexual orientations, and national ideologies. The essays examine romance and nationalism, relate historical romance to colonialism, and figure romance and/as genocide. They develop their arguments through readings of one or more narratives: novels, films, advertisements, stories, histories. Many of the essays include detailed and specific interpretations of texts as well as analysis of the cultures that produce them. Some of the essays reread literary classics; others read works that are popular bestsellers. Still other essays read narratives that are less well known or very contemporary. They reexamine discourses of race, explore dynamics of class and gender, and problematize the heterosexual family romance. In the process, they find new layers to romance as a critical metaphor.

READING ROMANCE, READING HISTORY

In organizing the essays in this volume, we have not followed the chronology of the writers or texts discussed in each essay. This collection does not pretend to comprehensive coverage of historical periods, and while it ranges widely, its inclusions and approaches do not aim at sequential completeness. Once history has been romanced, chronology goes out the window with linear causality; many of the fictional texts interpreted in this volume project backwards in time, explore relative overlappings of past and present, and meditate on history's fluidity. Similar boundary crossings make it inappropriate to organize the essays along divisions between "literary" romance and "popular" romance: even if the romances did not so vigorously resist such a division, the critical interpretations proceed too closely, situate themselves in the same theoretical grounds, and generate similar readings of cultural tensions appearing in romances of both kinds.

Our organization follows the resonances among topics, approaches, and readings that emerge in the essays. We begin with our own essays, which follow most closely from and extend thinking in this introduction about romance and history. Both essays develop implications for a critical reading practice out of the cross-pollination that comes from the historicizing of romance and romancing of history. The essays take allied approaches to contemporary women writers, both narrating love stories that are doomed and lost, with the haunting after-lives of the survivors. In both narratives, the lost love reflects the loss of certainty in the cataclysms of modern history. Enduring these definitive losses turns the protagonists to story, art, and poetry: to the creation of enduring romance.

Mary Paniccia Carden's essay, "Making Love, Making History: (Anti)Romance in Alice McDermott's *At Weddings and Wakes* and *Charming Billy*," argues that history and romance coincide in narrative scripts positioning heterosexual love and marriage as privileged metaphors for the processes of immigration that produce Irish American history. In McDermott's fiction, she finds, Irish American immigrants place the heterosexual romance plot at the center of their individual and communal identity, and because the narratives are metaphorically akin, the desire for romance becomes synonymous with the desire for historical destiny. Paniccia Carden exposes both the stakes in romance and the failures of and in romance to provide either the transcendence or the stability sought by characters and narrators who continue to yearn. This doubleness, she suggests, forms the epistemological ground of a culture's history.

In "History and the End of Romance: Danticat's *The Farming of Bones*," Susan Strehle interprets the 1998 novel by Haitian American writer Edwidge Danticat. Both love story and painful history of genocide, the novel sets romance against the background of the racially focused massacre of some 35,000 Haitians by Dominicans in 1937. The text juxtaposes sections of history, told in the preterit, with sections of romance, written in the present and printed in bold. Neither a romantic history nor a historical romance, the novel calls the ideological assumptions of both genres into question. By conjoining the love story with the historical account of genocide, the novel situates women's victimization in both realms as an outcome of their roles as passive observers. At the same time, romance turns the narrator to poetry, while Danticat's novel opens up possibilities for difference: the narrator bears witness in order to preserve the name of her beloved, and romance empowers her voice and artistry.

Romance reflects ideologies of nation, race, and gender, as the first two essays show; the possible, permissible desire allows individuals access to history. In the next group of essays, the excessiveness of romance emerges in the figure of miscegenation—the temptation to exceed cultural limitations and love the racial Other or hybrid—which complicates the ways in which history has been thought to unfold. Janet Dean reads *The Last of the Mohicans* as a reinscription of racism; as the hybrid offspring of mixed races, Cora cannot be tolerated and must be cloaked, silenced, and buried. Above all, she must not circulate in the American economy of love and marriage geared to reproduce a history of white male hegemony. Susan Blake finds a far more open reception of hybridity in *The Sheik*, whose orientalized exotic Arab is both the dark son of Spanish moors and an English lord. The racial mixture and the British heroine's romantic desire are both permissible, Blake argues, because of the class of the Sheik's relatives and because Hull's narrative manages to have it both ways. Exoticized like the Sheik as an oriental other, the Japanese man in Watanna's novel wins the love and desire of an American woman, but Huining Ouyang demonstrates that her attraction is disqualified throughout the narrative as mere coquetry. Desire must be diverted back inside socially acceptable boundaries and so, like Cooper's Cora, the impermissible Orito dies. Watanna's novel, in Ouyang's view, disrupts romance conventions even as it restores a historically validated patriarchal and racial order at the end.

Janet Dean's essay, "Stopping Traffic: Spectacles of Romance and Race in *The Last of the Mohicans*," rereads Cooper's foundational text in the light of what Gayle Rubin calls "the traffic in women"—the exchange of women between men as the basis for male control of property and power. Adding racial markers to the exchange on the frontier, Cooper's novel finds its limits in the fear of miscegenation, as the uncontrolled and mixed race Cora becomes a vector of romantic desires that can only lead to her death. On the frontier, Dean believes, the power of the female body rouses anxieties related to male control of race and gender. Cooper resolves the conflicts over women on the frontier with a funeral in which Cora's body is elaborately dressed for burial. After positing biracial harmony and interracial desire in an unstratified natural space on the frontier, Cooper concludes by restoring the dominant ideals of a progressive national history.

Susan Blake's essay, "What 'Race' Is the Sheik? Rereading a Desert Romance," interprets E. M. Hull's 1919 novel which became a publishing phenomenon and then a classic film, made in 1921 with Rudolph Valentino. While critics have long read *The Sheik* as a narrative about sex and gender, Blake finds the story of an Englishwoman falling in love with an Arab who turns out to be an Englishman also a story of racial anxieties. Situating Hull's novel in the context of the racial discourse of its era, Blake argues that the Sheik is both English, born of an abusive English father, and Arab, born to a Spanish noblewoman with Moorish blood. How other characters read his race depends on their view of culture: his aristocratic English lover sees him as an Arab, defined as a romantic aristocrat; his European manservant insists that the Sheik is English and therefore one of Us. The Sheik's dual identity, Blake concludes, allows the text to cross racial boundaries and to criticize English marriage from within the marriage plot.

In "Behind the Mask of Coquetry: The Trickster Narrative in *Miss Numè of Japan: A Japanese-American Romance*," Huining Ouyang analyzes the first romance novel in the Asian American literary tradition, published by Onoto Watanna in 1899. A woman writer of English and Chinese descent, Watanna complicates, interrupts, and accommodates the master plot to gain voice in the literary marketplace. Through a tricksterlike portrayal of the transgressive romance between a white American woman and a Japanese man, Ouyang argues, Watanna subverts white masculine dominance and disrupts modes of orientalist representation that eventually shut down the possibilities she raises. Set against the subgenre of exotic romance, Watanna's novel undermines the power structure implicit in the white man's domination of the willing, self-sacrificing Asian child-woman. Although Watanna eventually restores white patriarchal order, her sympathetic portrayal of cross-racial love stories disrupts, even though she does not entirely escape, the romance conventions that structure Western culture.

Transgressive border crossings problematize the intersecting conventions of romantic and historical narratives in the next two essays as well. In Josephina Niggli's novel, set in the borderlands between Mexico and Texas, the central character is both illegitimate and hybrid, blending a native heritage with Tex-Mex parentage. Crossings of narrative conventions place this novel as a feminine recasting of the masculine political novel about the Mexican revolution, focusing on private romance narratives, plural characters, and complex family relations rather than the single linear narrative of heroic exploits and battles. Rita Keresztesi creates the term "borderlands romance" for the kind of romance that (mis)translates between realms, forging a critique of conventional stabilities on either side of the border. Stephanie Burley uncovers the repressed homoerotic (and autoerotic) agenda of popular romance fiction, using Eve Sedgwick's theory of homosocial desire to "queer" the genre of romance. In a transgressive crossing of the boundaries of historically constructed heteronormative sexuality, Burley exposes the homoerotic desire evoked in—and deliberately marketed to—women readers who are pleased by the pens of other women and offered fantasies (and tools) to increase their reading pleasure; she also explores the elaborate strategies invoked to conceal this subterranean desire under appearances of heterosexual coupling.

Rita Keresztesi's essay, "Romancing the Borderlands: Josephina Niggli's *Mexican Village*," interprets an experimental novel published in 1945 by the Mexican-born daughter of Scandinavian American parents. Keresztesi argues that Niggli rewrites the historical and political story of the Mexican Revolution as romance, displacing the focus on the nation at large and subverting the patriarchal politics that accompany traditional accounts of the Revolution. Niggli's strategies expose both the United States' neocolonial imperialism in Mexico and the macho violence of the Revolution as these intersect in multiple love stories. While critics have read *Mexican Village* as a romantic precursor of Chicano literature, Keresztesi explores the fissures in its romantic vision, finding the novel an ironic borderlands romance that presents its subject as a colonized, industrialized, and culturally hybrid contact zone.

Stephanie Burley's essay, "What's a Nice Girl like You Doing in a Book like This? Homoerotic Reading and Popular Romance Fiction," exposes the discursive investment of popular romances in homoerotic imagery and the incomplete recuperation of these images into a heterosexual economy of representation. Queer theory, especially Eve Sedgwick's framework of homosocial desire, provides the ground for Burley's reading of popular magazines, romance novels, and academic discourse. Just below the surface of heteronormalizing narratives of romance reading, Burley finds, lie provocative counternarratives of adult female desire, same-sex identification and erotic affiliation, and fungible sexual identities. Burley replaces the apparatus of object relations theory used by Radway, Modleski, Thurston, and others to explain the psychosexual interactions of romance texts with a version of readers as adult sexual agents participating in an erotic discourse that threatens to exceed its heteronormative boundaries.

The authors of the last three essays envision a potential for constructive transformation of and by romance, as border crossings enable characters to break out of confining gender roles. The complex personality gained by appropriating traits of the other gender appears uniquely successful in the terms of both romance and history. In all three essays, characters who become trans-gendered, who learn the currency and language of the other gender, find happiness with those they love and good fortune on the stage of history. The characters in these historical romances remain emphatically heterosexual, but cease to be one-dimensionally male or female. In a reading of the economic ideology embedded in romance, Charles Hinnant interprets Kathleen Woodiwiss's bestselling novel as showing that the autonomous "alpha" man leaves behind the self-sufficiency and rugged individualism associated with masculine economic ideals and adopts more feminized traits of sociability, empathy, and interdependence. Karin Westman reads the Regency romances of Georgette Heyer as celebrations of women who appropriate the currencies in which men trade: money, sex, and wit. The heroines who cross these gender borders succeed in authoring their own stories. Rita Dandridge introduces three historical romances by contemporary black women, set amid nineteenth-century oppressions of race and gender. In the face of double challenges, the black women protagonists maintain independent professional aspirations, work for the uplift of their race, and insist on their own rights and values in romance. Dandridge's view of these characters' empowerment provides a strong, positive note on which to conclude.

In "Desire and the Marketplace: A Reading of Kathleen Woodiwiss's *The Flame and the Flower*," Charles Hinnant returns to the classic romance bestseller to explore the historical imperatives of economic ideology expressing itself in this and other successful romances. The conventional argument holds that desire is embodied in the autonomous male subject in the American economy, but Hinnant finds that in romance, the figure of the woman acts to generate, supplement, and vastly heighten desire. Woodiwiss's novel embraces a reinvigorated liberal market ideology, Hinnant argues, in the sense that freedom of choice and personal liberty extends to women as well as to men, while men give up the rugged self-sufficiency common to modern economic and gender stereotypes and become interdependent. The successful romance also represents the mutual benefits of progressive market exchange, which in turn reflects the complex interchanges among authors, editors, and readers of romance.

Karin Westman's essay, "'A Story of Her Weaving': The Self-Authoring Heroines of Georgette Heyer's Regency Romance," explores the fiction of popular British romance novelist Heyer, who published fifty-seven novels during a fifty-year writing career. Heyer's best known historical romances, set during the Regency period (1811–20), are carefully researched and layered with historical detail. Westman argues that Heyer's Regency heroines can achieve successful revisions to the expected script for women's lives, and in a sense "author" their own history, by learning the rules of patriarchal society; they must especially learn how to deal in three currencies of that society—money, sex, and witty speech. Reading several Heyer novels, Westman concludes that the Regency heroines gain autonomy and satisfaction through their worldly knowledge and verbal gifts; in contrast, the heroines of Heyer's four novels set in modern times lack control over their lives because they lack knowledge and wit.

In "The Race, Gender, Romance Interconnection: A Black Feminist Reading of African American Women's Historical Romances," Rita xxxiii ~ *Introduction*

Dandridge reads three African American romances of the 1990s, all set in the nineteenth century to highlight interactions of the dynamics of love with/in cultures of racism and sexism. For the three black heroines of *Indigo, Clara's Promise,* and *Sunshine and Shadows,* the challenges of romantic involvement include cultural oppression of both women and African Americans; all three need to establish self-sufficiency, Dandridge argues, in order to achieve romantic fulfillment. The heroines work at the racial uplift and communal betterment of their people, in part through self-definition and independence. At the same time, all three heroines find fulfillment in passionate love and marriage. Reading these romances from a black feminist perspective, Dandridge finds that they reflect both black women's activism and all that challenges it, both black women's sensuality and the forces in culture that would exploit and denigrate it.

We believe that critical thought about the intersection between romance and history will find important impetus in the rich variety and depth of insight in these essays. They affirm that when history is romanced and romance is historicized we can no longer view either as solid, self-evident discourses to which we have easy access. These essays further demonstrate that when history is romanced and romance is historicized many things change—cultures, nations, views of the norm, views of ourselves. As we edited them, we came to see untapped possibilities in love: as an organizing principle for teaching about cultural constructions of identity, for example, or for imagining new directions for and implications of gender studies. Because these essays cross boundaries between popular culture and literary studies, between British and American texts, and between the fantastic realm of romance and the grave realities of history, they invite readers to invent their own intersections and crossings, pushing further in the directions we have here begun to map.

Doubled Plots

Making Love, Making History

(ANTI) ROMANCE IN ALICE MCDERMOTT'S *AT WEDDINGS AND WAKES* AND *CHARMING BILLY*

—Mary Paniccia Carden

"Romance plots of various kinds, the iconography of love, the postures of yearning, pleasing, choosing, slipping, falling, and failing," Rachel Blau DuPlessis has observed, comprise "some of the deep, shared structures of our culture" (2). For better or for worse, the happily-ever-after expectations of the traditional heterosexual romance plot have done more than any other cultural ritual to solidify models for intelligible identities, construct interpersonal relations as signifiers of public priorities, and channel multiple and discontinuous currents of desire into predictable expressions, outcomes, and narrative frames.[1] From virtually all cultural directions—from music, movies, and fiction to the more personal accounts of friends and relatives—we are encouraged to seek and follow the path of redeeming love. Love stories establish our identities as men and women and secure our places in familial, communal, and national histories. But romance, we all know, does not always work and happily-ever-after endings remain notoriously elusive. As a "social script"

(DuPlessis 2), romance is both a triumph and a limitation, socially mandated and a function of individual chemistry, dearly cherished ideal and fodder for stand-up comics and television sit-coms. A shared goal that few reach, happily-ever-after offers a compelling yet conflicted ground for writers and readers seeking narrative and ontological truth.

Preoccupied as we are by romantic plotting, it should not be surprising to find the conventions of heterosexual romance permeating seemingly unrelated discourses. Even the driest historical text—rooted firmly in a tradition presented as factual and rigorous, in direct opposition to the sentimentality and fantasy ascribed to romance—shares some of the functions and assumptions of the most melodramatic of love stories. Like romance, history "appears to offer a means to an origin that provides both answer and explanation" (Roof xxviii). Romance and history both purport to teach us where we come from and how we might envision our ideal futures.

Historical narratives work to impose pattern and hierarchy over the vast and unpredictable field of human events, and the heterosexual romance plot does the same for individual lives. Leslie Rabine notes that "the traditional romantic quest narrative, which puts at its center the development of a single, individual hero, and which rests on strongly end-oriented, rationally ordered, monolinear chains of cause and effect, provides the conceptual form in which history is thought to happen" (3). Rabine is discussing the male-oriented quest plot, but we might make similar observations about the courtship/marriage plot: with its predictable movement from uncertainty and incompleteness to stability and reward, love plots follow the "monolinear chains of cause and effect" which parallel the "conceptual form" of an intelligible historical narrative. History gives order and meaning to events which may appear chaotic and threatening; romance gives significance and truth to lives which end in death. Joseph Allen Boone suggests that "English and American fiction has relied on a conceptualization of romantic love *in* marriage not only as an achievable goal, but as a practical and an imaginative necessity for the fully experienced life" (6). Stories that account for the past and stories that resolve the vagaries of human relationships structure the world, teaching

5 ~ (Anti) Romance in Alice McDermott

us to live successfully. Romantic and historical plotting proceed through a common set of narrative assumptions, a discursive complex framing knowledge, experience, subjectivity—in short, an epistemology.

I will address Alice McDermott's treatment of this epistemology in *At Weddings and Wakes* (1992) and *Charming Billy* (1998), novels which simultaneously invest themselves in and view with skepticism the romance plot's function in the formation of histories and identities. McDermott posits heterosexual romance as the primary but overdetermined metaphor for Irish immigration to America and for the subsequent rewards and burdens of family- and community-building—and ultimately for their attendant historical narratives. *At Weddings and Wakes* and *Charming Billy* conjoin heterosexual desire and historical desire, a uniquely personal romance and a unified, destiny-bound communal future; in McDermott's novels, immigrant histories find their expressive model in romantic couples. But as they trace the centrality of romantic scripts in individual and communal self-definition, these novels also track the anti-romantic failures and inadequacies of this mode of identification. *At Weddings and Wakes* and *Charming Billy* are composed of competing discourses of romance and anti-romance, and these conflicting narrative priorities expose individual and cultural stakes in romance as the privileged measure of personal and communal success, as pivot of and metaphor for history.

McDermott explores ideologies of love and of immigration as activities which direct their energy at the future, exploring the integrations and adaptations aimed toward happily-ever-after endings in an America built on and defined by happily-ever-after promises. Combined discourses of romance and immigration comprise one of the nation's central narratives, in which the conquest of the new world—expressed in metaphors of heterosexual desire and reward—is accomplished by immigrants striving for self-determination and security. There are, however, obvious seams in this narrative; ideologies of immigration and of national identity are often incompatible. Becoming American, Werner Sollors points out, "is often imagined as volitional consent, as love and marriage," while an immigrant's ethnicity appears "as seemingly immutable ancestry and descent"

(151): "Descent relations are those defined by anthropologists as relations of 'substance' (by blood or nature); consent relations describe those of 'law' or 'marriage.' Descent language emphasizes our positions as heirs, our hereditary qualities, liabilities, and entitlements; consent language stresses our abilities as mature free agents and 'architects of our fates' to choose our spouses, our destinies, and our political systems" (6). But notions of consent and descent and their applications are not absolute. "The realm of descent," for example, "is in itself subject to consent, to cultural choice and interpretation" (165), while the consent-based complex of "love-and-marriage" is frequently represented as a natural force (167) in line with the fate associated with descent.

In Sollors's analysis and in McDermott's novels, the alignment of romance with agency in the formation of American identity raises the question of the extent to which we can affect love-and-marriage and the extent to which it stands beyond the reach of choosing, where it, rather than individual will, works as "architect of our fates" and histories. Love-and-marriage serves as a primary metaphor for human being and doing, encapsulating assumptions about shared needs and desires. These assumptions—about sources of satisfaction, functions of the family, and measures of individual value—are couched in the language of both "nature" and "choice." At stake in the (very common) practice of positing heterosexual union as a template for other relations (immigration/romance, American identity/love-and-marriage) is an epistemology—a method, structure, and limit for thought and knowledge—that molds not only selfhood (whether in resistance, acquiescence, or enthusiastic agreement), but also the histories of communities and nations.[2] McDermott traces its ordering function in narratives of the Irish in America, exploring its constitutive yet contradictory presence in intertwined discourses of history and identity.

In the ten years during and after the potato blight in Ireland (1845–1855), a million and a half destitute Irish Catholics flooded American ports. The Famine Irish represented the first large-scale migration of a "white ethnic" people to the United States and were received with suspicion and alarm.[3] This population of Irish immigrants defined themselves as exiles.

7 ~ (Anti) Romance in Alice McDermott

Forced from their homeland, they made the treacherous crossing to the United States only to find virulent bigotry, grinding poverty, and signs reading "No Irish Need Apply."[4] These circumstances precluded rapid assimilation of the bourgeois lifestyle and gender-role performance that have come to represent the American dream as well as the outcome of romance.

McDermott situates her novels in New York City, where "the thick clustering of the Irish in massive numbers made it possible for [them] to create institutions to ease the difficulties of migration" (Diner 101). By the early twentieth century, the Irish were gaining ground on the American dream and easing the way for newcomers streaming into their communities. Following in the wake of the Famine Irish came waves of men and women who had been "raised ... for export" (McCaffrey 66). During "the Great Hunger," entire families often made the crossing together, but after the Famine individual men and women arrived in the U.S. via a process of "chain migration" fueled by "a ceaseless stream of cash ... and prepaid passage tickets sent by the Irish in America" (Miller and Wagner 69–70). At the turn of the century, these new Irish encountered poverty and prejudice, but also entered supportive communities, had access to established social and civic organizations, and were embraced by a welcoming Church. The discourse of exile seems to lose much of its urgency after the turn of the century, as Irish immigration patterns began to coalesce with the American master narrative of progress, a story of integration and reward following uncertainty and displacement.

Alice McDermott's Irish families trace their origins as Americans to this transitional period and, rather than diasporic bitterness and bewilderment, they emphasize faith, continuity, and investment in the American dream. They mythologize their immigrant pasts and imagine their American futures through the tropes of heterosexual romance; for them, romance functions as the privileged metaphor for meaningful history. However, they also view the happily-ever-after paradigm as an illusory and ironic model for conceptualizing history, negotiating culture, and formulating individuality. *At Weddings and Wakes* and *Charming Billy* unseat heterosexual romance as the privileged anchor of identity and history while allowing it to remain stubbornly in place, its epistemological force deferred but still powerfully present.

At Weddings and Wakes considers the ironies of romance in the lives of the Irish American Towne family. It focuses on women for whom love leads not to success but to loss, whose experience confirms all that romance denies—disappointment, futility, suffering. In At Weddings and Wakes, the events of a year long past (circa 1960) are narrated through the eyes of three children—two girls and a boy, now adults. The children's mother, Lucy Dailey, routinely takes them to Brooklyn to visit her sisters and aunt/stepmother, where they listen to her "lament" the "snagged and unsuitable happiness" (15) of her marriage. "She was feeling unhappy, she was feeling her life passing by. She hated seeing her children grow up. She feared the future and its inevitable share of sorrow" (18). Lucy is " 'not having the kind of life [she] wanted' " (24).

Lucy's voice joins a chorus of dissatisfaction voiced by her sisters, who speak from a sense of deprivation created by the early deaths of their parents, separate events which continue to define and shape their lives. Momma Towne greets their arguments, despairs, and cries for love with reminders of their father's losses and loss—" 'If your own father doesn't deserve a mention I don't know what I can ask.... Forgotten, I suppose' " (104). When the sisters respond with "tears" and "hushed pleas for peace and reconciliation," Momma proffers only "a taste of the silence of the grave" (104). From Momma, Lucy learns that "given the muddle of life, loss following as it did every gain, and death and disappointment so inevitable, anger was the only appropriate emotion; that for any human being with any sense, any memory or foresight, every breath taken should be tinged with outrage" (108–9).

Momma's outrage stems from two broken romances—her own and her sister's. Her sister Annie met Jack Towne by chance, " 'on the boat, both of them coming over from different parts of Ireland. A shipboard romance' " (68). Annie comes to America to escape her alcoholic father, Jack for political reasons, but romance makes immigration less a matter of desperation or politics and more a purposeful and promising plan for the future. They marry and begin a family, and when her father dies in Ireland Annie sends

9 ~ (Anti) Romance in Alice McDermott

for her sister. Annie dies two weeks later, as a result of childbirth, and Momma stays to care for her nieces; a year later, she marries her brother-in-law. They had, she tells the children, "'a fine marriage.... The only thing I ever held against him... was that he made me believe the worst was over'" (147). After less than a year of marriage, Jack dies in the hall outside their apartment, apparently of a brain aneurysm. Momma replays this scene endlessly to his daughters and grandchildren, reminding them that their lives in America are products of immigrant sorrow. The "strife and mournfulness" (92) of her household reinforce their debt to a bitter history of loss.

The sisters contribute to this environment of outrage with the "sudden anger" that possesses them each day, "somehow prescribed, part of the daily and necessary schedule" (31). Lucy's children remember that there was never "a gathering of any sort, when one of them had not disappeared, retreated to a bedroom or... torn off down the street" in order to "prove," apparently, "that like the dead their presence would be all the more inescapable when they were gone" (112). The sisters measure their possibilities against the absence of their parents and the apparent futility of love. Lucy's free-floating dissatisfaction and fear of the future reflect a history in which love is merely prelude and invitation to disaster. If romance serves to ameliorate the painful ironies of human life and its end in death, *At Weddings and Wakes* offers no happy couples to redeem disappointment and suffering. Instead, there is the outraged knowledge that while romance fails to produce its proposed outcome, little else seems worthwhile; Momma, Lucy, Agnes, and Veronica continue to define their lives through the love that they lack.

But May, an ex-nun and the sister "most determined to be happy" (21), attempts to distract Lucy from her romantic disappointments, urging her to appreciate everyday joys. Her unexpected, middle-aged love for a mailman named Fred affirms her embrace of life over death. She understands that this stance renders her vulnerable to disappointment as she steps away from "the old life" that had been "as immune to accident and irony as it was to too much happiness" (132). A rejection of outrage and mournfulness, her projected marriage repudiates the lessons Momma has spent a lifetime teaching. "Happiness," May muses, "put some people at risk: today, for the first time she could remember, she had . . . crossed the worn carpet of the landing and not thought for a moment of how on a fall afternoon over forty years ago her father had died there" (69). Forgetting her father's death, May steps outside family history. To Momma, one of the people put at risk by happiness, May's plans for a happily-ever-after future demonstrate her dangerously deficient understanding of the past. In the face of Towne family history, the assurances of the priest officiating at May's wedding that love "'sustain[s]'" us as we follow "'our own arduous way . . . toward death'" are at best ironic (172). May, however, accepts the "blessing" of love, attempting, perhaps, a new family history.

The children's father also attempts to evade Towne history, "bless[ing]" (38) his family with annual vacations to Long Island. Each year, he finds a place where they have "no history . . . no memory of another time . . . It was as if he stopped time for them . . . cut them off from the past and the future so that they had only the present in a brand-new place" (200–1). Each year, however, Momma "find[s] some reason" (52) to reclaim their attention for history, "to remind them all that they'd been dancing on graves" (204). But when her call comes in the days following May's wedding, it is to inform them that May has died, apparently of an aneurysm. Dying of her father's malady, May extends, after all, the family pattern of brief hope in romance followed by its end in death. Four days separate her wedding and her wake, an abbreviation that affirms Towne history.

As the Dailey children narrate their family's past, they enter into its history. The stories of their mother's dead parents and of Momma's losses are deeply inscribed in their thought processes, "part of everything they [know]" (84). As Momma offers her tragic romance as the frame for May's plans for a new life with Fred, it seems to the children that she "want[s] something from them but they could not give it, or even say what it was" (142). In the face of this unanswerable obligation to the past, the children are thrilled and alarmed by a cousin's off hand comment: "'Aren't you glad . . . that you only have to see your relatives at weddings and wakes?'" (194). Despite the "appeal" of this refusal of the "old lamentations" (195), the Dailey children nevertheless become narrators of the family story;

11 ~ (Anti) Romance in Alice McDermott

At Weddings and Wakes is composed of their attempts to position May's story and their parents' disintegrating marriage in the context of Towne family history. Their stories enjoin a master narrative of tragedy which subverts the happily-ever-after expectations of romance and of the progress-oriented immigrant story.

Charming Billy also centers in the conflicted imbrication of romance and anti-romance, but its multiple interpretations of romance-as-history produce a more complex set of responses. Narrated by the unnamed daughter of Dennis Lynch, the title character's cousin and closest friend, the novel begins at Billy Lynch's funeral luncheon. *Charming Billy* moves between 1945 and 1991, as the narrator explores the story of Billy's tragic romance and the ways it has defined not only a common Irish past but also future American generations. Gathered in "a small bar-and-grill" located in the Bronx, which "might have been a pub in rural Ireland" (1), the mourners struggle with the meaning of Billy's life and death. He had been an alcoholic who "had, at some point, ripped apart, plowed through . . . the great, deep, tightly woven fabric of affection that was some part of the emotional life, the life of love, of everyone in the room" (4). In order to "mak[e] something worthwhile" of their investment of affection and faith in him, they must make "something worthwhile" of his romantic story, and by extension of their own "li[ves] of love." According to Dennis Lynch's adult daughter, "You could not redeem Billy's life, redeem your own relentless affection for him, without saying at some point, 'There was that girl'" (5).

Billy meets Eva, "the Irish girl" (5), on Long Island as he and Dennis enjoy their post–World War II "hiatus . . . between their lives as they were and whatever it was their lives were to become" (63), repairing a cottage belonging to Mr. Holtzman, the man Dennis's mother married after his father's death. In *Charming Billy*, the Long Island house functions as a nexus of competing meanings around love. Dennis's mother is capable of "deflat[ing] the most romantic notion with a single word." She has "no patience for poetry, Broadway musicals, presidential politics, or the pomp of her religion . . . under her steady gaze exaggeration, self-delusion, bravado simply dried up and blew away, as did hope, nonsense, and any ungrounded giddiness" (39). To her the cottage represents stability, not romance; to Dennis and Billy it stands for the perfect union of the two. Having "been here, just like this, all the while [they] had been locked in the adventure and tedium of the war" (65), it represents a bridge to prewar normality and to the security of love and family.

At the beach, the cousins encounter two Irish au pairs; Dennis lays immediate claim to Mary, leaving her sister Eva for Billy. Billy "fall[s] in love" with her "before she had even come clearly into his view" (76). At their next meeting he falls "in love with the rest of his life, and that was better still" (76). It seems to him that like the cottage, "this golden future . . . had been part of the same life he'd been living all along" (76–77). Unable to see Eva "clearly," Billy imagines her as a kind of fetish of an extended Irish American history. In this space of upper-class privilege, Billy's "golden future" extends the possibilities of his working-class fathers, combining continuing immigration from Ireland with movement up the American social ladder. Billy starts toward this future by asking Eva to stay in the United States. She, however, feels impelled to return to her family in Ireland, prompting Billy's offer to bring them over, as well:

"That's how my father's family did it. Dennis's father came over first and then brought over his six brothers and his sister, and Lord knows how many more."
. . . "I'll send for you," he told her. . . . "as soon as I save the money I'll send for you. I'll bring you back. Can I do that?"
She shook her head only slightly and . . . whispered, "There's still my family."
"I'll send for them, too," he said, and because he heard her laugh a little, perhaps saw her smile, he added, laughing as well, "I'll send for them all, your parents and your sisters and the next-door neighbors if you want me to. Does your town have a pastor—I'll send for him. A milkman? Him too. . . . Is there a baker you're particularly fond of? Any nuns? Cousins? We'll bring them over. We'll bring them all over." (84–85)

This, he believes, is "what his life had held for him all along" (85); successful romance with "the Irish girl" would reestablish continuity by replicating his family's model for "creating a future" (30). Like *At Weddings and Wakes*, *Charming Billy* presents romantic love imbricated with the hopefulness of immigrant dreams and the possibilities of America, a romantic love that stands as metaphor for the historical processes that create Irish Americans.

But Billy receives word that Eva has died of pneumonia in Ireland and later marries the "plain" Maeve, a union that seems "a futile attempt to mend an irreparably broken heart. A moment's grace, a flash of optimism, not enough for a lifetime" (12). Billy's cousin and drinking partner, Dan Lynch, believes that had Eva lived, the family would be gathered to evaluate "'a different life'" (19). While Dan figures Billy's alcoholism in direct proportion to his loss, Billy's sister Rosemary points to the many alcoholic members of the extended Lynch family and argues that alcoholism "'isn't a decision, it's a disease, and Billy would have had the disease whether he married the Irish girl or Maeve.'" Her assertion that "'every alcoholic's life is pretty much the same'" (19) opposes Dan's view of Billy's romantic agency, his manly loyalty to one true thing.

While Rosemary focuses on Billy's "genetic predisposition" to alcoholism, to a fate he carried "in his genes" (22), Dan insists "'Say he was too loyal. Say he was disappointed. Say he made way too much of the Irish girl. . . . But give him some credit . . . for having a hand in his own fate. Don't say it was a disease that blindsided him and wiped out everything he was.'" (23). This exchange encapsulates the narrative conflict between romance and anti-romance, consent and descent, random fate and truths there all along. Billy's romantic plan to bring Eva, her family, and most of her village to America recapitulates the process of immigration that his community celebrates as the source of their own lives. His plan has failed, but his loyalty upholds the values and priorities that produced the Lynch family in America. While *At Weddings and Wakes* focuses on immigrant sorrow as outcome of history and model for romance, *Charming Billy* posits romance as the primary metaphor for the community itself, regardless, to some extent, of outcome.

Billy's romantic immigrant plan encapsulates communal history in its connections to the community's other hero, center of its other privileged romantic narrative—Dennis's father, Daniel Lynch. Continuously importing relatives from Ireland, Daniel replays an immigrant romance that makes him his community's patron "saint" (22) and revered patriarch.

When Billy "cri[es] in his beer that he would not have [Eva's] boat fare by summer," Dennis remarks, "'You're more like my father than my father was.'" "'In this family,'" Billy responds, "his glass to his heart, 'you couldn't say a kinder word'" (115). Even the outwardly cynical Dennis believes "in his own (his own father's) romantic heart" that the "consummation" of Billy's Irish romance "would become a small redemption for them all" (119). Perhaps this desire to redeem the lives constructed by Daniel Lynch's immigrant dream is behind the lie that Dennis tells Billy, a lie that both perpetuates and ends Billy's romance. Eva did not die young, beautiful, and tragic in Ireland. Instead, she marries a "hometown boy" and uses Billy's passage money for a down payment on a gas station (26). Dennis invents Eva's death because he believes it would be "better" for Billy to be "brokenhearted" than "trailed all the rest of his life by a sense of his own foolishness" (31). His lie preserves the model of masculinity central to the community's Irish American romance with history by preserving the dignity of the would-be patriarch.

The potential redemption Dennis had invested in Billy's successful conjunction of immigration and heterosexual romance occurs at the gaps in Daniel Lynch's story. His father had been a fisher of men, providing new life in a better place, a role that may have "made him Holy Father to a tenement's worth of Irish immigrants but kept his wife and son mostly impoverished and never—what with one wetback mick after another being reeled in from the other side and slapped down on their couch—alone in their own home" (39). Daniel's romanticized status is contradicted by the "dark fairy tale" (102) Sheila Lynch tells. Orphaned and alone, she marries Daniel hoping for security and recognition, but instead finds continuing dislocation in "one- and two-bedroom apartments that also served as permanent way stations for an endless string of penniless Irish immigrants" (104). Sheila wakes on "her second morning as a young bride" to find two such immigrants asleep on the floor and "never had [Daniel's] attention all to herself again" (108). Daniel's primary love interaction is with the new arrivals who provide the rewards and satisfactions of his life; his immigrant romance supersedes their romantic couplehood. Dissenting Daniel's myth, Sheila teaches her son the dangers of romantic

15 ~ (Anti) Romance in Alice McDermott

illusion "in the same careful and loving way another mother might tell a child that the aspirin was not candy and the laundry bleach not fruit punch" (88). So when Dennis prevents Billy from revealing his "rabid infatuation" (88) to Sheila, he protects not only Billy but also his own investment in Billy's dream, a dream that would renew and repair the romantic narrative disputed by his disappointed mother.

Billy misinterprets Dennis's suppression of the Irish girls, assuming that Dennis feels guilty for having had sex with Mary. *Charming Billy* continually reminds us that Dennis also had an Irish girl, insistently referencing an anti-romantic counter plot to Billy's story. But even as his experience shadows Billy's deferral of sexual fulfillment in immigrant desire, Dennis is seduced by Billy's "sweet romance" (90). Romance, it seems, is contagious in all its incarnations: after getting Billy the job and loan that will enable him to bring Eva to America sooner rather than later, Dennis "understood for the first time why . . . his father had bankrupted himself and estranged his wife and filled their tiny apartment with far-flung relatives from the other side: simply to know this power, this expansiveness. Simply to be able to say, as he said to Billy that day . . . 'Here you go.' Here's your life" (125). Caught up in this power, he decides to "give [Mary] a ring on the day Billy married Eva" (125). When Mary summons him unexpectedly, he believes she is pregnant and resolves to "marry her immediately," but also realizes that she represents "a future that he only understood now he never honestly wanted" (127). After she delivers the news of Eva's defection, he ends their relationship (127). Dennis's failed romance with "Irish Mary" (209) highlights the element of chance in Billy's relationship with Eva (what if Dennis had picked Eva instead?) and illustrates Dennis's ambivalent reception of his father's legacy. Mary stands at/as the start of another potential chain of immigrants, positioning Dennis to continue the work his father began. In the story he tells Billy he banishes her to Ireland, space of dead dreams.

Dennis is "stunned" at the "audacity" of his lie, well aware that "the workaday world, the world without illusion (except Church-sanctioned) or nonsense (except alcohol-bred) that was the world of Irish Catholic Queens New York, didn't much abide audacious and outlandish. Not for long, anyway" (32). But although his lie might seem outrageous, its effect is conservative—it preserves his community's romantic view of its history and adjoins its other ordering narratives. Even Dennis falls back on the view of Billy as a tragic hero of romance; as he tells his daughter the truth after the funeral luncheon, he adds that "'when Billy sets his heart on something there's no changing him. He's loyal. He's got this faith—which is probably why he drinks'" (35–36). Dennis, as we have seen, is not alone in this view. In *Charming Billy*, alcohol, romance, and religion converge on multiple levels.

A reviewer of *Charming Billy* characterizes Billy as a "priest of romance, a person who gave to earthly love the priest's loyalty to the divine" (LeClair 27). Romance, like religion, necessitates a leap of faith, an assurance of permanence that promises enduring meaning and reward. When Billy kisses Eva for the first time, it "[is] like inhaling the essence of some vague but powerful alcohol" (83) imbued with "the dark flavor of desire . . . for something he couldn't give a word to—for happiness, sure, for sense, for children—for life itself to be as sweet as certain words could make it seem" (84). Despite the powerful intoxicating effect of love (and gin), he also knows that "adrift in the same world that held their fine future there was accident and disappointment, a sickening sense of false hope and false promise that required all of God's grace to keep at bay" (85). Aware that romance might not be capable of withstanding a cold and random world, Billy seeks the supplement of grace—divine love—as its mirror and affirmation.[5]

As the day of Billy's funeral draws to a close, Dennis's daughter holds a drink (poured symbolically for Billy) and observes that "each sip raised a kind of veil that was both a warmth across the cheeks and a welling in the eyes. A way of seeing, perhaps. Perhaps the very thing that Billy would have found so appealing, had the drink been his" (177). This "way of seeing" alleviates the discordance between faith and disillusionment, between the promise of love and the experience of loss. When Billy drinks, he experiences "the force of his faith . . . a force he could only glimpse briefly while sober" (187). It becomes "clear and steady and as fully true as the vivid past or the as-yet-unseen but inevitable future. . . . Drunk, when Billy turned his

17 ~ (Anti) Romance in Alice McDermott

eyes to heaven, heaven was there" (187). Dan Lynch, who insists on the sanctity of Billy's loyalty to Eva, compares him to a priest who sacrifices all to enter "so fully into his faith that it changes the very fabric of his life" (172). In these interconnected locales of faith, the "way of seeing" offered by alcohol, the hopefulness of grace, and the promise of love keep fear and loneliness at bay by offering the assurance that individual lives matter.

While Billy might appear as a "priest of romance," McDermott and her narrator have one eye fixed on the contradictions of such a position—they come clear to Billy himself during his trip to Ireland to take the pledge (213). Dressed as a priest in order to carry a friend's license and drive his rental car, he sets out to visit Eva's grave. Instead, he finds himself visiting with Eva in her gas station/lunch room. Thirty years later, their summer on Long Island seems "part of a story now, and as story, it was nothing any of them had truly lived" (222). But, a "married priest" (213), Billy did "truly live" an illusion, and his masquerade reflects his competing identities: true to Eva and to Maeve, romantic hero and maudlin drunk, a "priest of romance" face-to-face with his "thirty years of misdirected prayer" (207). His broken romance, it turns out, was not a matter of fate but of choice; Eva chose Ireland. Her enduring shadow-romance with her hometown boy relocates love to the space Billy's community has left behind, throwing the romance of American lives—the foundation of Daniel's myth—into dispute. Marrying, having children, working in her small business, Eva lives a life quite similar to the life Billy offered. For his part, Billy does not stop drinking, does not tell anyone but Dennis about his encounter with his dead love, and does not die hoping to find Eva in "the sweet hereafter" (35), as his community believes. Billy has defined himself through his romantic faith, and dies with the knowledge that he has lived under false assumptions.

These assumptions are never abandoned by his community, despite the almost universal anti-romance which characterizes their lives. Dan Lynch, a reduced version of his namesake, clings to "the story" that he never married because he "was such a connoisseur of beauty and behavior that no flawed wife could have pleased him and no flawless one could have been found" (17). Sheila glories in her marriage of security, viewing Holtzman as "the embodiment of good sense, practicality, relief, the soundest investment she had ever made" (95). When she rents the Long Island cottage, site of Billy and Eva's projected honeymoon, her tenant's marriage falls apart. Dennis believes that "Mr. West would not have left his wife and three sons" if Sheila "had not been there offering a furnished rental at a year-round, reasonable rate" (49). Billy's sister Kate endures years of browbeating from her aspiring-lawyer husband and is now bejeweled and manicured but alone. Bridie "from the old neighborhood" (17) had "a crush on Billy" when she was young, a crush that "everyone" knew about; Billy, however, deflects her unrequited love by insisting that she "would have married Tim Schmidt if he'd lived" (31). But Tim Schmidt died in the war and the man she later married suffers from advanced Alzheimer's disease.

The narrator incorporates these and other stories into her reconstruction of Billy's, positioning ideals of romantic love beside unfulfilled desire, empty promises, and bitter disappointments. Her own parents' romance, she believes, "ran the typical course from early infatuation to serious love to affection occasionally diminished by impatience and disagreement." Their love, she feels, "is a given," but she also believes that "there were months, maybe years, when their love for each other might have disappeared altogether and their lives proceeded only out of habit or the failure to imagine any other alternative" (45). This acknowledgement of the mundane, even tedious, course of love integrates romance into the "nine-to-five" life that, according to Sheila, makes individuals "what [they] really [are]: one of the so many million, just one more" (92). Dennis views "wife children house" as "the extent of his success" (204), and, like his father before him, is "depend[ed] upon" by "scores of friends and relatives" (46). At bottom, this life does not seem substantially different from the future he rejected with "Irish Mary."

But this "good-enough . . . typical kind of mid-twentieth-century marriage . . . suddenly blossomed into something else in the year [Claire Lynch] was dying" (45), when the narrator's parents claim "their love, their loyalty to one another" as the source of their lives' fulfillment. As love and loyalty become "no longer a matter of chance or happenstance but a condition of their existence no more voluntary or escapable than the pace

19 ~ (Anti) Romance in Alice McDermott

of their blood" (45–46), Dennis and Claire view "their meeting, their courtship, their years raising children, every ordinary day they had spent together" as "merely the running start they had taken to vault this moment. To sail, gracefully and in tandem, across the abyss" (45). Affirming heterosexual union as completeness, their renewed love ameliorates failures, inadequacies, and twists of fate. Here, romance makes something "triumph[ant]" (46) out of ordinary lives, after all.

However, this narrative of successful, satisfying romance, Dennis and his daughter understand, has been belatedly imposed over a sometimes unruly and often disappointing experience. After his wife's death, Dennis could not

> convince himself that . . . the assurance that they had achieved something exclusive, something redemptive in the endurance of their love, had been any more than another well-intentioned deception, another construction, as unbelievable, when you came right down to it, as the spontaneity of a love song in some Broadway musical, the supposedly heartfelt supplication of a well-rehearsed hymn, the bearing any one of Billy's poems . . . had on the actual way any of us lived from day to day.
>
> He could not convince himself then . . . that heaven was any more than a well-intentioned deception meant to ease our own sense of foolishness, to ease pain. (211)

Taking stock of his life with Claire, Dennis rejects the romantic symmetry that, like the promise of heaven and his lie to Billy, serves to redeem our standing as just "part of the crowd." Later he recants, telling his daughter that "'it was only a brief loss of faith'" and that he "'believe[s] everything now. . . . Again'" (212). "Of course," she notes, "there was no way of telling if he lied" (212).

Even this ambivalent success is withheld from Maeve, whose name, "ironic[ally]," means "intoxicating one" (175). Her childless marriage to Billy seems firmly situated in the realm of anti-romance, only marginal "compensation . . . for what he had lost" (161). "Without [Billy]," Maeve "would have become a nun," and "having chosen this part," she "stand[s] steadily by as his future was formed for her" (134). She tends to Billy as she had to her alcoholic father, and now holds "in her memory . . . a thousand

and one moments she would never recount, things he had said to her, terrible things he had done, ways she had seen him (toothless, incoherent, half-clothed, bloodied, soiled, weeping) that she couldn't begin to tell" (157). Maeve's sisters-in-law praise her "loyalty," her "patience" and "endurance" (169), but most of the characters view this form of loyalty as anti-romantic.

Dennis's daughter considers the postcard Billy sent Maeve from Long Island after the Ireland trip. The card—a picture of "Home Sweet Home in East Hampton" (142) with the salutation "*beautiful friend*" (232)—may encode an ironic commentary on the romance associated with the Long Island cottage or a transformation of the anti-romance associated with Maeve, an honoring of other forms of constancy. Possibly, it demonstrates Billy's late acceptance of "yet another life, the one that had been waiting for him all along, even while he'd been busy imagining his life with Eva" (180). Or it might simply represent Billy's tendency toward the poetic. The card encapsulates the contradictions of Billy's life, an uneasy balance between his romantic mythos—represented in his loyalty to Eva—and his prosaic life—represented in his loyalty to Maeve. The "Home Sweet Home" card and its inscription in any case illustrate a powerful component of Billy's charm—his ability to make the unbeautiful beautiful, to narrate his life and the lives of others through poetry and prayer, through the language of love and faith. Despite his ugly death and the anti-romantic realities underlying his love story, Billy remains an attractive romantic figure who embodies his community's view of history.

The narrator cannot determine what her father intends that she understand from their exchanges about Billy, Sheila, and Claire, seeing in him "either the near-triumph of faith or the nearly liberating letting go of it" (155). It is also unclear why she repeats the story, interposed with those of other members of the community, to her husband and children. Dennis's daughter met her husband—a son of the Long Island tenant—in the same area Billy met Eva, but is "spared the memory of a first conversation on the same sunny bay beach" (61). Although she and Mr. West's son disavow the conventions of romantic love, "world-wise, open-eyed, without illusion," they "truly believed" then and "would believe on and off again for the rest of [their] lives" that the "whole history of Holtzman's little house" was, "with [their] own meeting, redeemed" (230). This belief positions their romance as the culmination of the familial and cultural histories that the house represents; this, she implies, is what their lives held for them all along. Because we know virtually nothing about the narrator's love relationship, her references to it add another level of complexity to the ambivalent textual view of romance: her (patchy) love plot both echoes and disavows Billy's and her parents'.

Observing that "the claim to exclusivity in love requires both a certain kind of courage and a good dose of delusion," she articulates history as a series of coincidences: "Irish Mary . . . would have been happy enough to accept my father's ring . . . had Eva not chosen to stay in Ireland. . . . My mother's first fiancé would have married her gladly . . . if my father hadn't beaten him home" (209). The narrator acknowledges similar factors of chance in her meeting with her husband, but also suggests that at their first greeting their children "must have pricked up their ears" (49). Dennis's daughter evokes a fated romantic couplehood to describe her relationship with her husband, yet notes that "there are a hundred opportunities . . . for a sense of falsehood to seep in, for all that we imagine as inevitable to become arbitrary, for our history together to reveal itself as only a matter of chance and happenstance, nothing irrepeatable, or irreplaceable, the circumstantial mingling of just one of the so many million with just one more" (209–10). As she tells her family's stories of (anti)romance, she acknowledges that love, the thing that we imagine distinguishes us from "the so many million," is the very thing that makes us the same.

Remembering and revising the foundational narratives of her Irish American community, the narrator reviews their lessons about love and history, about meaning and truth in human lives, but finds no satisfying answers.[6] *Charming Billy* concludes with the surprising and (to the narrator, at least) anti-romantic news of Dennis and Maeve's marriage. Dennis and his daughter do not examine this relationship in light of his earlier talk of truth and lies, leaving her to wonder "was it penance . . . compensation for an old and well-intentioned lie, for the life it had deprived her of? Or was it merely taking care . . . A hand held out once again to whoever happened to be nearby" (242). She does not consider that this might be what their lives had held for them all along. While the narrator does not perceive Dennis and Maeve's relationship as an alternate, perhaps more realistic, expression of love, McDermott leaves this possibility open. Noting that her father's "capacity for sympathy was no less than Billy's for self-denial," the narrator concludes that "their faith . . . was no less keen than their suspicion that in the end they might be proven wrong. And their certainty that they would continue to believe anyway" (242). Here, the narrator makes an unacknowledged transition, combining the lines of "faith"—romantic and religious—established through the text. Fusing faith in God's redemptive plan with faith in redemptive heterosexual union, she transfers both to a level of mystery that seems to transcend logic, philosophy, even experience.

Dennis says, "'every one of us is living proof . . . that it's a powerless thing, this loving one another, nothing like what [Billy] had imagined. Except in the way it persists'" (225). He marries Maeve in the church he attended during the Long Island hiatus, renamed from "St. Philomena's" to "Most Holy Trinity." Philomena had been "tossed out of the canon of saints . . . because some doubt had arisen about whether or not she had actually lived" (242–43). Dennis's daughter, however, is not convinced that "in that wide-ranging anthology of stories that was the lives of the saints—that was, as well, my father's faith and Billy's and some part of my own—what was actual, as opposed to what was imagined, as opposed to what was believed, made, when you got right down to it, any difference at all" (243). While the narrator views the romance that structures individual lives and cultural histories as "imagined," even illusory, she also finds that its "actual" truth or falsity does not diminish its force as "belief," as epistemological foundation of the various faiths that give lives meaning.

We have been taught that those who do not learn from history are condemned to repeat it. In McDermott's novels, as well as in a much of Western literature and culture, romance, which is endlessly repeated, stands as history. McDermott's characters understand their Irish American history as a reflection of the promises of the heterosexual romance plot, which creates the possibilities of their lives. Here, history is romance and romance is history. But this equation labors under the constant pressure of anti-romance, of the failure of heterosexual union to provide the transcendence it promises. The pervasive anti-romance of *At Weddings and Wakes* denies the power of love to redeem individual lives, while *Charming Billy* oscillates between hope and disappointment in heterosexual romance as a controlling metaphor. If romance stands as the historical screen upon which we project our lives, then McDermott's narrators have stepped briefly behind it. The screen, once dislodged, does not completely return to its original position, leaving the projection to play into the darkness behind. Fixed and de-centered, present and absent, true and false, romance-as-epistemology evokes yet continually defers solid meaning in individual lives and cultural histories.[7]

McDermott "writes beyond the ending" (DuPlessis 5)[8] by insisting that romance never resolves itself and that happily-ever-after dreams continue to recede before us. Love—situated as the privileged source of balance and stability for individuals and cultures—produces abiding uncertainty. In *At Weddings and Wakes* and *Charming Billy* McDermott melds romance and history into a single story, a story that is both necessary to individual and cultural self-definition and "nothing any of them had truly lived." Her novels center around efforts to sort "truth" from "story," but demonstrate that such a distinction is finally impossible, that those epistemological "truths" which structure our lives are a function of story. And romance is the story we seem to know best.

History and the End of Romance

DANTICAT'S *THE FARMING OF BONES*

—Susan Strehle

Edwidge Danticat describes her latest novel, *The Farming of Bones* (1998), as "a work of fiction based on historical events" (311). The novel appears at points to *be* a history, designed to engage the events of 1937 and to recall them forever from obscurity. In her acknowledgments, the Haitian American writer lists several sources she researched for the historical background on the massacre of some 35,000 Haitians by Dominicans in 1937. The endpapers of the hardback version of the novel reproduce a letter from Haitian President Sténio Vincent to U.S. Secretary of State George Leger describing the massacre: "*Evidemment on ne saura jamais exactement la quantité de gens qui sont morts.* (Evidently we will never know exactly the number of people who have died.)"[1] The novel focuses its telling of these events through one fictional character's experience; Danticat said in an interview, "What I am trying to do is tell the history through one voice. The monumental historical figures don't interest me as much as the ordinary person. An old woman in her 80s telling how she survived this event is more interesting than, say, a memoir of someone who knew all the players" (Shea 50). Just twenty-nine herself when

25 ~ *Danticat's* The Farming of Bones

The Farming of Bones appeared, Danticat had previously published a novel, *Breath, Eyes, Memory*, which appeared in 1994 and was selected for Oprah's Book Club, and a book of stories, *Krik? Krak!*, a National Book Award Finalist in 1995. Both previous texts addressed Haitian identities and histories—in fact, one story in *Krik? Krak!*, entitled "Nineteen Thirty-Seven," deals with the massacre. Nonetheless, *The Farming of Bones* is a more deliberate, extended, and elaborately researched historical fiction than any of Danticat's previous work.

For a novel designed to recover political history, *The Farming of Bones* makes a seemingly peculiar decision: it begins as a love story, full of the conventions of romance fiction. Indeed, the first third of the novel concerns itself with the domestic arrangements of families and romantic couples, rather than with the national events leading two Caribbean peoples toward cataclysm. The narrative begins in the timeless present of romance: "His name is Sebastien Onius. He comes most nights to put an end to my nightmare, the one I have all the time, of my parents drowning. While my body is struggling against sleep, fighting itself to awaken, he whispers for me to 'lie still while I take you back ... into the cave across the river'" (1). Sebastien appears powerfully masculine, "lavishly handsome," and compassionate in his response to Amabelle Désir's history of pain and loss (1). The ideal guide to an adult identity beyond the wreckage of her childhood, he can take Amabelle back in memory and imagination to the time before her parents died. Yet for all the desire focused on him and for all his seeming power, Sebastien disappears halfway through the novel. The romance hangs suspended; the closure of marriage is withheld. The love plot, with its destined ending in the union of opposites, the production of children, and the validation of patriarchy, remains unfulfilled.

Racism and genocide—the forces that send Sebastien spinning into eternity—also warp the conventional romance plot beyond recognition. *The Farming of Bones* poises the young romance of Sebastien and Amabelle against the slaughter of Haitians in the Dominican Republic. While Amabelle escapes to Haiti, maimed and scarred, to tell the story, Sebastien disappears, leaving only rumors of his death to filter back to Haiti. Early in the novel history, told in the preterit tense, alternates with romance, written in a timeless present and printed in bold; as the history of massacre displaces and almost obliterates dream-memories of romance, the text becomes all preterit. The time of ahistorical repetition becomes a lost past: "I thought of past Saturdays spent sitting in the house ... visiting Sebastien at the mill ... For so long this had been my life, but it was all the past" (184). From daily domestic activities, the text turns to singular events, mostly deaths, of history and revolution, as Amabelle flees toward the border and her own historic encounter with Generalissimo Trujillo outside a church in Dajabón.

The focus on momentous historical events of the middle of the book is not sustained, however, but rather gives way to a poetic gathering of scattered, momentary glimpses of the afterlives of the survivors through several decades. For this reason, the last third of the novel is problematic for reviewers, one of whom complains that the last section is "lacking the momentum of the book's earlier chapters" (Upchurch 13), while another notes that "the narrative loses a little steam" (Freeman C4). Like the romance narrative, the historical plot also fails to achieve the closure, finality, certainty, or rest we expect of traditional historical narratives. While time passes between the events of 1937 and the novel's end,[2] time does not bring clarity, recovery, or understanding of these historical events. In fact, the measurement of time drops away, and very few of the glimpses and conversations can be placed in any given year or even decade. The last third of the novel focuses on characters who have fallen out of both love and history; isolate, not fully sane, these characters look backwards with growing uncertainty: "Perhaps there was no story that could truly satisfy. I myself didn't know if that story was true or even possible" (305). As a narrative, the novel turns away at its end from the conventions that have appeared to define and guide it.

Danticat's novel presents a complex understanding of both history and romance as these two forces intersect in Amabelle's narrative. History—a brutal history of the subjugation, use, and murder of a racialized other—emerges with the postmodern recognition that histories are constructed by those who tell the story. Histories have a point of view, a language, and an excluded set of data beyond their chosen frame; for instance, the first account of the massacre was created by Trujillo, who claimed that an unorganized group of farmers arose spontaneously to drive Haitians out of the country, and only a few were killed. The problematic nature of historical representation poses special problems for those who have been marginalized and excluded from history—for those like Haitian American women writers—who must therefore acknowledge the constructed nature of historical narratives while finding a way to bear witness to historical events. Romance is also constructed, and like history it is most successful where it most fully expresses the needs and accomplishes the work of culture. Romance emerges from and expresses traditional constructions of gender, work, desire, narrative structure, and human worth. Romance seems to young Amabelle to be history's opposite and antidote, to bring comfort, and to provide a soothing counternarrative that enables a scarred caneworker and a haunted domestic servant to escape from the cares of their daily lives. But romance and history turn out to be more similar, more intertwined, and more reliant on each other than she has supposed.

The Farming of Bones is neither a romantic history nor a historical romance, but rather a new form created at the intersection of history and romance, calling the ideological assumptions of both genres into question and transforming them both in the process. *The Farming of Bones* writes the as-yet-unwritten history in order to expose what has been suppressed; it provides no explanation, causality, or resolution. The novel writes the romance that fails when the projected joy turns to tragedy, the lifelong marriage stifles the spirit, and the love relation ends in murder. At the same time, it narrates the unquenchable love that concludes in Amabelle's determination to preserve Sebastien's name and memory. In both historical and romance modes, it focuses on individuals and tells detailed stories in order to count the costs of large-scale losses. This remarkable novel exposes lines of affiliation between traditionally conceived history and romance as forms of narration whose orderings rest on and perpetuate the politics of patriarchy. The narrative also finds in these narrative forms, however, openings for resistance and renewal.

Danticat's interest focuses especially on the related ways in which both narratives construct women. Received narratives of history and romance rely on women's desire and women's labor; women are personally expendable in both narratives, but their symbolic and especially reproductive functions are central to both enterprises. In order to fulfill their functions in both, women are required to be passive and self-effacing, amenable to pain, as Michelle Massé has shown,[3] deferential before "masculine behavior in a world in which men learn to devalue women," as Tania Modleski has argued (60). By conjoining a fractured love story with a historical tale of genocide, the novel suggests that women's roles as lovers emerge from the same cultural values that express themselves in the historical slaughter of the racialized other, while women's roles as victims and observers of history bespeak the same cultural values that can make them the helpless mates of tyrannical men. But when an aging Amabelle turns to poetry in order to preserve the name of her beloved Sebastien, Danticat's novel opens up the space in which romance can empower and liberate women to assume a different role in love and history. As the novel ends, Amabelle's created vision of history and romance allows an open time, a naming that summons and changes the lover, and a renewal that gathers the past together.

Like her protagonist, Danticat writes a poetic counterhistory that is fragmentary, open, and unfinished. The novel tells what Molly Hite calls "the other side of the story," in part by granting privilege to the oral histories of witnesses and survivors (1–18); ironically, most of them remain unheard by the authorities who write down versions of this history. The text includes multiple details, seemingly trivial events, and incongruities to create what Foucault calls "genealogy"—the opposite of history in that it does not see from the end as a closed totality, but rather glimpses events from the midst. Genealogy, Foucault writes, recollects the past without trying "to restore an unbroken continuity that operates beyond the dispersion of forgotten things," but rather identifies "the accidents, the minute deviations—or conversely, the complete reversals—the errors, the false appraisals, and the faulty calculations" beneath phenomena (146). Danticat produces a genealogy of the events of 1937, not only using a single first person narrator to witness the catastrophes of this national tragedy, but also collecting the accidental moments—a nameless young

29 ~ Danticat's The Farming of Bones

woman's corpse rolling off a wagon pulled by oxen, a sandal dropping from a corpse hung in a tree, an empty black dress floating past in the river before a shot rings out—that comprise a senseless massacre. Her approach to history is fully postmodern, in the sense Diane Elam defines when she writes that the postmodern romance presents the past as "an excess over consciousness": "The postmodern romance re-members the past, re-situates its temporality, in order to make the past impossible to forget. To render the past in this sense unforgettable is to point out that it is impossible fully to remember, fully to come to terms with the past" (15). Rather than a history we can order, understand, and thereby forget, Danticat narrates the past that exceeds understanding and becomes unforgettable.

Danticat's approach undoes history as it has been written, exemplified most fully and surprisingly in the histories authorized by and about Trujillo. These narratives provide another dimension of totalitarian control and enforced closure. One of the sources Danticat acknowledges in her afterword is *President Trujillo, His Work and the Dominican Republic*. Written in 1936, this book by Lawrence De Besault glorifies the dictator. As Trujillo was planning the massacre of Haitians, De Besault wrote servile praise for "his good will, his prodigious generosity, his love and his patriotic faith, and his statesmanlike powers . . . without any other purpose than the satisfaction of doing his duty and without any other stimulus than his own conscience—with the point of view of the truly great, who know how to sacrifice themselves for the general welfare" (365).[4] The gilded leather cover of this book, with its raised portrait of Trujillo, makes the same point as the flattery it contains: Trujillo's control over the republic is presented as heroic. No detail escapes the author's tyrannical singleness of purpose; no disruptive hints intrude to suggest another version. De Besault's narrative voice claims absolute authority, certain knowledge, and superior access to immutable truth: he knows the inner mind and motives guiding even the most accidental and seemingly unrelated events.

Other approaches to this history exist, of course, including some that follow a method Foucault would call genealogical. Among the texts Danticat acknowledges, Ambassador Bernardo Vega's *Trujillo y Haití* contains detailed chronologies, stories of preceding and distant events, documents from the press and political archives, telegrams, letters, photographs of wounded survivors, a chronological table of rising estimates of the number of dead Haitians, and a lengthy summary of judicial declarations made by survivors who crossed the border and escaped to Haiti (348–60).[5] This way of telling history gathers detail and evidence, offers some conclusions, but leaves final acts of interpretation to the reader. It focuses on individual stories, multiple costs, and an intricate web of historical links. Vega's narrative voice differs vastly from De Besault's: he does not claim authority and certainty in the same ways, but rather collects and presents a multiplicity of facts, causes, and relevant details. His version of causality is far more complex than De Besault's, for where De Besault finds one cause (the dictator's heroic generosity) beneath all events in the Dominican Republic, Vega goes to great length to discuss global economic conditions, military attitudes, racial fears, and other contributing sources; a chapter titled "*Causas de la Matanza*" (389–412) describes a multitude of factors leading to the massacre. In his understated conclusion, Vega writes of the outmigration to the United States of both Haitians and Dominicans: "*En los barrios du Nueva York, haitianos y dominicanos, por primera vez se juntan en grandes cantidades fuera de la Española.... Esperemos que, en el caso domínico-haitiano, la trágica historia de ayer no se repita. Buscando ese propósito, es que se ha escrito este libro.* (In the barrios of New York, Haitians and Dominicans encounter each other for the first time in large numbers outside the island of Hispaniola.... We hope that, in the Dominican-Haitian case, the tragic history of yesterday will not repeat itself. Seeking this proposition, this book has been written [420, my translation].)" This voice considers a wide range of events and hopes that presenting research will stave off the repetition of tragedy. Implicitly, it is up to readers to draw their own conclusions and to create a different history. Danticat, a genealogical narrator herself, no doubt finds the method of Vega (and others like him) congenial: this is counter-history, empowering further narratives like *The Farming of Bones*.

The roles women play in history—indeed, the roles history constructs for them—are passive and symbolic. For the historical Trujillo, a notorious womanizer, women were defined as sexual vessels and bearers of children; he had dozens of mistresses and was known as the Goat.[6]

31 ~ Danticat's The Farming of Bones

He ordered the murders of the three Mirabal sisters who intruded into the realm of politics and history; then, once his police had transformed them to beautiful dead symbols, he is reported to have visited the site of their death and lamented, "Such good women, and so defenseless!"[7] Trujillo's view of women is, of course, neither unique nor personal; Danticat's novel shows that women in the culture viewed themselves in the same way. One memorable example can be seen in the self-effacing Señora Valencia: she marries a brutal lieutenant who carries out the massacre, and she makes excuses for him for the rest of her life, even to her Haitian servants, and even after he abandons her for other women. Passive and irrelevant in both history and romance, Valencia has served her husband as symbol and symbol-maker. She paints two pictures in her life, one of Generalissimo Trujillo who gives her husband a role in history, the other of the "bone-white baby boy" who gives her husband reproductive evidence of whiteness (294). As the "sister" who grew up close to Amabelle, Valencia reflects a different route to womanhood than Amabelle can take, and her journey leads to spiritual suffocation.

While history enters the novel as a destructive force, romance wears a softer and more pleasant face; it provides a soothing alternative story with more opportunities for a happy ending. Indeed, the romance elements of Danticat's plot appear at first to distract, provide escape, and create the illusion that the personal is neither political nor historical. But, as Donette Francis has astutely argued, "Danticat uses the universal medium of a love story to render intimate the personal cost of political oppression, and spends the final third of the novel portraying how the slaughter impacted the everyday lives of Amabelle and other Haitians" (171). Danticat appears interested in the ways a writer may cloak political analysis under the guise of romance. In an interview given while she was completing *The Farming of Bones*, she "points out that women often write what seems a romantic work on the surface, but beneath the text political themes are exploding ... 'You're throwing darts from hiding, and it's like rebelling but not being in the melee" (Shea 48).

The romance elements in this and some other contemporary women's texts are not only a way to personalize history and to conceal political themes: they function as a critique of history, exposing the power relations that structure love. One of the most surprising aspects of Danticat's latest novel is its suggestion that the seemingly perfect romance between Sebastien and Amabelle is actually part of the problem as well as a saving alternative. Amabelle experiences primarily the reassuring and comforting aspects of her romance, but the novel also explores forms of damage created by heterosexual love. For the Haitian characters, romance enables the illusion of escape from poverty, pain, and servitude under an oppressive and racist politics, and therefore actually keeps them in their place. For the Dominican characters, romance allows an indulgence in cruelty and injustice under the guise of routine domestic economies. Romance creates couples, children, families, weddings, households, and historical continuities; the lure of the ideal mate actually props up dictatorship, slavery, and genocide by making invisible and acceptable the power relations that give strong men control of their women, wealthy men control of their servants, and dictators control of their country. Romance also contributes in surprising ways to Amabelle's liberation late in her life; I will turn to that phase after I explore the ways romance limits and restricts freedoms in the novel.

In our introduction to this volume, Mary Paniccia Carden and I have explored some of the contradictions implicit in the romance as both validation of and dissent against patriarchal values and institutions. Two important critics are especially helpful in highlighting the ways in which romance reflects and perpetuates patriarchal values, on the one hand, while voicing women's dissatisfaction with them on the other. Janice Radway's landmark study, *Reading the Romance*, argues that the ideal romance "originates in the failure of patriarchal culture to satisfy its female members" and therefore expresses women's discontent (151). Romance focuses women's longing, however, back on the socially sanctioned goals of finding the right mate, learning how to read his true tenderness beneath his apparent indifference, and becoming the woman "required by patriarchal marriage and its sexual division of labor" (149). In effect, Radway believes, romance instructs women "about the nature of patriarchy and its meaning for them as women, that is, as individuals who do not possess power in a society dominated by men" (Radway 149).

33 ~ *Danticat's* The Farming of Bones

Rachel Blau DuPlessis focuses her critique in *Writing Beyond the Ending* on the ways twentieth century women writers challenge patriarchal definitions of women's proper role: "What then joins these writers is their desire to scrutinize the ideological character of the romance plot (and related conventions in narrative), and to change fiction so that it makes alternative statements about gender and its institutions" (x). The writers DuPlessis studies invoke the romance plot but, to a far greater degree than Radway's popular writers, displace, erode, and revise its writing of gender codes. Together, these important books measure the ways in which stories of romance have tended to reinforce traditional notions of gender, together with women's dissatisfaction over the boundaries constructed for dependent wives and mothers. In the more recent formulation of Lynne Pearce and Gina Wisker, "the radical potential of such reworkings . . . lies *not only* in the extent to which they alter the codes and conventions of traditional romance . . . but whether or not they *actively* interrogate and destabilise the institutions in which those conventions have become embedded" (1). In contemporary women's novels like *The Farming of Bones*, a radical revision of romance coincides with the interrogation of marriage-and-family plots, institutions, and narrative forms.

Amabelle has been fully inscribed by the discourse and ideology of romance. Her name, Amabelle Désir, defines her as the beautiful woman who loves to desire and desires to love. She interprets her desire for Sebastien in relation to its fulfillment of the needs that attract women readers to the genre: what Radway calls "the emotional bonding between hero and heroine [which] suggests that women still desire to be loved, cared for, and understood by an adult who is singularly capable of self-abnegating preoccupation with a loved one's needs" (84). In her memories, Amabelle dwells on Sebastien's attention to her, his questions about her past, and his voice "that speaks as if every word it has ever uttered has always been and will always be for me" (13). His physical features strike her as profoundly other—hard, strong, and masculine: "a handsome, steel-bodied man" with arms "as wide as one of my bare thighs. They are steel, hardened by four years of sugarcane harvests" (282, 1). Yet he embodies caring and tenderness in every memory she has of him; in her dreams, he appears to bring remedies for her wounds (282). This nurturing male figure with the body of steel is the product, as Radway shows, of women's desire: he emerges at the end of most popular romances, the fantasy goal of the narrative. Amabelle literally begins her narrative in his arms; all of *The Farming of Bones* then comprises what DuPlessis means by "writing beyond the ending." While Danticat's first novel, *Breath, Eyes, Memory*, led its young protagonist to love and marriage with a sensitive older musician, *The Farming of Bones* begins inside the marriage plot but leaves it behind. Amabelle loses her lover, if not her love, and all of her later business is with women who give her glimpses of worlds outside of heterosexual romance.

Amabelle's identity is founded on romance, however, and her fidelity to romance guides her throughout the narrative. The power of her attachment to Sebastien and to the hope for romantic fulfillment drives her choices. It leads her to refuse several invitations from Doctor Javier to leave the Dominican Republic to assist in a Haitian medical clinic. The doctor urges her to leave and hints of danger for those who remain in the Dominican Republic. She would receive a wage, he tells her, where she seems to receive none in Señor Pico's house (79). She thinks, "Perhaps I should seize this chance. But not unless Sebastien was prepared to leave also" (80). The world of work, while basic to Amabelle's life from her childhood onward, does not ever guide her choices; indeed, it appears irrelevant in comparison to the realm of romance and the defining, life-long choice of a partner.

Her ongoing attachment to Sebastien leads Amabelle to dreams and memories rather than action, and it leads the narrative to fragmentation and echoes rather than linear progression. Indeed, the complete absence of romance in Amabelle's life after 1937 is more remarkable than the fulfillment she finds in romance for a few years before 1937. Although she lives for decades after the massacre, she never marries, never enters another romance, and has no children. She has, instead, a long-term companionship with Yves, Sebastien's close friend and roommate, another spirit who is as broken as she is by the massacre. They escape from the Dominican Republic together; when they reach Haiti they stay together.

Yves' mother puts them to bed in the same room, perhaps hoping that Amabelle would "embrace her son and forsake Sebastien" (228). But they are both too scarred. They live together for twenty-four years as detached neighbors, speaking only "necessary prattle"; each has been made an isolated ghost by the massacre. Yves is as dead to romantic possibilities as is Amabelle. Although Amabelle "had often hoped that he would find a woman to love him and take him away from the courtyard" (270), and although she also "regretted that we hadn't found more comfort in each other" (274), they are isolated, distant, far less companionable or loving than their circumstances would predict.

Romance occupies stage center in *The Farming of Bones*, yet it has an absent presence. It is a marker for a place that remains empty, a measure for how much the massacre took away from the people it touched. Loving the dead, looking back, years pass in a flash. Danticat's narrative strategies resemble those studied by DuPlessis, who argues that modern women writers use these means "to deligitimate romance plots and related narratives. These strategies involve reparenting in invented families, fraternal-sororal ties temporarily reducing romance, and emotional attachment to women in bisexual love plots" (xi). Danticat's vision of Amabelle's later life minimizes these possibilities: romance is not temporarily reduced but permanently gone; the tie between Yves and Amabelle lacks the family warmth of most brothers and sisters; while Amabelle has women friends, there are no bisexual love attachments; and while she finds a friend in Yves' mother, she is not effectively reparented. Danticat uses many of the strategies identified by DuPlessis for writing beyond the ending, but the ending represented in the massacre proves to be so brutal and final that "beyond" lies only memory. Afterwards Amabelle feels aged and broken, no longer the sort of subject who can be the heroine of the romance plot: "I knew that my body could no longer be a tempting spectacle, nor would I ever be truly young or beautiful, if ever I had been. Now my flesh was simply a map of scars and bruises, a marred testament" (227). Like other Haitians blighted by the massacre, she turns to sleep, dreams, and memories.

Another way to read her romance with Sebastien, however, uncovers Amabelle's dedication to a love so strong and fulfilling that it leaves no room for any other. Her lifelong fidelity to Sebastien's memory merely carries out the promise she makes when she agrees to Kongo's request to "keep yourself just for him" (122). Similar commitments, lived out for all their lives, appear common among the Haitian characters in the novel, including Kongo and his woman, Amabelle's parents, Juana and Luis, Odette and Wilner. Love leads some of these characters to die with their beloved; Amabelle's distinction is to live for years with the vivid memory of her beloved. There is consolation in continuing to love and remember, as there is for the former Catholic priest, Father Romain, in renouncing the church for love and family. But for Father Romain, Amabelle, and all of the characters who survive, the comfort found in love appears entwined with inextinguishable sadness and loss.

Many of the stories surrounding Amabelle's provide commentaries on the failure of the romance plot. Amabelle's foil and figurative sister, Señora Valencia, lives out the public fulfillment of the conventional romance: she marries, gives birth to twins, and plays the role of the wealthy, faithful, supportive wife. She enters into, upholds, and reaffirms each of the institutions (heterosexual marriage, monogamy, the family) in which romance conventions issue, even as her story provides evidence for the problematic nature of those institutions. Her husband Pico is a tyrant, racist, murderer, but she deludes herself and excuses him. She lives with estranged and uneasy servants while her husband, a womanizer from his early years, lives in the city. Their daughter Rosalinda has married a young man "attired in a uniform like her father's" (293). Valencia's romance has performed its appointed function: it has created a social unit that survives through time despite its hollowness, a wife who is a monogamous prisoner within the walls of her home, and a daughter who replicates her mother's choices.

In this novel of a hundred glimpses, other stories emerge briefly to comment on the powerful inscription of the romance plot on the lives and values of women. Most of the minor women characters define themselves by the discourse of the marriage plot, or at the least by success in relation to their man. The quest for fulfillment in love drives women to risk great dangers; for example, two Dominican women, Dolores and Doloritas, join

37 ~ Danticat's The Farming of Bones

the exodus to seek the lost Haitian love who has been taken from the younger sister. The loss of her mate and partner leads directly to Odette's death by drowning as she crosses the river; although Amabelle believes she is responsible, Yves assures her that "Odette died when Wilner died . . . They killed her when they killed him" (249). As if Señora Valencia's story were the only fulfillment to which women can aspire, most women characters want the security she has despite its visible hollowness. In a powerful last look at Valencia and the young maid Sylvie near the end of the novel, Amabelle recognizes that

> in Sylvie's eyes was a longing I knew very well, from the memory of it as it was once carved into my younger face: I will bear anything, carry any load, suffer any shame, walk with eyes to the ground, if only for the very small chance that one day our fates might come to being somewhat closer and I would be granted for all my years of travail and duty an honestly gained life that in some extremely modest way would begin to resemble hers (305–06).

In the novel Danticat has written, women rarely achieve fulfillment through love and domesticity; but few women can imagine anything else to desire.

A different sort of desire animates Beatriz, sister of Doctor Javier, who rejects marriage in favor of freedom: "I would like to travel, escape, to go far away," she tells Valencia (150). Educated, a speaker of Latin in a culture that bases life or death on powers of speech, she sees through Pico's ambition to his opportunism and cruelty. She explains to Valencia why she rejected Pico's suit: "'There is a side to Pico that I never liked,' confessed Beatriz. 'He's always dreamt that one day he would be president of this country, and it seems to me he would move more than mountains to make it so.' 'He is a good man,' Señora Valencia said, using her customary defense of her husband. 'Many good men commit terrible acts these days,' Beatriz said" (150). Beatriz rejects the institutions that support men's right to commit terrible acts, and she speaks as if women have the right to question anything men do. Speaking to Valencia's father Papi as an equal, she asks questions "like a paid inquisitor" (77). This independent woman passes up several suitors and remains unmarried to the end; she succeeds in her dream of travel and escape, for Valencia later reports that Beatriz made it to Nueva York (298). Indifferent to romance, Beatriz gains the power to follow her dreams of self-fulfillment.

Yves' mother, Man Rapadou, rejects the conventions—and more radically destabilizes the institutions—of romance, as she defines the power of a woman patriot to place her conscience above her feelings of love. Amabelle's closest friend in her later years, Man Rapadou tells her extraordinary story to Amabelle near the end of the novel. She reveals to Amabelle that she murdered her husband:

> "I have not told this to anyone... but I believe there are many who suspect, even my son. The Yankis had poisoned Yves' father's mind when he was in their prisons here; he was going to spy on others for Yanki money after he left their jail. Many people who were against the Yankis being here were going to die because of his betrayal. And so I cooked his favorite foods for him and filled them with flour-fine glass and rat poison. I poisoned him... I should not tell you this about me. You might do the same to my son. But then you do not love him like I did Yves' father, but greater than my love for this man was love for my country. I could not let him trade us all, sell us to the Yankis." (277)

Man Rapadou feels romantic love for her husband, but chooses to sacrifice romance in favor of honor, loyalty to country, and love of her fellow citizens who would be betrayed by her husband. Man Rapadou sacrifices her own pleasure—her memories, security, family stability, and desire. She becomes an aging woman alone, like Señora Valencia, but where Señora Valencia exonerates her husband to the end, Man Rapadou faces her husband's guilt and takes the only action her conscience will allow. As fiercely independent as Beatriz, Man Rapadou shows even more courage in giving up what she treasures: she loves, enjoys, and then poisons the husband whose mind has been poisoned by the Yankis. In telling her story to Amabelle, Man Rapadou precipitates the last series of actions in the novel by which Amabelle transforms into the new (old) woman who becomes a storyteller herself. She helps Amabelle find her own courage, her own original way to speak in the face of love and history.

The real dramatic action in *The Farming of Bones* occurs during the last section: late in her life, Amabelle changes, becoming capable of narrating the poetic story we read. In the first section, she is an eager participant in a romance that, given the patriarchal nature of her culture, renders her passive and dependent. In the second section, she is a hapless victim of history. Under Trujillo, Señor Pico, and the hierarchy of soldiers, the Dominican patriarchy expresses its will; Amabelle flees, eats the parsley they feed her, and curls into a ball to escape the kicks. While she is in motion throughout this section, her motion is like that of the empty black dress floating in the river's current—itself a powerful image reminiscent of Tillie Olsen's "dress on the ironing board, helpless before the iron."[8] Amabelle watches and listens, absorbing the lessons to be learned from both romance and history. In the third section, the long aftermath during which she grows old, her main acts involve seeking news of Sebastien and waiting: "I waited for Doctor Javier's reply by feeling my wider, heavier body slowly fold towards my feet, as though my bones were being deliberately pulled from their height towards the ground . . . Yes, I waited for Doctor Javier's reply by growing old" (267). Throughout most of the novel, Amabelle is a sensitive witness but rarely an actor or a speaker.

Only at the end does Amabelle turn from a watcher to a seeker, questing after something ambiguously poised between extinction and rebirth, as she becomes a speaker of increasingly poetic language. While she feels that "New dreams seem a waste," she nonetheless turns in the next breath to a quest for new visions: "Still I think I want to find new manners of filling up my head, new visions for an old life, waterless rivers to cross and real waterfall caves to slip into over a hundred times each day" (281). These images contain suggestions of death—crossing the river Lethe, the cave as grave—but their connotations proclaim that this dire change will be a positive transformation: new perspectives, a river-crossing that will redeem the deaths in the Massacre River, and real caves to replace the lost remembered one. In the last of the bold-print sections with which the novel identifies memories, dreams, and timeless time, Amabelle tells Sebastien that she has decided to find him: "'Sebastien, the slaughter showed me that life can be a strange gift,' I say . . . I chose a living death because I am not brave. It takes patience, you used to say, to raise a setting sun. Two mountains can never meet, but perhaps you and I can meet again. I am coming to your waterfall'" (283). At the literal level, she has decided to return to the Dominican Republic to look for the waterfall where she and Sebastien made love for the first time. At a metaphoric level, she anticipates death: the setting sun rises again on the next day, or in another world—in such a place, with more courage than those who endure a "living death," Amabelle can find Sebastien again.

First, however, she travels back to the town of Alegría, to reconnect with her past. She goes in early October, on the anniversary of the massacre, and spends half a day wandering around the area looking for the stream and the waterfall. The place is too strange: "I felt as though I was in a place I had never seen before" (289). Significantly, she does not return to Alegría with any desire to see Señora Valencia; she only looks for her help in finding the waterfall. While she regarded the young Valencia as a sister after the deaths of her parents, helped birth Valencia's children and was valued by Valencia, Amabelle reflects now on the differences between their lives and thinks "I never truly loved her" (296). In their conversation, Amabelle shows a fierce need to prove her own identity, but no interest in Valencia's life and ideas: "all I wanted now was for her to tell me where the waterfall was" (296). After Valencia drives her to a waterfall she does not recognize, Amabelle leaves: "Sebastien, I didn't find. He didn't come out and show himself. He stayed inside the waterfall" (306).

This return to the scene of romantic promises and domestic harmonies of the first third of the novel exposes the shallowness of Valencia's lived-out version of romance. Valencia, the loyal wife, doesn't know what she saw with her own eyes. Utterly protected by her class and wealth, she can speak to two Haitian servants about the massacre as if it were a minor and distant trouble, a "*corte*" or cutting. "I did what I could in my situation," she rationalizes, and reflects philosophically that "We lived in a time of massacres" (299–300). Following only twenty pages after Man Rapadou's story of courageous conviction, Valencia's self-justification appears false and hollow, a desperate preservation of the privileges wealthy wives gain in patriarchy. Valencia's lifelong "romance" with Pico is a sham; the lies she has told herself in order to preserve her marriage have cost her integrity, honor, and truth. No wonder Sebastien hides inside the

41 ~ Danticat's The Farming of Bones

waterfall: Amabelle cannot recover the dream-memory of love when she sits beside the symbol of love's betrayal.

It is not the recovery of her youthful romance that Amabelle anticipates at the end, when she tells the driver to leave her at the river because "my man is coming for me" (308). Her man turns out to be the crazy "professor," an old man whose sanity has been blasted by the slaughter. This last, ironic patriarch calls forth visions of what Sebastien might be, had he survived, what Halle became, in Morrison's *Beloved*: the measure of a permanent, irredeemable shattering of identity and the proof that some cataclysms cannot be survived. Amabelle wants to call him by name and ask him "to gently raise my body and carry me into the river, into Sebastien's cave, my father's laughter, my mother's eternity" (310). But he has gone, and she does not know his real name; so Amabelle removes her own clothes and slips into the river at the novel's end. She enters warm, shallow water, and lies naked on her back. As the professor returns to watch her, she is "cradled by the current, paddling like a newborn in a washbasin." They are both, she concludes, "looking for the dawn" (310). Ambiguously poised between a peaceful death that reunites her with those she has loved and a baptismal rebirth that heals the wounds she carries, Amabelle ends suspended between two states. She is, at the last, under her own control, navigating her own course. If she waits, dawn will raise the setting sun. Meanwhile, she tells her story.

In this remarkable conclusion, Danticat leaves history for myth, patriarchal stability for feminine transformation. Amabelle the midwife finally births herself, whether to a new and different vision or to a tranquil death remains to be seen. The only witness to her transformation is a man who has gone beyond the reach of patriarchal codes and reasons, a shadow-man whose clothes drip the river, a "ghost with a smile on his face," whose eyes are "bright red like the inside of a flame" (309). This ironically named "professor" may see what lies outside rationality, history, and order. Unlike Sebastien Onius, he has lost his name, and he will therefore be one of the "nameless and faceless who vanish like smoke into the early morning air" (280). Nobody who loved him survived the massacre to tell his story and preserve the memory of his life. But he kisses Amabelle on the lips, and his kiss marks Amabelle as a kindred spirit, a poet and a prophet. A symbol for her final hopes, he reflects the creation of a different order, one that does not rely on patriarchal structures or domination.

In the way she has told her story, Amabelle has all along rejected the coercive orderings of traditional history and romance: she has included the seemingly extraneous detail, recorded glimpses of the seemingly irrelevant character, meandered, allowed the thrust of present time to be disrupted at will by the play of memory, and given wide scope to those elements of her tale that seemed beside the point. Her tale-telling is itself profoundly significant, for she preserves memories that have no place in any official script, and in doing so she takes a more active role than women traditionally play in romance. History and romance have both exerted considerable force to silence Amabelle: the force of history stuffs her mouth with parsley, breaks her teeth, and damages her mouth so severely that she can neither eat nor speak for weeks. When she goes to tell her story to the justice of the peace, she waits fifteen days without being allowed to speak, and then the justice leaves. In her romance, even with the sensitive and thoughtful Sebastien, Amabelle is also silenced: "lie still while I take you back," he says (1). At the end, however, Amabelle's voice and narration act to preserve Sebastien, to keep his name and memory alive—she takes the role of guide and guardian, while he lies still. Realizing that "Men with names never truly die. It is only the nameless and faceless who vanish like smoke into the early morning air" (282), she returns again and again, insistently, to Sebastien's name: she will be the one to save and preserve him. For this reason she wishes to call the professor by his "proper name" (309); she has found her calling in speech, narration, and naming. Her mode of telling creates a free space outside the bounds of traditional romance and in the face of traditional history. Her way of telling romances history, historicizes romance: it produces the newly self-birthed Amabelle of the end of the novel, who has a consciousness liberated enough to leave behind the rationalized narratives of history and the pleasant dreams of young romance. Amabelle ends poised on the brink of some other, better narrative—the one, in fact, we have just finished reading.

43 ~ *Danticat's* The Farming of Bones

Amabelle's is a love story first to last, but only at the end does the consciousness produced by a lifetime of experience become empowered to create the narrative. Her abiding, continuous love for Sebastien spurs Amabelle to create the narrative as an enduring monument to his name. In her lush, poetic language, we can read the trace of love's importance and its gilded energy. At the same time, it appears to have taken the experience of loss, and the surrounding narratives of women who survive romance, to enable Amabelle to produce her story. In these contradictions, Danticat finds her own way to renew romance while recalling a history the world should not forget.

Other women writers have turned to national histories for the subject of recent fiction, and their novels have simultaneously explored the ways women characters are inscribed by the expectations of traditional romance. Like Danticat, they tell history through individual figures and count the costs of political tyrannies in private, domestic lives. Indeed, each of them measures the price paid by women for patriarchal ambitiousness of the sort Danticat locates in Pico and Trujillo. Among others, these writers include Julia Alvarez (*In the Time of the Butterflies* tells of Trujillo's murder of the Mirabal sisters in the Dominican Republic), Arlene J. Chai (*Eating Fire and Drinking Water* fictionalizes torture and oppression under the Marcos regime in the Philippines), and Barbara Kingsolver (*The Poisonwood Bible* explores events in a small village in the Congo/Zaire as Lumumba is elected and then assassinated). Toni Morrison's *Beloved* and *Paradise* explore national histories of patriarchal oppression impressing themselves on women inscribed by the romance plot, as do Louise Erdrich's *Tracks* and *The Antelope Wife*. These novels depict women protagonists who lose what they hold most dear in the upheaval of history and whose stories rethink the institutions and values sustained by the romance plot. Each novel focuses on storytelling—bearing witness—as the woman's strongest means for intervening in history, restructuring love and romance, refusing the traditional institutions of patriarchy, and writing a text that not only gets out of patriarchal control but actively resists it.

Interrogating received history and rescripting the love-marriage-family plot have appealed to writers of every age, as this volume of essays suggests. Surely *Tristram Shandy* could be interpreted richly as an example of the narrative impulse to historicize romance. Nonetheless, for reasons having to do with the intellectual climate specific to the last twenty years, this impulse flourishes now among contemporary women writers. Poststructuralism made history both accessible and far more interesting for writers, with the exploration of how all language emerges from ideology; historical narratives are texts with no superior claim to objective truth. Feminism gave romance the same permeability, while exploring how the romance plot and the institutions it validates have inscribed women's choices. Indeed, with its exploration of women's subject positions, constructed in response to patriarchal codes, feminism has opened up the possibility of an altered positionality, spoken, written, and narrated with a difference. These two intellectual developments, meeting a flowering of excellent women writers of fiction, have led to several important novels allied by the common initiative to romance history, historicize romance. In that group, Danticat's *The Farming of Bones* stands out for its poetic language and lyrical vision.

Stopping Traffic

SPECTACLES OF ROMANCE AND RACE IN *THE LAST OF THE MOHICANS*

—Janet Dean

In the final chapter of Cooper's best-known novel, the body of Cora Munro is laid to rest in a bicultural ceremony that is at once funeral and wedding. Six Delaware women sing a burial song celebrating the posthumous romantic union of the English woman and Uncas, "the last of the Mohicans" (870). Having reassured Cora she will be safe in the afterworld with her Indian mate, the women step aside as psalmodist David Gamut sings a Christian hymn. Like the imagined marriage of Cora and Uncas, the two songs seem to transcend the racial and cultural impediments that would normally separate these communities. Though he doesn't understand the Delaware song, David Gamut is "enthralled" by its beauty, and the Delaware women listen to his English hymn "like those who knew the meaning of the strange words, and appeared as if they felt the mingled emotions of sorrow, hope and resignation they were intended to convey" (870, 874). Cross-cultural sympathy rises above language, and over the two graves the cultures of white and Indian mourners apparently merge. Colonel Munro, Cora's father, instructs Natty Bumppo to translate his gratitude to the Delawares in words that make explicit the suggestion of cultural union: "Tell them, that the Being we all worship, under different names, will be mindful of their charity; and that the time shall not be distant, when we may assemble around his throne, without distinction of sex, or rank, or colour!" (874).

Taken out of context, the funeral/marriage at the end of *The Last of the Mohicans* appears to deconstruct distinctions basic to nineteenth-century ideologies of the frontier, those presumed boundaries dividing pagan and Christian, white and Indian, "civilized" and "savage." But if the moment of transcendent unity seems to break down walls on the frontier, the conclusion of the novel reconstructs them. Standing over Cora's grave, Natty Bumppo cuts the lines of communication between the two groups: he refuses to translate Munro's description of a heaven without distinctions of gender, class, or race, because "to tell [the Delawares] this ... would be to tell them that the snows come not in winter" (874). Instead, Natty watches as the whites and Indians, deprived of the woman whose desirability brought them together in this particular frontier space, go their separate ways. Ostensibly a merger of warring cultures and races, the funeral/marriage is the beginning of the end of interracial cooperation and exchange.

The momentary union of two families, two races, and two cultures forged over the body of a woman calls to mind the paradigm Gayle Rubin famously terms "the traffic in women." Building on Claude Lévi-Strauss's theories of marriage as the basis of all social structures, Rubin describes a system of legal conveyance in which men exchange women in order to forge exogamous unions among themselves, consolidating their material and cultural property and power. For Rubin, as for Lévi-Strauss, marriage has little to do with romance and everything to do with relationships "between men" (Lévi-Strauss 116). In one sense, *The Last of the Mohicans* is chiefly about such exchange, as Cora and her sister Alice are alternately abducted by villainous Magua and rescued by Natty Bumppo and his Mohican allies against the backdrop of the French and Indian War. Cora, especially, is positioned to circulate in marriage: she admires Heyward, her white chaperone; Uncas loves her; Magua wants to force her to be his wife. Yet the "traffic" in Cooper's novel tests the implications of Lévi-Strauss's and Rubin's exogamous kinship economies by moving across racial boundaries, and the finality with which Cooper forecloses the possibilities of interracial exchange in the funeral scene suggests that the paradigm does not hold up on his imagined frontier. Magua's desire to make Cora his wife is an act of vengeance, not alliance. Heyward recoils from Cora's legacy of mixed blood. Uncas's potential romance with Cora ends in a scene of bloody interracial violence; their "marriage" can take place only in death. Indeed, the spectacle of Cora's *dead* body momentarily uniting cultures hints at the underlying urge to destroy the volatile exchange commodity that repeatedly brings the two groups together—to stop the traffic in women altogether.

That the closing ceremony of the novel is both marriage and funeral reflects the ways race profoundly complicates the traffic in women paradigm. The circulation of women in disputed territories can be more threatening than productive, and the violence infusing Cooper's text indicates that traffic in women is socially destructive on the frontier. In his discussion of the exchange of women, Lévi-Strauss remarks that incest "combines in some countries with its direct opposite, inter-racial sexual relations ... as the two most powerful inducements to horror and collective vengeance" (10). The passing reference to miscegenation begs the questions I address in this essay. How is the traffic in women managed when races and cultures collide? In the historical–fictional frontier, with its imperative for separation rather than alliance and for division rather than aggregation of property, how does what Rubin terms "the political economy of sex" change (183)? If miscegenation induces as much horror as incest, what is the effect on the traffic in women? And, finally, what happens to the women caught in the intersections of cross-racial traffic?

I want to examine the position of women "between men" in *The Last of the Mohicans* in order to interrogate and complicate the traffic in women paradigm. In the antebellum frontier novel, historical imperatives prohibit the establishment of a political economy among different races. The prospect of exchanging women does more than upset the sensibilities of white Americans horrified at the idea of white-Indian miscegenation; it also collides with white claims to power and frontier property, both material (in bodies and territories) and cultural. The depiction of the circulating, exchangeable woman thus reproduces and intensifies anxieties over control of the frontier itself. As dominant social structures work to contain the circulating woman, the female body becomes the object of an intense regulatory gaze. Efforts at containment build to a symbolic funeral scene in which the corpse of Cora Munro is enveloped in multiple layers of cover and closed off from the gaze of men, literally and figuratively taken off the market. The funeral puts an end to the exchange of women on the frontier and, according to Natty, in the afterworld, as well.

As it works to contain the female body, Cooper's novel also invests the frontier woman with the power to dismantle hegemonic social structures, an agency not accounted for by the traffic in women model. The explosive power of Cora's body is demonstrated as competing claims on it ignite nearly every violent confrontation in the novel, but her personal agency is equally evident in her tendency to mediate in the conflict between men, to forge her own bonds across racial divides. Collective anxieties about losing possession of the frontier can be exorcised partially through images of women brought under control on the imagined frontier. Yet Cora's racial indeterminacy and authority over her body confound efforts to control her, and the possibility of female agency she represents remains an explosive residue. Recognizing the volatile power of the mediating frontier woman as well as the dominant forces set in place to control her is an important step in appreciating the ways women function both within and against patriarchal systems of control.

FRONTIER TRAFFIC AND THE WHITE MALE GAZE

In *The Elementary Structures of Kinship*, Lévi-Strauss describes an economy of relations grounded in universal rules of reciprocal gift giving and in the incest taboo, an economy fueled by the circulation of women. Circulating daughters and sisters outside the family, clan, or tribe supports the social aim of exogamy and guards against incest, strengthening and extending relations among communities. In her influential essay "The Traffic in Women: Toward a Political Economy of Sex" Rubin focuses on the ways the exchange system helps to maintain an asymmetrical, gendered power structure where women are objects circulated among men. In such a system of legal conveyance, Rubin argues, women have no rights in themselves, since those rights are conferred on the men who "give" or "receive" them in marriage (183). "The traffic in women" participates in and maintains hegemonic constructs of material property, (re)production, and power, because, as Rubin notes, "kinship and marriage are always parts of total social systems, and are always tied into economic and political arrangements" (207). The exchange of women in marriage circulates not just the bodies of women, but blood and heredity, culture and tradition, and, frequently, material properties such as land and wealth. Marriage in these terms is a social system that allows men to construct economical and political ties with other men. Women are excluded from the economy and denied subjectivity; men are empowered and enriched by relationships forged with women as the conduit.

The economic and political motives of marriage and romance can be particularly overt on the frontier. Ethnologist Henry Lewis Morgan notes in 1859 how white male settlers "marry Indian wives and get adopted into the tribes and thus some few have gained farms, or the possession at least of valuable land" (28). He adds that "[t]he color of the Indian women is quite uniform, and is light. It shows that the white blood infused into them in the East has been well diffused throughout. The next cross with the white will make a pretty white child, of which I saw . . . a few specimens" (28). Marrying Indian women, white trappers control both territorial and biological property, participating in the national project of expansion, while the Indian female body, with its problematic racial difference, fades out of focus.[1] Economic and political agendas are reflected in discourse about traffic in white women on the frontier, as well. Yet here, women's bodies often are brought symbolically *into* focus in an effort to shift attention away from white male desire for territorial and cultural property and political power. Andrew Jackson used the image of a dark threat to the white woman's body as justification for the extermination of hundreds of Florida Indians and the appropriation of their territory in his "Proclamation on Taking Possession of Pensacola" of 1818: "The Seminole

Indians inhabiting the territories of Spain have for more than two hundred years past, visited our Frontier settlements with all the horrors of savage massacre—helpless women have been butchered and the cradle stained with the blood of innocence" (quoted in Drinnon 107). In Jackson's speech "taking possession" of the Florida territory is reframed as *re*possessing white women who have been forcibly moved across frontier boundaries. As in the circulation of Indian women, what is truly at stake in the transfer of white women across racial borders is the material and immaterial property of the frontier. The spectacle of the butchered woman and the bloody cradle—her lost reproductive value—cover over white motives. The desire for continental property is subsumed in woman's brutalized body.

The coalescence of gender, culture, and property that emerges in Rubin's illumination of the exchange of women suggests its applicability to understanding how gender operates on the imagined frontier, but like Lévi-Strauss, Rubin is concerned with social economies that work within a single race or culture.[2] As Luce Irigaray points out in her own reading of "women on the market," exonomy "requires that one leave one's family, tribe, or clan to make alliances. All the same, it does not tolerate marriage with populations that are too far away, too far removed from the prevailing cultural rules" (172). Lévi-Strauss's association of incest and miscegenation as "the two most powerful inducements to horror and collective vengeance" suggests that society guards against extreme endogamy and extreme exogamy with equal energy. Indeed, on the antebellum frontier, where the mandate for racial separation takes precedence over other forms of social organization, communal efforts aim at preserving a degree of endogamy in order to maintain the integrity of racial bounds. The drive for westward expansion disallows certain alliances among the disparate racial and cultural groups coming into contact on the fringes of European settlement; accordingly, the frontier social system requires the *constraint* of female sexuality and the *containment* of women's bodies within narrow limits. On the frontier, the exchange of women paradigm must be inverted: where relations "between men" are chiefly violent, stopping the traffic in woman becomes a cultural preoccupation.

White Americans visualized the termination of traffic in women in spectacular ways in the nineteenth century, producing countless variations of Jackson's brutalized white woman and her bloody cradle. In political rhetoric and journalism as in fiction and drama about the frontier, the white woman often served as spectacular substitute for the continent's disputed properties. Preoccupations with the body of the frontier woman—the victimized body, the sexual body, the reproductive body, the racial body—underlie struggles over the frontier itself. While the focus on the accumulation of territorial wealth and power obfuscates the racial difference of bodies exchanged in white male/Indian female marriages, the urge to contain white women who might circulate among Indian men stands in for anxieties over possession of land. On Cooper's imagined frontier, in particular, the circulation of women's bodies parallels even as it distracts from the volatile circulation of territory in the French and Indian War; as Cora changes hands across battle lines, the war for property rages on in the background.

The spectacular nature of frontier discourse points to the ways the traffic in women paradigm intersects with another familiar framework, that in which a scopic regime maintains hegemonic social order. Recognizing as Rubin does that "exogamy is an economic issue," Irigaray extends the logic of the traffic paradigm to see woman as a commodity whose value is extrinsic to her material, *visible* body (172). In the exchange "woman's body must be treated as an *abstraction*," "a transparent body, *pure phenomenality of value*"(174, 179; emphasis in original). Here, the woman on the market loses her very materiality: "In and of herself, she does not exist: she is a simple envelope veiling what is really at stake in social exchange. In this sense, her natural body disappears into its representative function" (186). Note the strikingly visual nature of this conceptualization: woman's body veils property; woman's body disappears into property; woman's body itself is an abstraction, a transparency. This movement of the primary object of exchange in and out of focus in the process of circulation is evident in the historical rhetoric on circulating frontier women: in Morgan's description of interracial marriage, property moves into focus as woman's body recedes; in Jackson's speech woman's body claims the foreground as property recedes. Such examples call for an integration of the exchange of women paradigm with important feminist theories of the gaze. Within the traffic in women, the privilege of seeing is a privilege of ownership, hence traditions such as that forbidding the groom from seeing the bride before the wedding. Producing a fantasy of possession, the gaze also restricts circulation: once taken "off the market," the possessed woman is an object for his eyes only. Stopping the traffic in women, then, involves careful surveillance; woman is no longer in circulation when she is virtually frozen in the singular male focus.

In *The Last of the Mohicans*, looking at women is a means of maintaining territorial, social, and national control. Natty Bumppo's preoccupation with "skin" and "blood," the presumed indicators of racial essence, reflects a system in which seeing and reading bodies imposes racial hierarchy. Natty's function as "scout" and tracker of the kidnapped women further demonstrates how regulating the traffic in women through surveillance is implicated in the practice of racial regulation. Natty's object is to keep the potentially circulating women ever in his scope of vision and to conceal them from the view of the racial other, thereby keeping power and possession squarely under white male control. Since Natty serves as master of the gaze (a role registered in his nickname, "Hawkeye") as well as primary regulator of racial interaction, he reveals the novel's synthesis of theories of racial and gender control.[3] My reading of the novel combines Laura Mulvey's influential concept of the "male gaze" as a means of insuring masculine subjectivity and feminine powerlessness with more recent scholarship on the "white supremacist gaze" that enforces racial and ethnic boundaries by reproducing spectacles of race as the subject of the regulatory gaze (hooks 50). As Shawn Michelle Smith demonstrates, visual technologies in the service of biological racialism emerge from and remain tied to concepts of gendered interiority in the nineteenth century, leaving racial paradigms enforced by the dominant gaze always "haunted by their gendered origins" (7).[4] The "male gaze" and the "white supremacist gaze" overlap more immediately across the ragged terrain of Cooper's imagined frontier. The regulatory gaze directed at women in the novel is a function of racial control; by the same token, the need to control racial others, to contain race, necessitates the surveillance of women. Race and gender become the mutually determining foci of the white patriarchal gaze.

In the traffic in women paradigm, women are conduits between men but never active mediators, never agents. Property is circulated, culture is perpetuated, citizens are produced "by means of," not by, women. The grammar of the traffic in women paradigm thus reproduces gendered asymmetries of power, leaving no room for female agency within the dominant social economy. But positing subject/object positions as flexible and mutually constitutive in the exchange, Karen Newman believes, may free woman from the trap of passivity. Similarly, film theorists who have objected to the seemingly intractable "active/male and passive/female" opposition produced by Laura Mulvey's masculine gaze (33), counter by theorizing the existence of the female spectator (Doane; Ellsworth; Modleski; Kaplan). Cooper's novel requires an adjustment of the traffic in woman paradigm to account for both the complications of race and the disruption of the subject/object dialectic evidenced in Cora's capacity to confound the gaze. Evading surveillance through her passing, Cora overturns the white patriarchal scopic regime upon which the traffic in women depends. Moreover, as a mediating woman Cora takes control in cross-racial and cross-cultural exchanges, asserting her subjectivity in a system that depends upon her being an object. Power circulates on Cooper's frontier, from male to female, white to Indian, subject to object, and back again.

NATTY'S "LOOK"

How can we account for Natty Bumppo's chilling refusal to translate Colonel Munro's words of racial reconciliation at the funeral? After all, Natty is known among many readers of the Leatherstocking novels as "a mediator between Indian and white" (Slotkin 105) whose lifestyle suggests the possibility of a harmonious commingling of races. Yet he is also the character most obsessed with maintaining established divisions of races and cultures. His cynical response to Munro's transracial ideal is typical, as is his disgust at the Delawares' suggestion of a *Liebestod* between Cora and

Uncas. If the Leatherstocking is famous for his friendships with Indians, he is equally known for his insistence that "kind must cling to kind, and country to country," as he argues in *The Pathfinder* (276). Throughout the Leatherstocking novels, Natty serves not as a mediator, but as a frontier border guard who restricts racial interaction. He lectures on the differences between whites and Indians and ruminates on the intractability of their "natural" distinctions. And he uses himself as a case in point; as he constantly reminds the reader, he is a white man who has lived among the Indians but remains "a man without a cross." As a "genuine white" in body and soul, he embodies "the irreducible minimum of white racial character" (Slotkin 91).

For Natty, bodily properties determine racial identity, and the body is in the foreground of the struggle for control on the frontier. He locates the basis for his own pure whiteness in the "whole blood of the whites" coursing through his veins (558). His repeated claims to whole blood are hardly necessary, since his whiteness is always self-evident: even "through the mask of his rude and nearly savage equipments," he exhibits "the brighter, though sunburnt and long faded complexion of one who might claim descent from a European parentage" (499). As a result, Natty boasts, "the worst enemy I have on earth . . . daren't deny that I am genuine white" (502). The physical body offers readable and reliable signs of difference; complexion reveals "blood," the presumptive truth of racial identity. Natty's supervision of relations among other people also hinges on bodily evidence of racial difference. His first act of rescue demonstrates the point: coming across the group of white travelers, he offers to determine whether their suspect Indian guide is trustworthy, as, he insists, "if it is a true Iroquois I can tell by his knavish look, and by his paint" (512). A summary glance is all Natty needs to identify Magua and to reestablish the boundary line between friendly Delaware and enemy Iroquois. "I knew he was one of the cheats as soon as I laid eyes on him!" he exclaims (513). By reading the empirical evidence of Magua's body, looking at his "look," Natty reinforces the divisions among peoples, saves the whites from certain disaster, and justifies his faith in what he later describes as "all the truth of signs" (707).

The reiterated reliance on outward physical signs for determining the "truth" of racial identity has its basis in what critics have called the book of nature, a concept Natty first describes in an argument with the scholarly David Gamut. Intellectual and effete, Gamut possesses the kind of "civilized" education that ill serves in the wilderness, and his dependence on the authority of Biblical passages evokes Natty's disdain for "bookish knowledge" (688) and produces this description of the gendered epistemology that separates them:

> "do you take me for a whimpering boy, at the apron string of one of your old gals; and this good rifle on my knee for the feather of a goose's wing, my ox's horn for a bottle of ink, and my leathern pouch for a cross-barred hand-kercher to carry my dinner! . . . what have such as I, who am a warrior of the wilderness, though a man without a cross, to do with books! I never read but in one, and the words that are written there are too simple and too plain to need much schooling." (604)

For Natty, written words, like apron strings and goose quills, are the inadequate tools used by the overcivilized. In his more masculine reading of the book of nature, the virile "warrior of the wilderness" gains unmitigated access to the truth through "plain" empirical evidence.

There are two circulating implications of Natty's epistemology. Control of racial boundaries depends on surveillance of a knowable, "natural" field of vision by an authorized masculine reader, a "true" man. At the same time, Natty's literacy in the book of nature is precisely what makes him a "true" man, uncorrupted by feminized civilization. Looking constitutes him as an empowered white male subject, his good rifle on his knee. The scheme creates a closed circuit of knowledge, subjectivity, and power: racial interaction is managed through vigilant reading of bodily signs by the most authorized—he who is both "genuine white" and unquestionably male—and authorization is granted through exercise of the gaze.

The link between such outward physical signs as skin color and the division of frontier property is made clear in a speech delivered by Magua later in the novel. Attempting to convince the Delaware tribe that he owns Cora, Magua expands Natty's concept of truth in nature to cast the distribution of property in racialist terms.

"The Spirit that made men, coloured them differently... Some are blacker than the sluggish bear. These he said should be slaves; and he ordered them to work for ever... Some he made with faces paler than the ermine of the forests: and these he ordered to be traders; dogs to their women and wolves to their slaves.... His gluttony makes him sick. God gave him enough, and yet he wants all. Such are the pale faces.

"Some the Great Spirit made with skins brighter and redder than yonder sun.... He gave them this island as he had made it, covered with trees and filled with game.... They were brave; they were just; they were happy." (819–21)

For Magua as for Natty, the body offers visible indications of an invisible order. Bodily signs maintain a natural, if unequal, system of property right: skin color betokens who owns and who is owned, who wins and who loses property. Importantly, despite Magua's characterization of whites as "traders," the racialized system he described is a closed economy. No transactions can take place here; rather, the usurpation of Indian property has already been accomplished in accordance with this racial system. Magua's language closes the frontier economy: his shift to the present tense in describing the whites ("he wants all") and use of the past tense for the Indians ("they were happy") reminds the Delawares of the injustices dealt them, but also rhetorically accomplishes their disappearance from the disputed territory. In short, Magua's speech naturalizes the historical imperative for white usurpation of frontier territory uttered in the phrase "the last of the Mohicans." Skin color acts as a reliable indicator of one's position in the already closed economy of the frontier.

While Natty reads Magua's "look" with care, he directs his gaze primarily on the female bodies he is assigned to monitor, tracking them when they are kidnapped by Magua and guarding them when they are returned to the possession of white males. At the same time, he works to keep the women out of the line of vision of the menacing Indian male, first concealing them in a cave and then behind the walls of the English fort. For if to gaze is to possess, the white woman's exposure on the frontier presents a profound threat to white male possession. Accordingly, the exposure of the English women elicits chaotic violence, while their (re)covery returns order, at least momentarily. Tracking and concealing circulating women protects white male authority to define boundaries between races. Women's bodies thus bear a strikingly iconographic force in the novel: moving across racial boundary lines, they stand in for the territorial, cultural, and racial power that is in circulation there.

CORA'S "SELF-COMMAND"

White patriarchal control of the frontier is emblematized in male surveillance of female bodies. Not surprisingly, then, the novel's first chapter subjects Cora and Alice to the penetrating gaze of the soldiers accompanying them as they journey behind battle lines to join their father. The episode at once defines Cora's and Alice's bodies as objects of value and draws a distinction between the sisters' susceptibility to surveillance, thus calling into question the pervasive authority of the white male gaze. Both sisters wear veils, but while Alice casually "permit[s] glimpses of her dazzling complexion," Cora "conceal[s] her charms from the gaze of the soldiery with . . . care" (488). The closely held veil mirrors the unreadable nature of Cora's body, for Cora is Natty's opposite, a woman with a cross. The child of a Scottish father and West Indian Creole mother, she has a lineage that cannot be unriddled by her "look," since her appearance obfuscates rather than reflects her racial identity. Accordingly, Cooper describes her in terms that suggest the uncertainty of her racial identity: "Her complexion was not brown, but it rather appeared charged with the color of the rich blood, that seemed ready to burst its bounds. And yet there was neither coarseness, nor want of shadowing, in a countenance that was exquisitely regular and dignified, and surpassingly beautiful" (488–89). Cora's complexion is not coarse, but also not without shadows; while she is "not brown," she is notably not *white*, either. And, significantly, hers is a permeable body: her blood seems poised to overrun the skin that would contain it, suggesting that Cora is destined to "burst . . . bounds" in ways that Natty, the border-crossing frontiersman, is not.

Cora's racial indeterminacy and her passing are literalized in her conscientious use of her veil.[5] In marked contrast to Natty's "mask" of wilderness accoutrements, only a transparent film over his pure whiteness,

Cora's veil stands for the racial indistinctness of the face beneath it. The veil differs substantially from the nearly farcical disguises donned by Natty, Heyward, Alice, Uncas, Gamut, and Chingachgook, which, as Jane Tompkins notes, "do not penetrate below the surface" to the true identity of the wearer; such costumes represent "boundaries . . . crossed with perfect impunity because the trespass is only an illusion" (116). Indeed, in a novel full of characters who apparently cross cultural and racial boundaries, only Cora's cross is material, rather than illusory. Natty is "pure," Chingachgook and Uncas are "unmixed" (504). Even Magua, whom Natty erroneously calls a "mongrel Mohawk" (513), is amalgamated through adoption, not heredity; his treason against the adoptive tribe proves that this mixture is less than skin deep. Cora alone inhabits a mongrel body produced by the physical transgression of racial boundaries. Cora's veil, like her complexion, makes "true identity" unreadable. If racial distinctions and property rights depend on readily visual markers of identity such as Natty's sunburned complexion and Magua's "look," then Cora's veil symbolizes how unreliable such markers can be. Like her skin color, it exposes the fiction of the book of nature.[6]

Because Cora's skin and facial features cannot be read in a system that depends on readable signs, her body poses a profound threat to the frontier order. That body, moreover, potentially enables further crossing of racial boundaries. Miscegenation, as Leslie Fiedler famously observes, is "the secret theme" of *The Last of the Mohicans* (205). The threat of what Heyward calls "the horrid alternative" of Magua's intention to make Cora his wife propels the plot of novel, and Cora's body functions as the volatile prop around which the drama unfolds. At the same time, Cora's admiration for Heyward and his ignorance of her racial identity in the first half of the novel raise the possibility, at least momentarily, of a marriage between black and white. The potential of miscegenation contained in Cora's passing body threatens not just racial divisions but the racialized distribution of many kinds of property. In the context of antebellum miscegenation law, Cora's descent from a Creole mother would consign her, as Munro puts it, to "that unfortunate class, who are so basely enslaved to administer to the wants of a luxurious people!" (653). Where Cora's passing blurs the distinction between black and white, it also confounds the system by which whites are owners and blacks are owned and subverts the social institutions set in place to regulate the transmission of nonhuman property among family members. In the antebellum U.S., passing threw into crisis the system of property distribution regulated by legal marriage and anti-miscegenation laws (Saks 39–69). The anxiety produced by such a crisis in the regulation and distribution of property is palpable in the horrified reaction of Heyward, a white southerner, to his discovery of Cora's race and to Munro's insinuation that Heyward might marry her (654). Cora's racial illegibility threatens not just the blood, but the material property of Heyward and his family.

More immediately, Cora's body, with its mixed blood and its potential further to mix blood, threatens the systems regulating the distribution of the territorial property of the frontier through surveillance. The menace of Magua's plan to make Cora "nurse the children of a Huron" lies in the possibility that it could reproduce—or, more precisely, multiply—Cora's pass. The offspring of a marriage between Cora and Magua would bear skin not definable as brown, or white, *or* red; even more so than Cora's, their appearance could break apart the presumably reliable correspondence between "skin" and "blood." Unreadable in terms of race, such triracial children would be ungovernable according to the laws of "natural" property distribution articulated by Natty and Magua, laws dependent upon the readable signs of difference. Cora's potential to reproduce and "remix" mixed races could thus perpetuate her boundary transgression and sabotage the frontier property system *ad infinitum*. The fact that Cora's reproductive body is in circulation on the frontier threatens properties of race, culture, and territory.

Cora's conscientious use of the veil does more than mirror the bodily properties it conceals. It deflects the white patriarchal gaze that would penetrate it. Throughout the novel Cora is remarkable for her "self-command," her refusal to relinquish control of her body (589). The quality most frequently invoked in descriptions of Cora is "firmness," an adjective that points to her physical control as much as her emotional resolve. While Alice tends to faint away at every hint of danger, to be carried around the frontier an insensible burden, Cora maintains authority over her body. Her self-command reveals fissures in white patriarchal power to regulate her movement across racial boundaries. Similarly, her use of the veil and the passing it represents are acts of self-command that unsettle the racialized scopic regime. Taking possession of her body by refusing to allow it to be read, she subverts the system upon which Natty Bumppo depends to regulate her circulation on the frontier.

Cora does not just deflect the gaze, she also reclaims it. She insists on looking, and in her interracial interactions she revises the gaze by rejecting the "plain signs" of complexion as indicators of identity. Of Uncas, she asks "[w]ho, that looks at this creature of nature, remembers the shade of his skin!" (530). And where Natty insists on a correlation between Magua's outward appearance and his essential being, Cora scolds "[s]hould we distrust the man because his manners are not our manners, and that his skin is dark!" (491). Her egalitarian sympathy defies the correlation between skin color and identity fundamental to the divisions Natty enforces, but it also grants her a measure of agency not permitted by the white patriarchal scopic regime. Hence, she has "an intuitive consciousness of her power" over Uncas (561) and a "secret ascendancy" over Magua (589). To the white men she is remarkable for her boldness and fortitude; Natty declares "I would I had a thousand men . . . that feared death as little as you!" (633). Since the gaze and its agency are attributes of white masculinity, Cora's appropriation of the gaze and her self-command amount to a kind of transvestism.

Cora's self-command constitutes the very essence of her threat, since the woman in command of her self is the female body out of control. And Cora is beyond control in more than one sense: her body's unreadable surface eludes the categories set in place to subjugate nonwhites and her refusal to judge by appearances sets that body in unchecked circulation. While Cora demonstrates no sexual attraction for Uncas, her ability to see past "the shade of his skin" makes her an eligible bride for the brave. Uncas responds to Cora's admiring comments with a demonstration of his own affection for her (533). Cora's unprejudiced trust in Magua makes her vulnerable to his vengeful plan to force her to marry him. Liminal, transgressive, racially undefined, Cora constantly evades the asymmetrical divisions of the frontier. Accordingly, her presence on the frontier is not socially normalizing, as the traditional understanding of feminine presence on the frontier would have it, but socially destructive. By breaking bounds of representation on a number of levels, Cora explodes the structuring myth of a racialized power and property hierarchy.

REPOSSESSING THE FRONTIER WOMAN

Cora's concealment behind her veil subverts the scopic regime set in place to regulate her, but, as we have seen, her exposure to the non-white male gaze can be equally disruptive, since it shifts agency from the white to the Indian male. Fittingly, another English woman's exposure sets off the novel's most spectacular scene of frontier violence and its most devastating instance of white male disempowerment. The scene, at the structural and thematic heart of the novel, is based on the historical massacre at Fort William Henry. As the English file away from the fort under a surrender agreement with the French army, the English women and children are particularly vulnerable.

The savages now fell back, and seemed content to let their enemies advance, without further molestation. But as the female crowd approached them, the gaudy colours of a shawl attracted the eyes of a wild and untutored Huron. He advanced to seize it, without the least hesitation. The woman, more in terror, than through love of the ornament, wrapped her child in the coveted article, and folded both more closely to her bosom. Cora was in the act of speaking, with an intent to advise the woman to abandon the trifle, when the savage relinquished his hold of the shawl, and tore the screaming infant from her arms. Abandoning every thing to the greedy grasp of those around her, the mother darted, with distraction in her mien, to reclaim her child. The Indian smiled grimly, and extended one hand, in sign of willingness to exchange, while, with the other, he flourished the babe above his head, holding it by the feet, as if to enhance the value of the ransom.

"Here—here—there—all—any—every thing!" exclaimed the breathless woman; tearing the lighter articles of dress from her person, with ill-directed and trembling fingers— "Take all, but give me my babe!"

> The savage spurned the worthless rags, and perceiving that the shawl had already become a prize to another, his bantering, but sullen smile, changing to a gleam of ferocity, he dashed the head of the infant against a rock, and cast its quivering remains at her very feet. (671–72)

The attacker then kills the mother, sparking a frenzy of bloodletting against the English prisoners, as the French troops stand by.

The sensational murder of the woman and her child functions as a model for Cooper's larger plot: a white woman is terrorized by an Indian man, and their violent encounter spawns more violence. Cora's attempt to intervene confirms her role as mediating figure and emphasizes her bond with the woman. She is also linked to the victimized white woman through her own maternal role: on more than one occasion Cora protects Alice from Magua by "fold[ing] Alice to her bosom" in precisely the same way the attacked woman attempts to protect her infant (568), and Alice shows "infantile dependency" on her elder sister, whom she thinks of as "my mother" (593, 602). The attacker's deception and desire tie him to Magua. As if to underscore the thematic connection, Magua's and Cora's actions immediately following the attack precisely reproduce it: Magua "lay[s] his soiled hand on the dress of Cora," then extorts Cora's cooperation by seizing and threatening to harm her sister; Cora begs him to "release the child!" then sacrifices her own safety to protect Alice (674–75). The primary triangular relationship of Magua, Cora, and Alice is replicated in the overdrawn encounter of the nameless man, woman, and child outside Fort William Henry.

This episode forces to the foreground the tensions engendered by the circulation of the exchangeable woman, whose exposure makes her susceptible to the gaze and the possession of the racial other. As she leaves the cover of the English fort, the woman's sexuality and her reproductivity become accessible to the racial other; she enters the market. The equivalency of the female body with nonhuman property invoked by the traffic in women paradigm is readily apparent here: the Huron desires the woman's shawl, but when he sees it taken by another warrior he claims the woman and her infant instead. More importantly, the description emphasizes the way possession of the exchanged woman is visually determined.

The woman's shawl "attract[s] the eye" of her attacker, and as she strips off items of clothing in a desperate attempt to save her child, the woman unwittingly exposes herself to a more deeply penetrating gaze. The performance is the inverse of Cora's careful veiling, yet both gestures have similar effects on the white power structure. Both mark a moment in which white men no longer have the power to determine who sees and who is seen.

The woman's exposure to the Indian male gaze results in a breakdown of the correlation between outward signs and meanings and a profound loss of order. The Huron *looks* willing to exchange the infant for the shawl, but his smile belies his murderous intentions. The Hurons "inflicted their furious blows long after their victims were beyond the power of their resentment" (672), while the French troops display "an apathy which has never been explained" (676). In this utter dissolution of social controls, neither the unwritten code of warfare nor the written contract between the English and French is upheld. Even familial ties seem to evaporate: Munro appears to hear the cries of his frightened daughters, but fails to come to their rescue. In the moment that the white female body is open to the gaze of the Indian male, white men find themselves curiously unable to act. The scene deteriorates into bedlam, where the constructed economy of power on the frontier is overturned and white male rights to property are alienable.

Unseating the authority of the white male gaze, the episode reflects the complexity of Cooper's deployment of visualization as a means of frontier control. On the one hand, the spectacular massacre scene depicts the presence of "other" gazes that threaten the integrity of white male control on the frontier. Just as Cora's "look" and her looking undermine Natty's ability to "read" and manage racial difference, the gaze of the Indian attacker disrupts the system of readable signs upon which white male authority depends. On the other hand, the very spectacle of violence to women simultaneously works to help white men reclaim agency. Like Andrew Jackson's invocation of the brutalized white female body, Cooper's representations of woman's victimization were circulated in a closed market of white novel readers, in a culture pursuing the extermination of Indians and the appropriation of territory. While it exposes weak spots in the white patriarchal scopic regime, the novel also returns woman's body to a regulating gaze outside of the frame of the text.

Linked as she is to the white woman in the massacre scene, it is not surprising that Cora becomes a spectacle of female victimization as she succumbs to the knife of one of Magua's men in a dramatic cliff-top struggle. Still, because she exhibits an agency denied her as a female and a nonwhite, because her body presents so profound a challenge to the white patriarchal scopic regime, Cora's disruptive presence must be brought under control not by making her a spectacle for the white male gaze, but by removing her from the visual field altogether. As her body is prepared for burial, it receives multiple layers of cover: placed "under a pall of Indian robes" it is "concealed in many wrappers . . . *her face shut forever from the gaze of men*" (866; emphasis added). Burial further encases the body in a coffin-like shell placed in a close grove of trees then ceremoniously covered with earth, leaves, and "other natural and customary items" (873). The nearly obsessive covering of Cora's body parallels the figurative containment realized by her death. Dead, Cora ceases to be a threat to the boundaries drawn between races and cultures. She functions only as the symbol of her father's vision of a time "without distinction of sex, or rank, or colour" and as the subject of the Delaware women's romantic stories of union between an English maiden and a Mohican warrior.

The death of the circulating woman in *The Last of the Mohicans* presents an opportunity for redrawing, this time more deeply, the lines separating races and cultures. Cora's death sets in motion the separation of races, as all the whites except Natty immediately depart for the nearest British army post. Her death also clears the way for Munro's surviving child to marry Heyward, thus insuring the racial integrity of his bloodline. Alice is taken away from the liminal territory of the frontier, "far into the settlements of the 'pale-faces'" where, presumably, she will bear children of unmixed blood (876). The rhetoric of Indian disappearance resounds in the last lines of the novel, as in its title: "The pale-faces are masters of the earth, and the time of the red-men has not yet come again," concludes Tammenund. "In the morning I saw the sons of Unâmis happy and strong; and yet, before the night has come, have I lived to see the last warrior of the wise race of the Mohicans!" (878). In narrative terms, Cora's concealment makes this particular moment of removal possible and inevitable, "the will of Heaven," as Munro laments (875). Cora's body, the volatile subject of cultural conflict, the explosive threat to hegemonic order, has been finally shut off from the gaze of the racial other. Accordingly, Cora's burial reestablishes the boundaries between races and reinstates the racialized system of property distribution, now signified as Indian removal and white expansion. As Cora's funeral concludes, Indians begin to fade from the narrative, and white men are (again) "masters of the earth."

As it reiterates the boundaries between whites and Indians, Cora's death also confirms Natty as guardian of those boundaries. Natty asserts his authority when he refuses to sanction the Delaware women's fantasy of interracial marriage in the afterworld. In the absence of the volatile circulating woman, Natty becomes the "medium" for whites and Indians on the frontier, "serv[ing] for years afterwards, as a link between [the Delawares] and civilized life" (875). His brand of intercultural and interracial exchange, limited and regulated according to the plain signs of racial difference, replaces the culturally destabilizing presence of the woman "between men." The closing scene features the sentimental union of Natty and Chingachgook forged *without* exchanging women: "Chingachgook grasped the hand that, in the warmth of feeling, the scout had stretched across the fresh earth, and in that attitude of friendship, these two sturdy and intrepid woodsmen bowed their heads together, while scalding tears fell to their feet, watering the grave of Uncas, like drops of falling rain" (877). The handshake across Uncas's dead body mimics the interracial accord kindled by Cora's funeral, but its ramifications are local rather than global, personal rather than political. Childless men, with "no kin, and . . . no people," Natty and Chingachgook cannot form the broad social alliances engendered by the exchange of women (877). Their friendship has no particular social meaning and thus poses no threat to the fundamental division of races. Accordingly, the silence that follows Chingachgook's and Natty's handshake is summarily broken by Tammenund's parting words and Cooper's eulogy for "the last of the Mohicans."

Cooper's novel thus exposes fissures in the dominant ideology only to paper over them in the final scene. The exaggerated covering of Cora's body, like the spectacular scenes of violence to women, hints at the anxiety evoked by the presence of women on the frontier. Women stand for the possibility and the threat of interracial commingling, a threat Cooper's hero, described by D. H. Lawrence as "womanless," is determined to put down (64). Yet it is important to recognize Cooper's admiration for the self-regulating frontier woman as well as his interest in the hawk-eyed frontier man. Cora is quite unlike the women Cooper condescendingly warns away from his novel in its preface, those "young ladies, whose ideas are usually limited by the four walls of a comfortable drawing room" (472); her mobility on the frontier is at the heart of her appeal. In Cora, more importantly, Cooper reveals discomfort with white expansionist strategies. Cora's disruptive, unreadable body exposes the defects of the book of nature and undercuts the idealization of its chief spokesman, Natty Bumppo. Her presence in *The Last of the Mohicans* demonstrates the patent artificiality of the racialized code of the frontier, the code that makes "natural" the territorial claim and cultural ascension of those with white skins. With Cora, Cooper begins to demythologize white claims to North American territory.

Still, Cora's death suggests that Cooper writes within a culture that would not accommodate the radical possibilities represented by the circulating, mediating woman and her uncontrolled body. Killing off Cora, Cooper instantiates the system intent on containing woman and endorses the white patriarchal project of asymmetrically dividing the frontier. Cora is sacrificed to the promise of white civilization embodied by Alice, who retreats to the white settlements, "where her tears had, at last, ceased to flow, and had been succeeded by the bright smiles which were better suited to her joyous nature" (876). The sacrifice enables the racially segregated happy ending that her white sister, and by implication white culture, will enjoy.

What "Race" Is the Sheik?

REREADING A DESERT ROMANCE

—Susan L. Blake

A willful young Englishwoman, rich, titled, and twenty-one, pooh-poohs the advice of her brother and other guardians of her virtue and undertakes an unchaperoned Algerian desert tour. On day one, she rides into exactly the fate her advisers have implied but been too discreet to spell out: capture and rape by an Arab sheik. She comes to love the sheik and makes him realize he loves her. He is revealed in the end to be no Arab at all, but an Englishman in disguise, and all signs indicate that the lovers will live happily ever after in the desert.

This story so captured the twentieth-century imagination that it is familiar today to people who don't recognize its title, never heard of its author, and haven't seen the movie. E. M. Hull's *The Sheik* created a sensation when it was published in Britain in 1919 and the United States in 1921. In America, it was the first novel to appear on the bestseller list two years in a row; by 1965, it had sold 1,194,000 hardback copies, long-term sales comparable to those of the canonized school texts *Elmer Gantry* and *The Sun Also Rises* (Hackett 123, 125, 235, 237). It was reissued in paperback in the 1920s, '40s and '60s. The story achieved a worldwide audience through the 1921 film adaptation, which made Rudolph Valentino a star and generated the term "sheik" for a man with sex appeal.[1] The story's success inspired a sequel, *The Sons of the Sheik* (1925), also filmed with Valentino, and countless imitations, variants, and parodies still circulating in secondhand bookstores. Recent critics credit *The Sheik* with establishing the formula not only for desert romances of the 1920s (Melman 91; Anderson 189) but for the mass-market romances that flourish today (Raub 123). Recent editions, from Barbara Cartland's 1977 condensation inaugurating her "Library of Love" series to a 1996 edition from Virago, suggest that the novel lives on not only as formula but as romance. Kate Saunders's introduction to the Virago edition concludes, "Enjoy."

From the scandalized reviewers of the 1920s to feminist scholars of the last two decades, critics have read *The Sheik* as a story about sex and gender. In 1921, the *Literary Review* identified as the "central idea" the fact that the heroine, Lady Diana Mayo, comes to love her captor and rapist, and pronounced it "poisonously salacious." The *New York Times Book Review* found it unrealistic and regressive: "to swallow the facts" it would be necessary "to revert to the old caveman ideal, to admit that women may be beaten into spiritual submission by strength" (24–25). An early feminist critic, Rachel Anderson, repeated the point in 1974: "*The Sheik* is the most immoral of any of the romances ... because of the ... totally unprincipled precept that the reward of rapists is a lovely English heiress with a look of misty yearning in her eyes" (188). Recent feminist critics, reading the novel in the literary context of the seduction novel tradition and the social context of attitudes toward female sexuality in the 1910s have followed the lead of Beatrice Hofstadter, who views Diana's submission to her captor as a paradoxical victory—"not the one Mrs. [Elizabeth Cady] Stanton had fought for, but ... a distinctly female triumph" (114). In contrast to the traditional seduction novel, Carol Thurston observes, *The Sheik* permits the heroine "to be both seduced and virtuous" (38). In a world governed by the double standard and haunted by fear of women's sexual emancipation, Billie Melman argues, it allowed a woman to "pursue pleasure without being punished for her presumption"(93). Further, Patricia Raub points out, the heroine's submission is only half the story: Diana also makes the Sheik love her. Thus union with her captor and rapist gives Diana power, both through the Sheik, as she becomes the consort of an autonomous ruler, and over him, as she converts his sexual aggression to love (125–26).

Whether they have found *The Sheik* immoral or empowering, all these critics focus on sex and gender. But the story of an Englishwoman falling in love with an Arab and an Arab turning into an Englishman is equally, and relatedly, a story about race. If the seduction plot is central to *The Sheik*, so is the miscegenation plot. If the spectacle of an Englishwoman falling in love with her rapist violated 1920s readers' mores, so did that of an Englishwoman falling in love with an Arab.[2] If the novel is a document about the self-perception of women in a patriarchal society on the brink of women's suffrage, it is also a document about the self-perception of white women in an imperial society whose racial foundation was beginning to crack.

In one sense, *The Sheik* fits predictably into the imperial ideology of race. Its "Arabs" are colonial representations of "good" and "bad" natives, where the "good" are childish and worshipful and the "bad" are projections of the colonizer's fear of his own sexuality. Its "good" Arabs are associated with Europeans: the Sheik's best friend and his valet are both French. Its "bad" Arabs are associated with "burly" Nubians, who despite their burliness are so weak the captive Diana commands them with an imperious look. The fact that the autonomous ruler of an Arab clan and the one man an English woman can fall in love with turns out to be English himself underscores imperial-patriarchal ideology: English superiority will out. The "Arab" qualities approved in the English hero—imperiousness and complete freedom—reflect an Orientalist discourse that serves the interests of an English aristocracy that claims these privileges for itself. While our Sheik demonstrates independence of the French colonial administration in Algeria, the image of an English ruler over devoted Arabs serves the interests of English colonialism both in general and in competition with the French. In fact, the dual character of the hero neatly negotiates the paradox of Britain's official stance toward Arabs at the time of the novel's publication, when its post–World War I division of the Ottoman spoils with France required thinking of Arabs idealized as allies during the war as now unfit for self-government. Like T. E. Lawrence, famous by the end of the war as a leader of Arabs, Sheik Ahmed Ben Hassan, né Viscount Glencaryll, represents both the idealized Arab and the English grip on actual power.[3]

Analysis of *The Sheik* as a buttress of imperial ideology is both textually grounded and necessary. Yet it does not account for what I find the most startling facts of the text: in a culture that divided humanity into biologically fixed and hierarchically ranged races, *The Sheik* creates a character who "is" both Arab and English. In a culture terrified of miscegenation, it permits an English lady not only to fall in love with a man she believes to be Arab, but to continue to think of him as Arab after his "real" identity is revealed and to settle into implied marriage with him in an Arab environment. As a popular novel, *The Sheik* necessarily supports the prevailing ideology of its time, but the nonconforming facts raise the question of what else it is doing. It has become a truism that, in Fredric Jameson's words, every form of mass culture has a dimension that "remains implicitly, and no matter how faintly, negative and critical of the social order from which, as a product and commodity, it springs" (144). Recent readings of race in colonial texts explore how these texts support and indeed constitute the prevailing social order. But how do the dissenting dimensions of popular texts work? Feminist readings of *The Sheik* and the whole romance genre changed when critics began to measure romance texts against the gender assumptions of their social contexts rather than a feminist ideal. The reading of *The Sheik* as a buttress of imperial racial ideology outlined above measures it against a nonracialist ideal. I will read it instead against two issues of its own time that coalesce in a romance where the heroine abandons English patriarchy for the "Arab" hero: race and divorce.

THE DISCOURSE OF RACE IN THE 1910s AND 1920s

In 1911, W. E. B. Du Bois summarized the prevailing trans-Atlantic racial philosophy as follows: "The central idea of that philosophy has been that there are vast and, for all practical purposes, unbridgeable differences between the races of men, the whites representing the higher nobler stock, the blacks the lower meaner race. Between the lowest races (who are certainly undeveloped and probably incapable of any considerable development) and the highest, range the brown and yellow peoples with various intermediate capacities" (59). In Britain, imperialists and anti-imperialists alike asserted or assumed the unbridgeable gulf between races and the duty of the lighter to govern the darker. The casualness of this assumption is conveyed in remarks like *The Spectator*'s argument for the postwar allocation of Syria to France: "Somebody must own it. That being so, we must obviously want to see it owned by a friendly power" ("Future of Syria"). Advocates of colonial education aimed to preserve racial distinction by making "of the African a better and more efficient African and not an imitation white man" (Lugard 64; Ormsby-Gore 247–50). Socialists condemned economic imperialism as "rapacious . . . exploitation" but defended European government in Africa as guardianship of "non-adult" races (Woolf 354; Webb).

Fixed as racial boundaries seemed, however, they were subject to the stresses of a changing world. Indian, African, and Arab nationalism, the growing power of "coloured" Japan, the presence of colonial students in Britain, allied dependence on colonial and African American troops in World War I—all tended to undermine racial certainties. In the 1910s race and especially "race relations" were topics of intense inquiry and debate. Du Bois's summary of the prevailing philosophy of race appears in his review of a 1911 international congress on race, which provided a forum for a liberal humanist challenge to the eugenicist position that races were biologically distinct and would be degraded by mixing. The First (and last) Universal Races Congress brought together two thousand academics, government officials, and moral leaders from Europe, Asia, Africa, and the Americas (Biddiss 37–38). Its published *Papers* reveal both the avant garde of contemporary racial thinking and the limits of liberal thought. A questionnaire included in the proceedings identifies the scientific questions at issue: whether physical differences imply mental differences; whether physical and mental characteristics are inherited or conditioned by environment and thus whether they are fixed or subject to change in the short or long term; and whether "so far at least as intellectual and moral aptitudes are concerned, we ought to speak of civilisations where we now speak of races" (Spiller xiv–xvi).

Most, though not all, of the anthropological papers argued that mental differences between human groups reflected environment rather than biology and that so-called races were already the product of mixture and change; some drew the explicit conclusion, which Congress organizer Gustav Spiller imposes on the whole collection in his preface, that, in the words of Franz Boas, "the old idea of absolute stability of human types must . . . evidently be given up, and with it the belief of the hereditary superiority of certain types over others" (103). The logic of individual papers and the harmony of the Congress broke down, however, at the question of practical race relations in the present. While Indian and African speakers argued for changes in colonial administration that recognized the humanity of nonwhite peoples (Rich, "Baptism" 544), many European speakers retreated from the implications of their own analyses. Cambridge psychologist Charles S. Myers, for example, opened his Congress paper with the assertion that there was no essential mental difference between primitive peoples and European peasants, but closed it with the assertion that the environmental changes necessary to bring the lowest races up to the level of the highest would take "many hundreds of thousands of years" (73, 78).

In popular and political discourse, practical race relations often boiled down to sex. Travel writer Mary Gaunt admitted that the gulf of knowledge and culture between black and white "might [be], and sometimes is bridged," but insisted on "that other great bar, the barrier of sex" (*Alone* 16). Political discourse constructed miscegenation as the alternative to European colonial rule. Abandon colonialism and you get miscegenation; allow miscegenation and you get black supremacy: "That there should be any mingling of the races is unthinkable; so I hope that the white man will always rule Africa with a strong hand," said Gaunt (16). Just how easily the least suggestion of African autonomy could be interpreted as advocating miscegenation is apparent in the rhetorical question with which

73 ~ What "Race" Is the Sheik?

Sir Harry H. Johnston introduced the issue at the end of an address recommending territorial segregation in South Africa as a way of fostering racial harmony. "So," he said, anticipating the assumptions of his audience or projecting his own upon them, "you will say I am advocating miscegenation" ("Race Problems" 612). Stephen Black's 1919 essay, "Black Men and White Women," lays bare the three-way connection among antimiscegenation discourse and colonial and gender politics. The ironically named Black condemned the marriage of the great boxer Jack Johnson to a white woman and "the monstrosity of importing for the war thousands of black, red, and yellow males from Africa, Asia, and America . . . to taste for the first time the fleshpots of France," but approved what he represented as the German practice of colonial concubinage because it affirmed the white man as "the conqueror—the male animal who takes possession of the female." What he found "repulsive" in the union of black man and white woman was "the idea of such an affair being an equal match" (357, 356)—that is, that the black man's gender superiority would balance the white woman's racial superiority and make a mockery of white supremacy.

Colonialism and miscegenation are further linked by a rhetoric of threat and protection, whose repeated adjustments raise the question, Who is protecting whom? Liberal colonial rhetoric cast the empire as protector of the native against the venality of indigenous rulers and the greed of European traders. Antimiscegenation rhetoric cast the white man as protector of the white woman against the sexual aggression of the native. Thus the "black peril" of political resistance to white rule in South Africa was expressed as the threat of assaults by black men on white women, which justified segregation and antimiscegenation laws.[4] Similarly, E. D. Morel campaigned against what he considered the unfair punishment of Germany and empowerment of France in the Treaty of Versailles by linking it to the threat supposedly posed to German women by French African troops of occupation (Cline 126–29). He also cast his campaign against the use of African troops as a means of protecting Africans from contamination by Western culture (Rich *Race* 41–42).

Anxiety about miscegenation gave practical urgency to the question of how to classify persons of apparently intermediate or ambiguous race.

What race were Arabs, Indians, and other non-African but also non-European peoples? Confident contradictions abounded. In his Universal Races Congress paper in 1911, Sir Harry Johnston identified Arabs, along with Persians and Afghans, as "white men" in contrast to the "brown and yellow peoples of Asia" ("World-Position" 334); in his 1924 address on South Africa, he considered Arabs members of a "whitey-brown" or "half-white Negroid (*not* Negro)" race that also included Berbers, Egyptians, Hamites, Fula, and Hindus ("Race Problems" 602–3, 612). At least three discourses of Arab racial identity circulated in Britain in the 1910s. As Edward Said demonstrates, hardline imperial discourse, represented by the rhetoric and policy of Lords Balfour and Cromer, assumed a binary division of humanity that bundled Arabs and other "Orientals" with sub-Saharan Africans as "subject races," understood to be culturally "opposite to" Europeans or "ruling races" (31–39). This binary division effectively constructs subject races as "black." Johnston's eventual identification of Arabs as intermediate between white and black represents a liberal three-part division of races that ultimately implies continuity, transition, even mingling, rather than distinction, between black and white, subjects and rulers.

A third discourse, practiced by Lady Anne Blunt and Richard Burton among others, idealizes "true Arabs" for the very qualities the English aristocracy claimed for itself, "superiority in point of birth" and "absolute independence."[5] This romantic-aristocratic discourse constructs Arabs as worthy of admiration and imitation by whites (literally, as Burton and T. E. Lawrence assumed Arab identity) and separates character from color, but preserves the idea of pure races and sidesteps the question of miscegenation. Lady Anne Blunt illustrates this side step in her description of the well-known Damascus couple Lady Jane Digby and Sheik Medjuel el Mezrab (whose marriage may have inspired the fictional union in *The Sheik*). Lady Anne devotes six pages to admiration of Medjuel, whose "dark olive complexion" she pronounces a sign of his "good Bedouin blood," but barely mentions "the strange accident of his marriage with an English lady," except to assure the reader that it has "not estranged him from the desert" (8–9). The judgment of Richard Burton's wife Isabel on the same marriage illustrates the more conventional imperialist attitude toward intermarriage. Lady Burton finds it "incomprehensible . . . how [Jane] could have given up all she had in England to live with that dirty little black—or nearly so—husband," even though "he was a very intelligent and charming man in any light but as a husband. That made me shudder" (Wilkins 394–95).

In the context of early twentieth-century racial discourse, Hull's story of an Englishwoman who falls in love with an Arab and an Arab who turns into an Englishman poses the key racial questions of its time: What is an Arab? What is race? How should the races interrelate? *The Sheik* dramatizes these questions in the language of a popular discourse that had reduced them to a simultaneous fear of and fascination with miscegenation.

RACE IN *THE SHEIK*

"He is not an Arab," replied Saint Hubert with sudden, impatient vehemence. "He is English."
Diana looked up at him swiftly with utter bewilderment in her startled eyes. "I don't understand," she faltered. "He hates the English." (243–44)

How we read race in *The Sheik* depends on how we read the race of the Sheik, which depends in turn on whether we hear more clearly the male voice of Raoul de Saint Hubert or the female voice of Diana Mayo and whether we pay more attention to the plot, which turns the Sheik English in the end, or to the story, which tries out a series of racial positions.

The evidence that Ahmed Ben Hassan is English is the story of his parentage that Raoul tells Diana late in the novel. Ahmed's mother was a young Spanish noblewoman, who, like many of the Spanish nobility, had "Moorish blood" in her veins (244), which, with his desert upbringing, accounts for the Sheik's "pure Arab" appearance (249). The Spanish noblewoman was married at seventeen, "without any regard to her own wishes," to the Earl of Glencaryll, who "had a terrible temper," drank too much, and made "her life . . . one long torture" (247–48). After one particularly horrific episode on a desert expedition, she ran away, pregnant, and was found by followers of Sheik Ahmed Ben Hassan. She refused to identify herself until she was dying, two years later, lest she or her son be returned to the husband whose "periodical drinking fits made him a very fiend of cruelty," but whom she nevertheless "loved . . . loyally to the end" (249). The childless Sheik adopted her son, named the boy after himself, and raised him as his heir. When the young Ahmed was told his story at the age of twenty-one, he became "the cruel, merciless man he has been ever since" (256) and undertook vengeance on all the English, vengeance that has led him to crave possession of Diana.

There are several points to note about this story beyond its revelation of Ahmed's European parentage. First, it is told by one of two principal voices in the novel, and its conclusions are never fully accepted by the other. Second, it contradicts the terms of the racial ideology it is meant to satisfy. Finally, it is a story of wife abuse by an English lord.

Broadly speaking, Raoul voices a biological understanding of race, Diana a cultural one. But neither is consistent. The novel enlists Raoul to bring a love affair between an English girl and an Arab sheik into conformity with an ideology of racial purity. But firmly as Raoul asserts that the Sheik is "English," his explanation of Ahmed's racial origin contradicts the principles of biological racial purity. He considers Ahmed "English" despite "Moorish blood" and "pure Arab" appearance and excuses the miscegenation that would have occurred if the elder Sheik had married Ahmed's mother with the statement that "even my father, who has a horror of mixed marriages, was impelled to admit that any woman might have been happy with Ahmed Ben Hassan" (247). Though Raoul's role is to free the love story from the barrier of miscegenation, he seems to understand race as a matter of social status rather than genetic inheritance. The elder Sheik's nobility would have made him a fit husband for the white woman, even in the view of one who "has a horror of mixed marriages," and the younger Ahmed's Moorish ancestry is apparently neutralized by the Spanish nobility through which he has inherited it. The contradictions in Raoul's explanation betray the necessity to make the romantic hero safely English while distancing marital impropriety through the victimized and deserting wife's Spanish nationality and the cruel husband's Scottish title.

77 ~ What "Race" Is the Sheik?

Diana never accepts Raoul's conclusion that the Sheik "is English." By the time Raoul tells his story, near the end of the novel, she has long since fallen in love with Ahmed as an Arab:

> He was a brute, but she loved him, loved him for his very brutality and superb animal strength. And he was an Arab! A man of different race and colour, a native; Aubrey [her brother] would indiscriminately class him as a "damned nigger." She did not care. It made no difference. A year ago, a few weeks even, she would have shuddered with repulsion at the bare idea, the thought that a native could even touch her had been revolting, but all that was swept away ... (133–34)

In this passage, Diana accepts the idea of racial difference based on color, but denies that difference matters. (Though she accepts male brutality, she does not tie it to Arab identity; the *and* between "he was a brute" and "he was an Arab" and the exclamation point after "Arab" separate the two identifiers.) Like Johnston, she positions "Arab" midway between white and black. Though she considers her brother Aubrey, who apparently takes Lord Cromer's binary view, wrong to conflate Arab and black, the Sheik is still a man of a "different race and colour," a member of the subject race of "natives," a man whose touch would make Isabel Burton shudder.

When Raoul reveals Ahmed's European parentage, Diana does not give up the idea that he is Arab, but adopts the romantic-aristocratic definition of Arab:

> The proud, fierce nature and passionate temper he had inherited, the position of despotic leadership in which he had been reared, the adulation of his followers and the savage life in the desert, free from all restraint, had combined to produce the haughty unconventionalism that would not submit to the ordinary rules of life. She could not think of him as an Englishman. The mere accident of his parentage was a factor that weighed nothing. He was and always would be an Arab of the wilderness. (258–59)

Here, "Arab" identity is a matter of culture rather than birth, but even more a matter of choice—of refusal to conform to English social conventions. In her first declaration, Diana has accepted difference and insisted on union. Now that the barrier to union has been removed, she insists on, even invents, difference. In the end, the "Arabness" of Diana's Sheik is the same quality she heard in his voice before she met him (when he serenaded her, unseen, outside her hotel in Biskra) and called "strangely un-English" (13). As Raoul needs the Sheik to be English, Diana needs him to be Other, the antithesis of English.

Although both Raoul and Diana voice elements of the romantic-aristocratic definition of Arab identity, their disagreement about whether the Sheik is English or Arab positions them on opposite sides of the underlying question of practical race relations: can cultural Others be our equal? Both want to consider the Sheik exceptional and acceptable. Raoul implicitly defines acceptability as identity: the Sheik is acceptable; therefore he is us, "English." The impossibility of being both Other and us produces the contradictions in his story. Diana insists on acceptance of difference: he is "Arab" and she loves him. Raoul's identification of the Sheik yields to the pressure of imperialist discourse to identify any Other as inferior (as in Lord Cromer's racial binary). Diana's insistence that the man she loves is "Arab"—Other and equal, if not superior—resists that pressure and thus functions as a counter discourse.

CRUELTY, DIVORCE, AND THE PARADOX OF PATRIARCHAL PROTECTION

The tension between male and female voices in the discussion of race is paralleled by a tension between plot and story in the narrative. By *plot* I mean the sequence of events that take place in the narrative present; by *story*, the entire sequence of events, including those in the past that motivate and explain the present action. In the plot, motivation is implicit and conventional; the absence of history allows us to supply explanations we already know. The complete story, however, provides specific motivation and historical situation, the raw materials of an alternative explanation of events. In *The Sheik*, while the plot marches on replacing "wrong" ideas with "right" ones, the story retains contestatory ideas. While the plot replaces Diana's Arab lover with an English one, the story muddles the meanings of English and Arab identity. The fact that Raoul tells Diana a story to prove that the Sheik is English advances the plot. But the story he tells complicates and undercuts it.

The story that an English boy became—and remained—an Arab man because an English lord abused his wife generates multiple challenges to the linchpin of patriarchal-imperialist racial discourse: the construction of "native" as sexual threat to, and white man as protector of, white woman. The plot evokes this construction when Diana walks into the anticipated trap of capture and rape by an Arab sheik and reinforces it in the masochistic opening of Diana's first declaration of love: "He was a brute, but she loved him, loved him for his very brutality and superb animal strength. And he was an Arab!" (133–34). The plot allows the reader to identify the brute who captures, rapes, and sexually awakens the English girl as "Arab" and the honorable man who repents of his conquest and selflessly stifles his declaration of love until the lady shows she would rather kill herself than leave him as "English." But the story rebuts the plot. The information that the captor and rapist is not Arab but English and has come to live as an Arab because of his English father's wife abuse attaches sexual violence, not once but twice, to the English. The story of another unprotected European woman, Ahmed's mother, whose abuser was English and rescuer Arab reverses the stereotypical racial roles, linking the sexual violence attributed to the Other to marital violence committed within the family. The plot provides enough tremulous anticipation of Arab violence to satisfy patriarchal expectations, but the story undermines the patriarchal premise that sexual threat comes from the Other and protection from the English. In Jameson's terms, the plot reinforces the social order; the story accommodates those wayward elements that criticize and negate it.

The challenge to the patriarchal discourse of threat and protection is articulated early in the novel in Diana's analysis of the arguments against her desert expedition as men's means of manipulating her for their own convenience. Her brother Aubrey's objection to her trip, she understands, might reflect "some latent feelings with regard to the inadvisability of her behavior, . . . but it was thoughts of his own comfort [that is, her assistance on his own "hunting trip" for a rich wife to give him an heir] that were troubling him most" (29–30). The timid suitor Arbuthnot personifies empty protective rhetoric, as he employs the arguments and rhetorical strategies Diana deconstructs:

"It isn't safe," persisted Arbuthnot.
   She flicked the ash from her cigarette carelessly. "I don't agree with you. I don't know why everybody is making such a fuss about it. Plenty of other women have travelled in much wilder country than this desert."
   He looked at her curiously. She seemed to be totally unaware that it was her youth and her beauty that made all the danger of the expedition. He fell back on the easier excuse.
   "There seems to be unrest amongst some of the tribes. There have been a lot of rumours lately," he said seriously.
   She made a little movement of impatience. "Oh, that's what they always tell you when they want to put obstacles in your way. The authorities have already dangled that bogey in front of me. I asked for facts and they only gave me generalities...." (9)

In revealing Diana's ignorance of sex, the passage supports the patriarchal assumption behind Arbuthnot's frustration: if Diana understood sex ("her youth and her beauty"), she would understand the danger posed by the Arabs. But it also pits the historical achievement of women travelers ("plenty of other women") against a myth of female vulnerability and interprets a stereotype of Arabs ("unrest amongst the tribes") as a device to manipulate women's behavior. Arbuthnot's silences and euphemisms illustrate Diana's point that patriarchy protects women from "facts" in order to control them. At the same time, the passage itself practices a protective propriety by refraining from spelling out the connection Arbuthnot implies between race and sex. Like the novel as a whole, the passage conforms to the requirements of patriarchal discourse as it challenges them.

   The story of Ahmed's father's wife abuse provides, near the end of the novel, a reminder of patriarchal control of women that is both more serious than the control Diana complains about in the beginning and safely situated in the past. The story of wife abuse is not necessary to explain how an English boy became Arab: Ahmed's parents might have been murdered by bandits or, as the film has it, abandoned by their guides to die of thirst, leaving a baby boy to be found by the elder Sheik's men. The story of wife abuse is required to explain why Diana needs her lover to be un-English. It provides a safely extreme and distant example of the patriarchal control of women that her expedition revolts against.

The ingenious explanation of Ahmed's cruelty toward Diana as revenge on "the English" for his father's cruelty to his mother paradoxically gives Diana access to the anger that social and literary convention requires both her and Ahmed's mother, who in Raoul's story "loved her husband loyally to the end" (249), to renounce. By giving up her anger against the Sheik, Diana gains access to a son's sanctioned anger against his father for abusing his mother. Both Ahmed and Diana displace anger against gendered behavior, male abuse of women, onto race, "the English": Ahmed, because he is male himself; Diana, because she must marry a man. If sexual violence is perpetrated by "the English" and Ahmed is "Arab," Diana need have nothing to fear.

In Britain in 1919, wife abuse must have stood not only for patriarchal control of women, but also for the specific control exercised by unrealistic and discriminatory divorce law. The term Raoul uses for the old earl's treatment of his wife is "cruelty," which, despite its euphemizing generality, is a legal term, interpreted well into the twentieth century as physical violence (Biggs 21–50). At the time of the novel, men and women had unequal access to divorce, and both needed to prove adultery. Husbands could petition on the ground of adultery alone; wives needed to prove adultery and an aggravating ground. Cruelty was a ground for legal separation and a secondary, but not sufficient, ground for divorce; a battered wife could not obtain a divorce for cruelty without also proving adultery.

The gap between divorce law and marital reality was a topic of acute public awareness. A Royal Commission on Divorce, appointed in 1909 in response to public pressure, had conducted seventy-one hearings over two years, at which it heard the testimony of 246 witnesses, many of whom represented organizations that had polled or petitioned their own members, and whose testimony was reported in the press (Harris 72–73). From 1906, when the controversial case of *Dodd vs. Dodd* broke a taboo against discussion of divorce in the press, until the war diverted attention, divorce reform inspired an outpouring of publication, from editorials to novels.

But even though the Commission delivered a report in 1912 recommending that grounds for divorce be equalized for men and women and broadened to include cruelty among other causes of marital dissolution, none of the recommended reforms was enacted until 1923—when women gained the right to petition on the ground of adultery alone—and grounds other than adultery were not recognized as sufficient cause for divorce until 1937.

In the 1910s, then, awareness of the constraints of divorce law was keen, and cruelty would have represented a particularly painful reminder of its entrapment of women. The story of Ahmed's parents—buffered by their not-quite-English nationality and their location in the past—permits the novel to reveal both practical and symbolic violence at the heart of the supposedly protective patriarchy and explains why Diana needs the Sheik to be un-English. The fact that the old earl is someone Diana knows, a friend of her father's, a well-known member of the tight circle of English aristocracy, associates domestic violence with both the peerage and the patriarchal structure of English society as a whole. As "Arab," the Sheik provides the heroine with an alternative to, and a protest against, English patriarchy. The fact that the "Arab" alternative is even more patriarchal than English society reveals the limits of imagination but does not negate its function as alternative. The dual identity of the Arab English Sheik allows the novel to criticize English marriage from the safety of the marriage plot.

We are back to reading *The Sheik* as a story about gender, but one that cannot be told without reference to race. What enables the symbolically Arab Sheik to function as alternative is the racial ideology that constructs Others as "opposite" to the English. The ideology that constructs white women as weak to paint black men as predators, black men as predators to justify patriarchal control of white women, and thus black men as opposite to white men's own self-justifying self-representation as protectors, gives the white woman both an injury to protest and an alternative to prefer. The interdependence of race and gender in racial ideology determines that gender rebellion will have racial implications. In its contortionist exercise of critiquing patriarchy through the marriage plot, *The Sheik* creates a reality in which "race" is not self-evident, but socially constructed, the English have no monopoly on virtue, and both threat and protection apply to both "English" and "Arab."

WHAT "RACE" IS THE SHEIK?

The Sheik's critique of racial discourse, of course, like its critique of English marriage, takes place within the frame of the ideology it protests. The novel is dual on every level. The Sheik is and is not Arab. Diana rejects English patriarchy and marries an earl. The debate between Diana and Arbuthnot practices the same protective evasions it has Diana expose. The novel is both a captivity narrative in which the captive chooses her captor and one in which she is rescued by her own people. The question is, which story, or stories, do we read? The twist that turns the Sheik English at the end functions like the tag, "And then she woke up." It creates a framework of denial, or deniability, for the story within. Does the framework erase or permit the story it denies? Does the voice of Raoul the European male interpreter correct or coopt or coexist with that of Diana the rebel daughter? Is the Sheik English or Arab?

If Raoul's version of events overwrites Diana's, the Sheik is English, Diana is rescued (from racial heresy as well as miscegenation), and the novel, like a skillful argument, questions racial boundaries only to prove their validity in the end. If Diana's perspective prevails, the Sheik is symbolically Arab; what is rescued by the revelation of his English parentage is not Diana but the story of an Englishwoman falling in love with an Arab; and we can read the story as an expression of either the desire to cross racial boundaries or the fetishization, the other side of demonization, of nonwhite sexuality. But if we see both these possibilities, hear a dual narrative, then the Sheik is Arab *and* English, and the interplay between alternative realities dramatizes the questions variously raised and repressed in the racial discourse of the time and the tension between male and female experience of the interdependent myths of race and gender.

ROMANCE AND HISTORY

Though singular in its success, *The Sheik* is not unique as a fantasy of miscegenation. In the 1920s, in the wake of the war, the women's suffrage movement, and accumulating challenges to racial hierarchy, countless novels sent plucky young Englishwomen into desert and jungle to experience metaphorical or literal encounters with blackness en route to reconciliation with patriarchal expectations. These romances implicate race in a fantasy of female identity as imperial adventure stories implicate race in a fantasy of male identity. Discussing the mixed, ambiguous messages about race and gender in the Tarzan stories, Marianna Torgovnick observes: "In any remaking of social orders and power relations, there must be two stages: first, the telling of stories . . . that make it possible to think new things, and then the painstaking transferal of the thoughts into actions. At some point in the process a certain key question arises: who will gain and who will lose power in the projected restructuring?" (69). Paradoxically, the very consistency of formula fiction enables it to tell stories that "make it possible to think new things" because the formula itself serves as a disguise: confidence in a safe ending permits both storyteller and reader to stray along the way. The same Mary Gaunt who declared "any mingling of the races . . . unthinkable" in her West African travel narrative wrote two adventure-romances that take interracial romance seriously before coming to their conventional conclusions.

Romance is particularly adapted to envisioning social change because its goal is to create a new social unit from the reconciliation of opposites. The project of romance, to bring about the union of sexes it constructs as opposite, is a metaphor for the purpose of the Universal Races Congress, which aimed to "encourag[e] between [the races] a fuller understanding, the most friendly feelings, and a heartier co-operation" (Spiller xiii). Further, the project of romance is motivated by dissatisfaction with existing social relations. As Janice Radway reminds us in *Reading the Romance*, "all popular romantic fiction originates in the failure of patriarchal culture to satisfy its female members" (151). Patriarchal culture fails to satisfy because it requires women to choose between autonomy and intimacy. The miscegenation plot is a logical extension of the standard romance plot: it ties the opposition between autonomy and intimacy that the romance plot attaches to the gender binary to the racial binary as well, and in challenging one opposition, confronts the other. The miscegenation plot plays with exactly what would be repulsive to the patriarchal sensibilities so baldly expressed by Stephen Black: "the idea that [an interracial encounter] would be an equal match," rather than an example of "the male animal who takes possession of the female." And precisely because it upsets such patriarchal sensibilities, the miscegenation plot offers a tempting if temporary alternative to the unsatisfactory structure of gender relations.

The second, more troublesome, stage of social change, "the painstaking transferal of the thoughts into actions," really depends on the "key question" of "who will gain and who will lose power in the projected restructuring." In the case of Tarzan, it is clear that, if perpetuated, the "fleeting images" the stories offer "of significantly altered relations between whites and blacks, men and women," would deprive their primary audience, white men, of "the hegemonic power they have enjoyed in traditional Western culture ... the power they have traditionally exercised over women and blacks" (Torgovnik 69). The fantasy of racial border crossing in *The Sheik* is ambiguous and ideologically inconsistent, but its primary audience is white women, who stand to gain as well as lose by alterations in gender and race relations. If history is made by the incremental negotiation between gain and loss, the ambiguity between gain and loss for women that is distilled in romance and symbolized in the dual identity of the Sheik is an instance as well as a metaphor of that negotiation. *The Sheik* reveals complexity in the fantasies it invokes, especially in the dream of escape. The fantasy of escape from English patriarchy participates—and involves its millions of readers—in both the social debates of the early twentieth century and the ongoing process of restructuring race and gender relations.

Behind the Mask of Coquetry

THE TRICKSTER NARRATIVE IN MISS NUMÈ OF JAPAN: A JAPANESE-AMERICAN ROMANCE

—Huining Ouyang

In *Writing beyond the Ending* (1985), Rachel Blau DuPlessis identifies "a poetics of rupture and critique" central to the project of twentieth-century women writers (32). Calling this poetics "writing beyond the ending," she defines it as the "transgressive invention of narrative strategies . . . that express critical dissent from dominant narrative," interrupting both the ideology and the structure of the romance plot and "[making] alternative statements about gender and its institutions" (5, x). I would like to extend DuPlessis' concept by examining challenging interventions in orientalist constructions of race, gender, and sex in the novel of exotic romance. Reading Onoto Watanna's *Miss Numè of Japan* (1899), the first (romance) novel in the Asian American literary tradition, I examine how Watanna, as a woman writer of English and Chinese descent, complicates, interrupts, and accommodates the master plot in her attempt to achieve voice in the turn-of-the-century American literary marketplace. I argue that although she operates within a received cultural form and thus does not transcend white patriarchal values and outcomes, through her tricksterlike portrayal of the transgressive romance between a white American woman and a Japanese man, she challenges white masculine dominance and ultimately disrupts orientalist means and practices of representation. Through this focus, I hope to contribute to the understanding of romance as a site in which race, gender, sex, and other power relations intersect to produce cultural knowledge. Exploring Watanna's complex negotiations with orientalist discourse, I affirm the positive potential of appropriating dominant discursive forms as an effective means of cultural resistance, but I also demonstrate the limitations and problematics of such appropriations.

To contextualize Watanna's subversions of dominant narrative, I begin with a critique of the master trope of exotic romance. A turn-of-the-century popular genre that originated with the "Oriental" novels by Pierre Loti, a French naval officer and writer,[1] exotic romances operate according to a major orientalist discursive strategy: the use of heterosexual romance to signify, legitimize, and naturalize Western masculine dominance. Set in the far reaches of the Orient, most frequently Japan, and usually authored by white male writers, this fiction invariably describes love between a white man and a native woman. The paradigm of white-male/Asian-female romance underlies some of the most popular "Oriental" fictional narratives of the time, including Pierre Loti's *Madame Chrysanthème* (1887), Clive Holland's *My Japanese Wife: A Japanese Idyll* (1895) and its sequel, *Mousmé: A Story of the West and East* (1901), John Luther Long's *Miss Cherry Blossom of Tokyo* (1895), and, most notably, Long's novella, "Madame Butterfly" (1898), as well as its adaptations, including David Belasco's Broadway play *Madame Butterfly* (1900–1905) and Giacomo Puccini's opera *Madama Butterfly* (1904).

The pattern of romantic reciprocity in these narratives thinly veils the unequal power relation between the interracial couples. However they culminate, the romantic liaisons rest upon a hierarchical structure of submission and domination, realized through the stereotypes of the willing, self-sacrificing Asian child-woman and the amorous but manipulative and condescending white "knight." In these orientalist fantasies, the Asian woman is figured as no more than the white hero's object of desire, generating aesthetic and erotic pleasure and yet herself remaining impassive and undemanding. In Loti's novel, for example, she is alternately portrayed as a "perfectly exquisite" mousmé and an insensate, soulless doll.[2] In Holland, she is referred to by the narrator-protagonist as "my mousmé," "my little Eastern wife," or "my little butterfly," and she is characterized as "a child-woman" who "[plays] at life with the dainty grace of Japan" and "[creeps] into the inmost recesses of [his] European heart" (*Wife* 1–2; *Mousmé* 38, 207). In Long, she appears as the ideal Cherry Blossom, modernized yet still feminine and submissive; or the "deliciously pretty" Butterfly, who is described as a picture from a fan and a "pretty-plaything" (57, 80). In addition to the objectification of the Asian woman, the sadomasochistic structure underlying the exotic romance is further reinforced through the trope of Asian female self-sacrifice. Epitomized by Madame Butterfly, the Asian woman readily sacrifices all—her family, religion, country, and even her life—for the sake of her white lover. Clearly, this recurring narrative enunciates the white male fetish for the exotic, ultra-feminized object of desire and suggests an attempt to naturalize access to Asian women.

Inextricably linked with the libidinal, however, is the Western colonial desire to feminize and subjugate Asia. The interplay between nation and sexuality, imperialism and desire has long been noted by critics. As Edward Said emphasizes, in orientalist representations, the sexual domination of Asian women by white men not only sustains "a male power-fantasy" but also figures as a Western metaphor for "dominating, restructuring, and having authority over the Orient" (207, 3). In a recent study, Traise Yamamoto also underlines orientalist conflations of the metaphoric and the literal—"feminized nation/female body, geographic landscape/orientalized woman"—through which "the body of the Japanese woman ... becomes a metonymic representation of Japan itself" (23).[3] In exotic romances, the convergence of sexual domination and colonial rule is perhaps most explicitly avowed in Loti's *Madame Chrysanthème*, in which the narrator-protagonist's desire and aversion for the title character also signify his ambivalent flirtation with Japan. Under Loti's mastering gaze, Japan becomes a land of "frivolous pleasure" and "pretty little trifles" (134, 169), and like its women, it is rendered desirable and dismissable at the same time. Thus, as the protagonist throws a faded lotus into the vast grave of the Japanese sea at the novel's end, he is casting off both Chrysanthème and her country. In orientalist discourses, erotic desire avowedly intersects with other colonial desires, and sexual asymmetries serve as tropes legitimizing and naturalizing other hierarchies of power.

The symbolic meaning of white-male domination and Asian-female submission acquires further resonance when we look at the particular historical era in which the exotic romance appeared. According to historians, the final decades of the nineteenth century saw a resurgence and eventual ascendancy of Western imperialism as European nations acquired sovereignty over one-fifth of the earth's land area and one-tenth of its population (Thomson, Stanley, and Perry 96). Toward the end of the century, the United States joined its Western allies in expanding into Asia territorially, commercially, and culturally and emerged as a colonial empire (94, 101).[4] While Western nations began to carve Asia into colonies, however, Japan embarked upon an era of modernization and militarization under the Meiji government in its efforts to reconstruct domestic order and fend off the threat of the Western colonial powers. During the 1870s, '80s, and early '90s, with its annexation of nearby strategic islands, its forced opening of Korea, and its winning of all the privileges enjoyed by the Western powers in China, Japan rose as a competitive imperial power (69–70, 135–37). The white-male/Asian-female romance thus serves as an orientalist discursive strategy to legitimize and maintain Western colonial authority through racial, gender, and sexual asymmetries. Because Japan was no longer willing to play the role of an apprentice to the West but became a serious colonial rival, it must be objectified, feminized, and subjugated in the orientalist imagination.

In the exotic romance, white masculine dominance is achieved through the subordination of white as well as Asian women and Asian men. By excluding and marginalizing the white woman, the white-male/Asian-female relational paradigm also articulates the gender politics of imperial cultures and underlines what Ann Stoler calls the "ambiguous positions" of white women, "as both subordinates in colonial hierarchies and as active agents of imperial culture in their own right" (634). Absent from the exotic land of lovers, the white woman in Loti's and Holland's novels is far away in the European metropolis as the intellectual but asexual patroness to whom the author dedicates his book, or she is the masculinized New Woman dreaded and avoided by the white male protagonist. Similarly, in Long's *Miss Cherry Blossom of Tokyo*, the two white American sisters are ambiguously positioned. Bearers of racist beliefs who encourage racial distinctions, they are determined to separate the Japanese female protagonist and her American lover. However, although they are subversive to white masculine authority, the sisters are in the end recuperated within white patriarchy through marriage or moral, spiritual transformation.

Such recovery depends on the thorough circumscription of white female sexuality. Whether the white woman entertains modern ideas about the advancement of women or exemplifies True Womanhood, her love interest invariably revolves around a white man, thus reflecting the anxiety underlying white patriarchy in both domestic and colonial contexts. The Asian man, on the other hand, stands for the masculine, aggressive, and competitive Japan that must be contested, emasculated, and subjugated. He is represented sometimes as an asexual, loyal servant (*Chrysanthème*), sometimes as a native playboy (*Wife*), and more often as a villainous rival threatening the white man's access to the Asian woman (*Yellow and White* and *Blossom*). The paths of the white woman and the Asian man never cross in the master narrative of exotic romance. The regulation of white female and Asian male sexuality also speaks to a deep-rooted fantasy in Western culture. As Gina Marchetti observes, "Within American [and European] popular thought, the Anglo-American female represents hearth and home, the continuation of white-defined and dominated culture. If stolen or seduced away from white men, she represents a challenge to white male identity and authority" (141–42).

Although Euro-American representations attempt to present white male hegemony as legitimate and stable, they also bring its authority into question and crisis through their portrayals of self-willed, intractable white women and recalcitrant, belligerent Asian men. The textual instabilities in exotic romances reveal that the master narrative is by no means uniform; rather, it is ambivalent, contradictory, and vulnerable to challenge.

Trickster Narrative in *Miss Numè of Japan*

One example of challenging interventions in the dominant narrative is represented by Onoto Watanna (Lillie Winnifred Eaton). Born in 1875 in Montréal, Canada, three or four years after her parents migrated from England, Watanna was the eighth child of an English father and a Chinese mother. Like Sui Sin Far (Edith Maude Eaton), her now better-known sister, she began her career as a journalist in the West Indies but for most of her life resided in the United States, where she became a celebrated fiction writer. Living and writing in an era when Chinese immigrants were excluded and persecuted, Watanna devised strategies of survival both in the literary marketplace and in society at large. While Sui Sin Far adopted a Chinese pen name to assert her Chinese heritage and write sympathetically about Chinese immigrants from the perspective of a cultural "insider," Watanna created a Japanese writing persona not just to escape the oppression of her mother's race but to exploit the turn-of-the-century orientalist exoticism, particularly the Western fascination with an exoticized Japan. As Onoto Watanna, a writer of allegedly Japanese descent born in Nagasaki, she published with major firms, such as Macmillan and Harper, about a dozen "Japanese" romance novels, many of which became best sellers. The exotic setting of Watanna's romances, their Japanese-looking cover and print designs, and the simple, spontaneous style, along with the author's various attempts to authenticate her Japanese roots, convinced many of her readers and reviewers that she was indeed a writer of Japanese origin.[5]

Watanna's enactment of a Japanese authorial identity links her with the practice of tricksterism, a major cultural tactic deployed by those on the social margins. Although culturally specific, the concepts of trickster and trickstering share universal meanings. Typically characterized by disguise, ambiguity, disruption, and adaptation, tricksterism describes rhetorical and cultural strategies practiced by the powerless to achieve some vindication, validity, or balance of the scales. American literary tricksterism, as Annette White-Parks suggests, grew out of the marginalization and exclusion of women and minority writers and has come to serve as a means of "achieving voice and visibility in a context of oppression, even of overturning the established hegemony" (2). Watanna's tricksterism included reappropriating the formula of exotic romance, a successful genre in the literary marketplace of her time, while subverting many of the ideologies and stereotypes in this fiction. In the reading that follows, I examine how Watanna both borrows and deviates from the dominant narrative in her first novel, *Miss Numè of Japan: A Japanese-American Romance* (1899). I argue that through various trickster rhetorical strategies, from the appropriation of oriental exoticism to linguistic masking, she challenges white masculine authority by bringing to the surface the culturally repressed—the forbidden romance between a white woman and an Asian man—and thus disrupts the paradigm of white-male/Asian-female romance underlying the master plot.

In her introduction to the 1899 edition of *Miss Numè of Japan*, Opie Read writes:

Onoto Watanna plays upon an instrument new to our ears, quaintly Japanese, an air at times simple and sweet, as tender as the chirrup of a bird in love, and then as wild as the scream of a hawk. Mood has been her teacher; impulse has dictated her style. She has inherited the spirit of the orchard in bloom. Her art is the grace of the wild vine, under no obligation to a gardener, but with a charm that the gardener could not impart. A monogram wrought by nature's accident upon the golden leaf of autumn, does not belong to the world of letters, but it inspires more feeling and poetry than a library squeezed out of man's tired brain. And this book is not unlike an autumn leaf blown from a forest in Japan.

Read's language not only speaks to the "Japaneseness" of Watanna's style but also characterizes her art as natural, unstudied, and spontaneous. One can imagine Watanna's delight in realizing that she was successfully playing the role of the orientalized other. From its elaborate "Japanese" design to its travel-guide discourse and laudatory introduction, the elements of Watanna's novel are carefully constructed to mimic the novel of exotic romance and to exploit readers' orientalist fantasies.

With an elaborate "Japanese" design, the physical presentation of the book rivals and even outmatches that of the most popular exotic romances of the day.[6] Embossed in gold letters, the auburn cover features an Oriental fan painted in bright color. The fan is partially unfolded to reveal a young Japanese woman perched on a rickshaw against the backdrop of Mount

Fuji, her lilac Victorian dress in sharp relief against the rickshaw man's black uniform. While the "Oriental" subject on the cover blends the exotic and the familiar, the frontispiece accentuates the exoticism with another picture from a fan, a small portrait of a kimono-clad and parasol-toting Watanna, beneath a color illustration featuring three similarly dressed Japanese women. The illustrations in the novel further enhance the illusion of an authentic representation of Japanese women with various black and white, photographic portraits of the title character and her young geisha friends, invariably subdued-looking and childlike, against the background of a domestic interior or a teahouse. While the design of the novel attempts to increase sales by appealing to readers' desire for things "Japanese," it certainly complements the tricksterlike tactics that Watanna devised to authenticate her Japanese writing persona. While authors such as Loti, Holland, and Long present the Orient through the eye of a Western visitor, Watanna claims to offer an authentic experience of Japan from the vantage point of a cultural "insider."

She also mimics the travel-guide discourse of the exotic romance. Playing the role of a local tour guide, the narrative voice simultaneously gratifies and mocks Western cultural voyeurism. The central narrative location of the novel is Kyoto, "the most picturesque city in Japan" (54), and in a number of chapters, readers are introduced to local histories and customs and invited to participate vicariously in the American characters' excursions to tourist attractions. At the same time, the novel signifies its difference from its Euro-American counterparts with the author's ironic detachment. On several occasions Watanna satirizes her characters' orientalist gaze, including the white women's belief that the Japanese male protagonist can "secure them the entrée to all desirable places in Japan" (24), Mrs. Ballard's complaints about "those queer Japanese" and "this strange place" (54, 55), and the American heroine's desire to take back "a little Japanese maid" because "they are so neat and amusing" (56). Watanna's subversion of orientalist exoticism can be also seen in a chapter entitled "A Barbarian Dinner." On the surface, she appears to amuse her readers with a Japanese geisha girl's troubles with "the barbarian [American] food" and to poke fun at Japanese ignorance and xenophobia (125). In effect, however, she parodies the Euro-American exoticization of Japanese food. Readers may recall Mrs. Ballard's fear about Japanese cuisine several chapters earlier: "I have heard such funny tales about their queer cooking . . . " (56). Challenging Western cultural normalcy and superiority, Watanna has Koto's American hosts apologize to the Japanese girl for having forgotten that she is not used to their food and assure her that "the Americans were just as foolish when they had eaten Japanese food" (125).

Watanna's trickstering appears most tellingly in her subversion of Euro-American representations of interracial sexuality. While the white-male/Asian-female relationship is romanticized in the master narrative, romantic relationships between white women and Asian men are never represented, for such relationships threaten the racial and gender status quo and disrupt the fantasy of white masculine dominance. With the energy and impulses of a trickster, Watanna subverts dominant conventions and ventures into the forbidden domain of Asian-male/white-female romance. As her title suggests, she does not discard the normative paradigm, but she complicates it with a parallel plot—the romantic entanglements between a white woman and a Japanese man. After the opening chapter of exposition about the Japanese main characters, the plot unfolds as Cleo Ballard, a blonde young American woman, meets Orito Takashima, a Harvard-educated Japanese youth, during their voyage to Japan. They fall in love despite the fact that he is betrothed to his childhood sweetheart, Numè Watanabe, and she is engaged to Arthur Sinclair, the American Vice-Consul in Kyoto. When Orito proposes to Cleo, she wavers, but eventually rejects him after months of indecision. To defend his honor, Orito commits suicide. Regretting her lost love, Cleo reforms her "coquettish" ways and returns to America, where she marries her cousin, Tom Ballard. In the meanwhile, Sinclair chooses the child-woman Numè over the American coquette, and they eventually marry and settle happily in Japan.

The plot of Watanna's novel invokes and revises a major convention of the Western romance: the device of parallel love stories. Janice Radway writes that in a typical romantic narrative, "the significance of heroine and hero as ideal feminine and masculine types is established by the existence of two abstract foils who embody those features of the female and male personalities that must be eradicated if women and men are to continue to love each other and fill one another's needs" (131). The depiction of parallel lovers may signify more than just conflicting gender beliefs, however. As Marchetti indicates, the device of parallel pairs of lovers with opposed fates can also resolve conflicting ideologies concerning race, class, gender, and sexuality. Appropriated in Hollywood film narratives of interracial romance, the two couples provide tragic punishment for those who break racial taboos and a liberal happy ending for those who can be assimilated into the mainstream culture (125). Long's *Miss Cherry Blossom of Tokyo* uses parallel love stories to achieve similar ends: the innocent, self-sacrificing, and yet modernized title character and her white knight, the American Secretary of Legation, overcome obstacles to their love and sail triumphantly to America as a newly wed couple; their foils—the worldly, calculating American New Woman and the egotistic, philandering American naval officer—must settle for a loveless marriage even though they do not meet a tragic end. In Watanna's novel, the trope of parallel lovers is repeated with a difference. Although her plot suggests another variation of the narrative of "tragic" and "transcendent" love, Watanna is far more subversive than she appears to be. While the transcendent couple undermines rather than reinforces the melting-pot image of America (for Numè and Sinclair, the land of love is not America but Japan), the tragic couple, reversing the white-male/Asian-female relational pattern, challenges rather than confirms the racial and gender status quo. Admittedly, by according the love between Cleo and Orito a tragic end, Watanna avoids overturning the established white male hegemonic order. However, her sympathetic representation of mutual romantic desire between Cleo and Orito constitutes a performative act that disrupts the master plot. Because a sympathetic portrayal of such a romantic relationship suggests a marked deviation from narrative conventions and poses a serious threat to white patriarchal order, the subject requires covert handling, a plot within and against a plot.

The title of her novel, *Miss Numè of Japan*, recalls Long's *Miss Cherry Blossom of Tokyo*, published only four years before. This is the first of a series of masking devices that Watanna deploys. Mimicking Long's orientalist exoticism (her "Miss Numè, or Plum Blossom" echoes his "Miss Cherry

Blossom"), Watanna's title seems to forecast another version of the romantic story of a white American man and a Japanese woman. Indeed, her novel incorporates several key elements of Long's text, including the parallel love story and similar character portrayal. Like Long's novel, Watanna's features an American diplomat who plays the role of a romantic, protective white knight; a half-Americanized Japanese child-woman who has been betrothed to a Japanese man but falls in love with the white hero; a worldly American young woman who competes romantically with the Japanese ingenue; and a meddling American older woman who persuades her Japanese protegé to sacrifice her love for the happiness of the American heroine. While no evidence exists that Watanna was consciously imitating Long, close resemblances between the two texts suggest that she might well have had Long's novel in mind when she wrote *Miss Numè of Japan*. By the time Watanna was writing her first "Japanese" romance, Long had already achieved renown with his novella, "Madame Butterfly," and other stories about Japan, so she was surely familiar with Long. In fact, another important detail in her novel, Orito's Japanese suicide, obviously points to the title character's ritual sacrifice in Long's novella. She was to become a conscious rival of his in 1902, when she accused Long and his coproducer, David Belasco, of plagiarizing in their second Broadway play her novels, *A Japanese Nightingale* and *The Wooing of Wistaria*, which she had recently submitted to Belasco for production. The matter was eventually settled a year later, and *A Japanese Nightingale* was produced on Broadway and briefly shared the limelight with Long/Belasco's first play, *Madame Butterfly* (1900–1905).[7] Although Watanna borrowed many features from Long's writings, she also deviated from them in significant ways. For the first time, the Japanese man and the white woman are no longer sidelined or demonized as they have been in Long and his fellow exotic romancers; instead, they become sympathetic central characters in a potential romance. However, by foregrounding the normative love relationship between an American man and a Japanese woman, the title of Watanna's novel ingeniously cloaks the transgressive white-female/Asian-male relationship that she also depicts.

Rhetorical play in the form of linguistic masking characterizes Watanna's narrative language, which negotiates, often painstakingly, between desire and repression. Her description of the initial meeting of Orito and Cleo at sea, for example, dramatizes the couple's romantic passion with a metaphoric language that simultaneously reveals and conceals their mutual desire. As Orito fixes his eyes on Cleo's face, "as though thoroughly fascinated with its beauty,"

> A sudden wind came up from the sea and caught the red cape she wore, blowing it wildly about her.... It was a sudden wild wind, such as one often encounters at sea, lasting only for a moment, but in that moment almost lifting one from the deck. The girl, who had been clinging breathlessly to the railing, turned toward Takashima, her cheeks aflame with excitement, and as the violent gust subsided, they smiled in each other's faces. (12)

While Cleo's red cape, breathlessness, and blushing cheeks signal her passionate response to Orito's romantic interest, the "sudden wild wind" foreshadows the couple's short-lived but overpowering passion. At the same time, the narrative language attempts to disguise their desire with an innocuous description of the weather.

However, Cleo's and Orito's romantic feelings do not so quickly subside as the cessation of the "violent gust" seems to suggest (12). In subsequent chapters, Watanna not only depicts the couple's increasing attraction to each other but also associates their relationship with romantic love. Simultaneously, to mask the American heroine's (and her own) transgression of sexual and racial boundaries, she obscures and defers her apparent meaning, a trickster rhetorical strategy that Henry Louis Gates, Jr. identifies in *The Signifying Monkey*.[8] According to Gates, meaning is not proffered but deferred when "the relationship between intent and meaning, between speech act and its comprehension, is skewed by the figures of rhetoric or signification"(53). Such rhetorical play characterizes Watanna's depictions of Cleo's romantic sentiment with the language of trickery that achieves direction through indirection.

Linguistic masking is clearly evident following Orito and Cleo's first meeting, as the narrative explains away Cleo's expression of desire by dismissing it as a flirtation. Indeed, echoing Tom Ballard's earlier warning to Orito that his cousin is "a flirt" (13), the narrator begins: "Cleo Ballard was a coquette; such an alluring, bright, sweet, dangerous coquette" (15).

Although she will "go miles out of her way" to gain new admirers, she enjoys breaking their hearts "gaily, thoughtlessly," "unscrupulously and impetuously" (15). "Who can analyze a coquette?" the narrator then asks rhetorically, reiterating the chapter title. The labeling of Cleo as a frivolous and irresponsible coquette blames the woman for instigating the interracial love, thus making "woman" the locus of perversity, the ultimate culprit of racial and sexual transgression. As Tom sighs, "Woman! woman! incorrigible, unanswerable creature!" (17). By essentializing Cleo, the label apparently trivializes and even disqualifies her attraction to Orito, thus removing the possibility of a sincere love relationship between them.

The narrative further masks Cleo's desire through her own denial. While she is obviously touched by Orito's undisguised admiration and jealous of the real or imagined rivalry from Numè and fellow American female passengers, she dismisses her attraction as merely a result of her coquettish and "womanly" nature. Revealing Cleo's inner thoughts, the narrator observes:

> It was a refreshment to her now to wake the admiration—the sentiment—of this young Japanese... Not for a moment did she, even to herself, admit that it was more than a mere passing fancy she had for him. She could not help it that he admired her, she told herself... That Takashima could never really be anything to her she knew fully well; and yet, with a woman's perversity, she was jealous even at the thought that any other woman should have the smallest thought from him. It is strange, but true, that a woman often demands the entire homage and love of a man she does not herself actually love, and only because of the fact that he does love her. She resents even the smallest wavering of his allegiance to her, even though she herself be impossible for him. (22–23)

Racial, sexual, and gender myths intersect in this passage to explain away Cleo's forbidden desire. It is possible and even inevitable for an Asian man to love a white woman, suggests the passage, but not vice versa. If Cleo is interested in Orito, it is only because the Japanese man is an exotic "passing fancy" of a "tired, bored" coquette and because with "the usual vanity [and perversity] of a woman," she wants to monopolize the most coveted object of desire (22, 24). Nor is Cleo alone in invoking dominant cultural myths. Her fellow white women passengers also dismiss her interest in Orito as no more than a coquette's "little game" and "outrageous flirtation" (25, 26).

Yet Watanna deliberately creates ambiguity: because these women are Cleo's "gentle enemy," their assumptions may result from their "malicious jealousy" rather than discernment (24, 25).

The repressed, however, will inevitably and repeatedly return. Under the camouflage of such chapter titles as "Jealousy Without Love," "The Man She Did Love," and "Merely a Woman," Watanna allows the unorthodox to emerge by revealing what is behind Cleo's mask of coquetry: her rebellion against patriarchal regulation of her sexuality and her preference for the sincerely devoted Orito over her indifferent, noncommittal white fiancé. When Cleo attempts to articulate to herself her transgressive desire, her dismissal of her attraction to Orito is simultaneously confirmed and contradicted. She asks Orito not to think of her as merely flirting with him, as "the coquette in her was subdued, and the natural liking, almost sentiment, she had for Takashima was paramount" (31). Later she is overjoyed to learn that Orito does not really love Numè; while the narrator remarks, "coquettes are essentially selfish" (34), Cleo is more ambiguous: "she kept telling herself that [she and Orito] could never be anything to each other, and that she already loved another, yet, after all, was she so sure of her heart?" (34–35). The same ambivalence occurs two pages later: "It was impossible that she was in love with Takashima, for she already loved another; and yet she could not understand why she felt so keenly about Takashima, nor why it hurt her—the idea of his caring for anyone else. Was it merely the selfishness and vanity of a coquette?" (37). Coquetry, though part of her character, does not entirely explain her feelings for Orito.

Indeed, the subsequent portrayal of Cleo's relationship with Arthur Sinclair reveals her pursuit of a romantic relationship with Orito not only as an assertion of her desire for love but also as an act of defiance against the sexual double standard in white patriarchy. Although Cleo had been a perpetual coquette who believed that "man is woman's natural plaything," her masculinized, deviant impulse is restrained when she meets Sinclair. "[An] ideal lover—always considerate, gentle, and tender," he subdues Cleo's "imperious nature" and refeminizes her, transforming her from "a coquette" into "a loving, tender woman" (39). However, the "ideal lover" is less than ideal. On the very night after his "passionate declaration" of love to her, he begins to doubt his own heart (39). Moreover, because Sinclair perceives himself as a knight rescuing Cleo from her sexual excess, his passion is quickly spent when he is assured of her exclusive devotion. His appointment as American Vice-Consul at Kyoto thus conveniently delays their marriage. Although neither of them is poor, as Cleo reminds him, he tells her that they should wait till he can afford to "keep my wife as I would like to keep you"(40). While she waits patiently out of "overmastering love" for him to send for her, he lapses into inattentiveness and indifference. What has been carefully buried is allowed to surface when the narrator reveals that Cleo's "proud" heart "rebelled" against Sinclair's double standard—his insistence upon Cleo's devotion on the one hand and his unwillingness to commit himself on the other (41). Later Cleo's awareness of this double standard resurfaces. As she remembers, "Sinclair had once told her laughingly that he gave her carte blanche to flirt all she desired. In his secret heart, like most men, he was opposed to this pastime (for women). Not that he was entirely free from it himself. By no means ..." (84). Thus, "It was with a feeling as much of hunger for sympathy and love, as of coquetry," the narrator concedes, "that [Cleo] had started her acquaintance with Takashima" (41). Even here, the linguistic equivocation, the seemingly equal emphasis on Cleo's romantic desire and her flirtatious impulse, indicates Watanna's attempt to disguise the young woman's challenge to white patriarchal control.

Because Cleo transfers her desire not just to another man but to a man of color, the language of trickery becomes all the more necessary for author and heroine to carry out their subversion of white masculine dominance. Comparing her fiancé with Orito, Cleo reflects: "the gentle young Japanese ... loved her—not as Sinclair had done, with a passion of a moment that swept her from her feet, but with deference and respect, and yet with as strong a love as she could have desired" (42). While this language seems to reinforce the racial/sexual stereotypes perpetuated in the master narrative by constructing a binary schema of the passionate, masculine white lover and the deferential, effeminate Asian admirer, it actually subjects this construct to ironic reversals. Sinclair is passionate, and yet his is "a passion of a moment." Orito is gentle, and yet he is by no means passionless. If we read this passage against earlier scenes when Cleo first meets the two men, the collapsing of the binary is all the more telling. While "half of [Sinclair's] passion [is] spent" once she reciprocates his love (39), Orito's love, strong enough to sweep Cleo off her feet, as the wind metaphor suggests, never dissipates. The contrast between the strength and sincerity of Orito's love and the weakness and falsity of Sinclair's becomes more prominent as the novel develops. Unlike Sinclair, who sees his engagement to Cleo as "bondage" and avoids talking about her "whenever it was possible"(89, 97), Orito "did not attempt, even from the beginning, to hide from her the fact that he admired her so intensely" (16). During their voyage and after their arrival, he "let her understand, in every conceivable way in his power, that he had not lost faith in her" despite her constant evasion and ambiguousness (96). Cleo may be unsure of her own heart, but she is not mistaken about Orito's. As he firmly declares to his and Numè's fathers, he loves Cleo "with all [his] heart" and he is ready to sacrifice his life for her (107).

Just as she subtly dismantles the binary opposition between Sinclair and Orito to suggest the Japanese man's superiority as a lover, Watanna engages in rhetorical play to further subvert white male dominance. Describing different degrees of love that Cleo feels for her white fiancé and her Japanese suitor, the narrator writes:

> Even a woman in love can put behind her easily, for a time, the image of the one she at heart loves, when she replaces it with one for whom she cares (not perhaps, in the same wild way as for the other, but with a sentiment that is tantamount to a flickering, wavering love—a love of a moment, a love awakened by gentle words—and perhaps put away from her after she has reasoned it out to herself); for it is true that the best cure for love is to try to love another. (43)

The circuitous, self-contradictory language registers Watanna's attempt to negotiate between the expression of transgressive desire and the claims of white masculine dominance. Since it is taboo for a white woman to express love, let alone preference, for a man of color, Cleo must dissociate her feelings for Orito from genuine romantic love. Thus, she equivocates. She tells herself at one moment that "I am not in love with him.... A woman cannot be in love with two men at once" (44). And yet in the next moment, she concedes that "I don't believe there are many girls who would admit it—and yet it is true—that we can love one man and be 'in love' with another" (44). While Numè will be able to acknowledge her love for Sinclair openly when she describes her dilemma of being "betrothed to one man and in love with another" (122), here Cleo must distort the nature of her conflict and qualify her love for Orito. She resumes the mask of a coquette and concludes that her selfishness and vanity, after all, make her desire Orito's exclusive devotion. However, this conclusion hardly corresponds with her attraction to Orito's sincerity and her resentment toward Sinclair's lack of commitment. As she herself admits, "I don't understand myself tonight" (45).

Cleo continues to vacillate between desire and fear, expression and repression, after Orito's marriage proposal. On the one hand, "she would look unspeakable longings into his eyes" and join him in envisioning their future together (52). On the other hand, she is also "frightened" by the prospect of life with him and avoids giving him a definite answer (53). Even her later "confession" to her friend Jenny Davis simultaneously expresses and represses desire. She has indeed encouraged Orito, she says to Mrs. Davis, but only because she is a "wicked, cruel woman" who "wanted to see how a Japanese would act if he were in love" (109, 111). A moment later, however, she admits to her friend, albeit hesitantly, "it was true, almost," that she does "care for" Orito (112, 113). Still, Cleo suggests that her prolonged delay results from her lack of courage to reject him (she is frightened, we are told, by Orito's determined pursuit) rather than from the conflict between her love for Orito and her obligation to Sinclair. The answer she eventually gives to Orito, however, clearly reveals her dilemma even as she attempts to conceal it: she cannot marry him because "I—am already betrothed—to Mr. Sinclair" and because "I never could love anyone but him" (185). By proclaiming her undivided devotion to her white fiancé, she flatly denies her attraction to the Japanese man. On the other hand, she also suggests that her betrothal to Sinclair prohibits her from loving and marrying another man, let alone a man from a different race and culture. Indeed, the inner crisis that she experiences after declining Orito's proposal reveals the truth behind her pretenses.

Not until after she is rejected by Sinclair and learns of Orito's death does Cleo finally discard her mask of coquetry. Only then can she acknowledge that Orito is "better than the other" and that "[she] must have loved him all along" (209). And only then does she confront Sinclair with "the truth" that she loved Orito although she did not know "till *it was too late*" (211, 212). Rendering Sinclair speechless, agitated, and contrite, if only for a short while, Cleo's "heart-breaking" and "tragic" confession stands as a direct challenge not only to her former fiancé but also to white masculine dominance (212). However, that she speaks the truth only after Orito's suicide ultimately absorbs and weakens the subversive power of her challenge.

Orito's tragic end, evoking Madame Butterfly's ultimate sacrifice, reinscribes rather than changes the existing racial and gender order. To be sure, Watanna's portrayal of Orito's self-sacrifice differs significantly from Long's of Butterfly's. Where Butterfly deifies Pinkerton in her last thoughts and sacrifices herself to defend her newly acquired Western notions of romantic love and the American way of life, Orito renounces Cleo and seeks "an honorable death" to "atone for all the suffering" he has caused his family and to prove that he has not forgotten his Japanese sense of duty (192, 193). While Butterfly's ritual sacrifice approximates the beauty, passion, and catharsis of high tragedy, Orito's suicide, accompanied by Numè's and his own fathers' self-destruction, is presented in melodramatic fashion, and its bloody and horrific effects are intensified by the ensuing terror and grief of their servants and relatives. Nonetheless, the representation of Orito's self-sacrifice, like Butterfly's, affirms white masculine hegemonic power. The triple Japanese suicides not only clear the path for Sinclair's pursuit of Numè but permanently sever her ties with her Japanese family and culture. Preventing his union with Cleo, Orito's death also removes the danger of white-female/Asian-male miscegenation and thereby preserves the purity of white women and restores the authority of white men.

Similarly, Cleo's return to America and her reintegration into the traditional white domestic circle at the novel's end also reveal Watanna's conciliatory stance. The novel closes with Sinclair and Numè's wedding in Japan and Cleo's union with her cousin, Tom Ballard, in America. Invoking the multiple-wedding denouement of a romantic tragicomedy, the ending of Watanna's romance signals the restoration of the moral and social order in white patriarchy. While Numè's Christian wedding assimilates her into the dominant white American culture and fulfills white male fantasies of a Japanese doll-wife, Cleo's lily-white marriage subjects her once again to the moral and social constraints of the American society. Her union with Tom not only confines her to the bourgeois domestic space and thus eliminates her sexual excess as a woman, but it also suppresses her desire for the Asian other and ensures the rigid racial and cultural boundaries between white and nonwhite.

Cleo's marriage to her cousin can hardly be imagined as happy. While Watanna describes Numè and Sinclair's wedding ceremony and their subsequent domestic bliss, she gives no detail about the Ballards as a newly wed couple other than mentioning the "strange news" of their marriage that Sinclair hears from his American visitors (220). And "strange" it is, for Cleo once laughs at the possibility that she will ever marry Tom, who often calls her "sis" or "little sis," because "[it] would be too much like marrying one's brother" (50). Indeed, readers have been informed earlier that Tom, orphaned at the age of twelve, was taken into his uncle's family and brought up with Cleo. Moreover, after the death of his uncle, "he had stood to the mother and Cleo as father, brother, and son in one" (48). Thus, not only is Cleo's marriage *not* based on romantic love but it also smacks of something close to incest. To Watanna's readers, marrying one's brotherly cousin may have seemed more acceptable than marrying a man from a different race and culture. Despite its apparent closure, then, the ending conjures up uneasy feelings for those who see Cleo's and Orito's fates as the unfair sacrifices of white female and Asian male desire. The narrator's sarcastic report of Sinclair's response to Cleo's sorrows in the penultimate chapter ("He could afford to be generous now that his own happiness was assured"; "When one has present happiness, it is not hard to forget the sorrows of others" [211, 213]) clearly register Watanna's sympathy for the tragic couple and belie the ideological certainty of the denouement.

The problematic resolution points to the complexities of Watanna's revisionist practices. By appropriating the novel of exotic romance, she represents the nonrepresentable, destabilizes established power relations, and suspends white masculinist fantasies. However, to have her book published and to avoid upsetting the racial sensibilities of her white middle-class readers, she must resort to accommodation and compromise. On the other hand, despite its final restoration of white male dominance, the novel also allows many of its narrative complications to remain problematic, as is evident in the textual gaps of the ending. That Watanna does not smooth over these gaps underscores her complex negotiations with the dominant discourse. In writing about narrative outcome as "one of the great moments of ideological negotiation in any work," DuPlessis states: "Any resolution can have traces of the conflicting materials that have been processed within it. It is where subtexts and repressed discourses can throw up one last flare of meaning; it is where the author may sidestep and displace attention from the materials that a work has made available" (3). Just as nineteenth-century fiction often resolves women's conflict between love and quest by repressing the latter through marriage or death, the ending of Watanna's novel attempts to reconcile racial and gender ideologies by deflecting attention away from her transgressive narrative of Asian-male/white-female romance. Yet at the same time, textual instabilities reveal traces of the ideological conflict.

Miss Numè of Japan is a milestone of sorts not only because it is the first Asian American novel but also because it exemplifies turn-of-the-century minority women's literary tricksterism. While white-male authored exotic romances overwhelmingly seek to maintain white male dominated colonial order in their constructions of orientalized others, Watanna challenges white masculine authority by venturing a sympathetic portrayal of romantic love between a white American woman and a Japanese man. Moreover, she manages to get away with it through trickster strategies. Although she does not in the end overturn the existing racial and gender order, her very attempt to disorder the order, to reconstitute terms and relations, is in itself a form of resistance to received cultural texts and conventional readings.

Writing the exotic romance in an adverse cultural and racial climate, Watanna had to negotiate the same questions that DuPlessis believes face certain women writers, with their acute sense of "the untold story, the other side of a well-known tale" that has been repressed (3). By producing a trickster narrative, Watanna has indeed "[written] beyond the ending." On the other hand, her inability to transcend the narrative outcome of the romance plot points to the limitations of her tricksterism. Working with an inherited literary genre, she inevitably retains some of the stereotypes and ideologies that she wished to challenge. Years later, she would regret that reliance on the romance formula led her to compromise her artistic vision and integrity: "My success was founded upon a cheap and popular device . . . I had sold my birthright for a mess of potage!" (*Me* 152–53). The limitations in Watanna's novel also have to do with her ambiguous racial and cultural positionality. She was able to exploit her identity as the racial other, and yet, as Ling and White-Parks acknowledge about Sui Sin Far, she "could not help but imbibe some of the orientalist notions and terms of her place and time" (5). Therefore, while we celebrate women and minority writers' subversive power, we should also remember that subversion cannot always entail a transformation of the ideological status quo, for nondominant articulations are vulnerable to the powerful insinuations of the very cultural assumptions they question. As Lisa Lowe observes, while the heterogeneities in the dominant discourse enable "counterhegemonies and resistances," nondominant discourses are also composed of heterogeneous sites, and "each site is already multiply constructed" (5). Although Watanna speaks from emergent spaces of opportunity, the intertexuality of her narrative suggests that her opportunities are also strongly inhibited by dominant constructions.

For all its limitations, Watanna's text represents an important voice of cultural resistance in her own time and beyond. That she was a household name in the early twentieth century and has now received increasing critical attention despite decades of near oblivion confirms her place both in Asian American literature and turn-of-the-century American fiction. Finally, the fissures and contradictions in Watanna's novel bear out the premises of today's cultural criticism that nondominant discourses, like their dominant counterparts, are complex, uneven, and irreducible.

Romancing the Borderlands

JOSEPHINA NIGGLI'S *MEXICAN VILLAGE*

—*Rita Keresztesi*

> *Here is a microcosmic bit of Mexican history being played out in terms of family rather than of nation.*
> —JOSEPHINA NIGGLI[1]

Josephina Niggli (1910–1983) was born in Monterrey, Nuevo Leon, Mexico, to immigrant American parents. Her father, Frederick Ferdinand Niggli, whose Swiss and Alsatian forebears immigrated to Texas in 1836, moved to Mexico in 1893 and worked as the manager of a cement plant in the village of Hidalgo, not far from the industrial city of Monterrey; her mother, Goldie (Morgan) Niggli, was of Irish, French, and German descent. Josephina Niggli grew up in Mexico and her childhood was indelibly influenced by Mexican culture and the Mexican Revolution of 1910: she grew up bilingual and bicultural, identifying as both Mexican and American. She symbolically acknowledged her strong connection to Mexican culture by changing her name from Josephine to Josephina. Her early books were published under the name of "Josephina Niggli," while her later works bear her name with another, less Anglophone, spelling "Josefina."[2]

After the 1913 assassination of Francisco Madero, the leader of the Mexican Revolution against Porfirio Diaz's dictatorship, Niggli and her family left Mexico for San Antonio, Texas. For the next seven years Niggli's family roamed the southwestern United States, never finding a home until they moved back to Mexico in 1920. Because of the continued violence in Mexico, Niggli was sent back to San Antonio where she finished her high school education. At fifteen, she enrolled at Incarnate Word College in San Antonio, Texas, where she started writing poems and short stories. She went on to study playwriting at the University of North Carolina at Chapel Hill, graduating in 1937 with a master's degree in drama. Before she published her most famous and influential piece, *Mexican Village* (1945), she had published a collection of poems, *Mexican Silhouettes* (1931), and several plays including *Soladadera* (1937). All of her works were written in English. Later she published another novel titled *Step Down, Elder Brother* (1947), and her last significant literary work, *Miracle for Mexico*, was published in 1964. Niggli taught at the University of North Carolina from 1942 to 1944, and then at Western Carolina University from 1956 to 1975. When she died in 1983 she was considered one of the most influential Mexican American authors of the century.[3]

Although Niggli's work is not well known within the American literary canon, critics of Mexican American and Chicano literature have celebrated *Mexican Village* for years; they value the text as a "transitional work" in the development of Chicano fiction.[4] In Raymund A. Paredes's assessment:

In its sensitive evocation of rural life, its emotionalism, and affectionate portrayal of exotic experiences and personalities, the book culminates the romantic tradition in Mexican-American writing. But *Mexican Village* also pointed forward to an emerging school of realism, confronting such issues as racism, the oppression of women, and the failure of the Mexican Revolution. Before Niggli, no writer of fiction in the United States, with the exception of Katherine Anne Porter, had so vividly depicted the fundamental tensions in Mexican life: the sometimes volatile interaction of Spanish and Indian cultures, the profound sense of history and traditionalism pulling against the fascination with that which is modern and voguish. (55)

While Paredes emphasizes the literary historical significance of Niggli's novel in preparing the road for contemporary Chicano writers, I focus on Niggli's reworking of the romance genre to create a hybrid genre that I call "borderlands romance." The novel retells the complex story of the Mexican Revolution's aftermath between 1920 and 1930 in a culturally and racially hybrid and historically layered romance plot, in order to explore connected narratives of family and nation within the locale of the Mexican-American borderlands.

I read *Mexican Village* in the context of historical narratives about the Mexican Revolution of 1910 and within the culturally hybrid political locale of the Mexican-American borderlands. While the events of the Revolution are often told in the popular and masculinized genre of the Mexican "political novel," I argue that Niggli rewrites the plot as a "borderlands romance." Rather than reproducing the bloody details of the Revolution's aftermath in the naturalistic form of the political novel, which normatively "couples" the ideology of patriarchy with that of the nation, Niggli subversively rewrites and intentionally "mis"-translates the genre as a feminine and transnational borderlands romance. She injects interlocking narratives of the United States' neocolonial imperialistic penetration into Mexico and the macho violence of the Mexican Revolution into the domestic romance narratives of multiple, interracial, transnational love stories. In the process, she paints a historically layered composite picture of Hidalgo in the 1920s: she situates her story in the locale of the politically contested and racially/culturally hybrid contact zone between Texas and Nuevo Leon, between the United States and Mexico.

When protagonist Bob Webster arrives in Hidalgo as the new quarry master of the local cement plant, he is surprised by the simultaneous modernity and anachronism of the place. The startling view juxtaposes Indian cave dwellings with skeletal New York tenement houses, creating an uncanny double-exposure where the present and the past coexist in a narrative bricolage:

He followed Don Anselmo around the curved slope, and then paused in speechless astonishment. The quarry was a deep, ugly wound in the mountain side, but above it, small ledges for walking having been carefully retained, was row after row of cave openings, so that the towering wall had a cynical resemblance to a New York apartment house sheered through the center. (9)

Webster's arrival in the Sabinas Valley is a simultaneous step back to Mexico's repressed precolonial past and a step forward to its neocolonial modernity. He is more familiar with the icons of the modern cityscape than with the architectural landscape of a traditional village. His point of reference for making sense of cave dwellings, by mistranslating and recoding them into his own idiom, produces the image of immigrant quarters in a New York tenement house.

Niggli repeatedly disinters multiple layers of historical realities. In another example, she balances the sinister image of American industry creeping across the border to Monterrey, "that strange city of contrasts, which industry had transformed into a Texas suburb" (462), with the visually and linguistically rich image of the local Indian witch's animal sacrifice. The mostly invisible Malicheño Indian population of Hidalgo is foregrounded in the text's description of an ancient secret ritual:

> As she swayed and dipped and turned, her feet made no noise on the moss-grown trail. There was silence everywhere—in the sky, in the mountains, at the crossing of earth and water.
>
> Then a whisper of sound came from the woman, so faint, so nebulous, that it was no sound at all. But the awareness of sound was there, and the sound became a word, a word in the language the Spaniards thought they had destroyed with the death of the last Malicheño Indians in the closing year of the seventeenth century.
>
> The mountains remembered the word, and echoes tossed it back to the woman, so that her voice rose and other words came, and the old names: Juquialán, Pitale, Corianúa.
>
> The chant grew wilder and higher in pitch. The dancing jumps came faster and faster. There was a sudden swing of the right hand towards the cock's throat and red blood spattered on the corn threads in the dish—corn threads along which traveled as on a highway the desire of the worshiper to the minds of the sleeping gods. (91–92)

Niggli recovers and reproduces the almost foreclosed language and rituals of the local Malicheño Indians. Tía Magdalena, Bob Webster's housekeeper, performs the bird-sacrifice in order to keep him in the Sabinas Valley. Seen as a witch, Tía Magdalena conjures up the "residual"⁵ memories of an Indian past that have survived several hundred years of Spanish colonial rule.

In Hidalgo life is conducted in Spanish, which Niggli then translates into English, but the truly important events are only accessible in the "lost" language of the Malicheño Indians. When the author describes the ritual bird sacrifice, she not only translates the words from the indigenous language to Spanish and then to English, she also acts as a cultural mediator who has access to dormant Indian languages and rituals preceding the Spanish Conquest. Niggli thus positions herself among the secret society of Hidalgo witches, including Tía Magdalena the eagle witch, Nimfa the herb woman, and Lolita the gypsy's daughter. Niggli occupies the position of a cultural translator who negotiates between the precolonial past and the neocolonial present in Mexico. Her position as outsider who travels between borders, languages, and cultures allows for a unique vision. As a strategically positioned "borderlands subject," much like her protagonist Bob Webster, she is not blinded by the intense nationalism and patriotic fervor of either side on the Mexican-American border. Moreover, she is able to project the still-lingering indigenous voices of pre–Columbian Mexico.

In a passage near the end of *Mexican Village*, Bob Webster picks up a popular political novel about the Mexican Revolution, Guzmán's *La sombra del caudillo* [*The Shade/Shadow of the Commander*].⁶ After reading the opening paragraph of Guzmán's novel, Niggli's character impatiently tosses aside the book, which he considers to be just another partisan and fictionalized retelling of the political intrigues of the Revolution's aftermath. This passage also implies Niggli's own critique of the patriarchal nationalist paradigm so often fictionalized in Mexican literature:

"Forgive me, señor. You are a frontier man? I am sure that your general must have been very grand."

... The grand generals, Bob thought with amusement. How consumed Mexico is with its own history. All its paintings, its sculpture, its literature born from its history. He pulled a new novel from his bag and looked at the title: *The Shade of the Commander*, by Martín Luís Guzmán, and read the first paragraph:

"The cadillac of General Ignacio Aguirre crossed the streetcar tracks on the Avenue of Chapultepec and came to a stop a short distance from the headquarters of the Insurgents..."

He shut it with a snap and tossed it on the bed. Another story born of the Great Revolution. Guzmán had been one of the Intellectuals who had found themselves trapped between their two commanding geniuses: Zapata in the South and Villa in the North. If I had been in Mexico then, Bob wondered, whom would I have followed? ... The boy was right. I am a frontier man. (459)

Bob Webster's derisive gesture signals Niggli's own critical commentary on telling the story of the Mexican Revolution as a politically polarized, extremely violent, and exclusively male nationalist narrative. In popular novels of this genre, "political power and violence were inextricable" (Gyurko 545). In Guzmán, an "initial atmosphere of superficial cordiality and unity ... adumbrate[s] a horrendous cycle of violence begetting increased violence" (Gyurko 548). Niggli rejects both the violence and the polarization; Webster situates himself as a "frontier man," or in modern terms a "border subject," who does not identify with either of the political factions in Revolutionary Mexico. He prefers the position of an outsider who can freely move between borders, nations, and cultures.

Mexican Village makes the locale of the Mexican-American border zone its central theme against the backdrop of the Mexican Revolution. In the microcosm of the small Mexican frontier town of Hidalgo Niggli sets the stage for romantic encounters between Spanish colonial aristocrats and Indian aborigines and between Mexican villagers and North American neocolonial industrialists. Instead of telling the history of the Mexican Revolution through the heroic and often violent actions of Mexican soldiers within the setting of the nation state, and thus recreating the male political novel, Niggli redirects her focus to romantic liaisons between members of different families, villages, nations, and cultural/racial groups. She tells the story of modern Mexico through multiple, historically layered stories of local and foreign families whose romantic affairs often result in miscegenation.

Niggli thus writes a domestic and historically burdened counterdiscourse, in which the Mexican Revolution appears only in traces, as a poignant absence. Such a shift in perspective and plot allows the author to explore the less visible familial relations behind the more readily available public arenas. While the political novel tells its story through a straightforward realist narrative plot, Niggli's story constitutes a more opaque narrative, the historically layered and ideologically coded genre of the borderlands romance. This genre accommodates the intercultural, interracial, international, and historically determined personal encounters that make up what Fredric Jameson calls the "political unconscious" of a nation: the borderlands romance tells a love story taking place across international borders and often across racial categories over time. Niggli's racially and culturally ambivalent characters localize distant collective memories of Mexico through the narrative recovery of the three coexisting layers of Mexican history: the indigenous Indian presence before the conquest, the era of Spanish colonial rule, and finally, the neocolonial aggression of American imperialism—Niggli's present.

Niggli's borderlands romance depicts the decade succeeding the Revolution between 1920 and 1930. She breaks the plot into ten interpolated tales, each focusing on a different character or romantic liaison. The diverging plots are contained by the locale of the Sabinas Valley, which is situated in the Mexican-American borderlands, and by the centrally positioned (but often disappearing) character of Bob Webster. Niggli subverts the linear narrative of the Revolution's aftermath by layering her story diachronically and then reassembling the pieces synchronically. Thus, the story of the ten years Bob Webster spends in the Sabinas Valley is inscribed over the implicit narratives of Mexican history and recent international events. The xenophobic nationalism and macho violence of the Mexican Revolution are displaced as Webster occupies a place on the transnational European, American, and African stages of the era: before moving to Hidalgo, he lives in Texas, travels to Europe, to Ireland and France, and then to French colonial Morocco. Instead of participating in the Mexican Revolution, like the heroes of the political novel, Webster is notably somewhere else. He does not visit Mexico until 1920, ten years after the Revolution.

Each of the ten chapters of *Mexican Village* starts with a title page and a design (by Marion Fitz-Simons), and each story bears a date and a Mexican proverb as epigraph. The first chapter is dated "March 1920," while the last one is from "December 1930." Each story refers to a sequential year between 1920 and 1930. While the surface structure of the book follows a linear pattern through the decade, the stories cover a much longer period: Webster's family history goes all the way back to the middle of the nineteenth century, and the story of Hidalgo also includes the history of Mexico's Indian populations.

Niggli's novel makes the hidden historical layers visible by foregrounding the "forgotten" contexts of miscegenation and neocolonial American imperialism. Bob Webster is the "product" of an illicit union between the Spanish Isabella Castillo and the Indian Mariano Menendez, even though the Castillo family represses the story of Isabella's abduction by and subsequent marriage to Webster's Indian great grandfather. Niggli thus reaches back historically to Mexico's indigenous cultures which still coexist with the Revolution's aftermath. She also keenly observes that in the 1920s the United States was increasingly involved with moving some of its heavy industry south of the border. Her narrative dialectically contains both "structures of feeling" of romantic nostalgia—for a simpler and seemingly organic past she sees in the Malicheño Indians' language and rituals—and modern ironic ambivalence over the neocolonial proliferation of multinationals. Niggli's novel is a nuanced fictional recoding of the ideological and textual ambivalences that characterize the borderlands in the decade after the Mexican Revolution.

The mass production of goods and commodities has corresponding effects on a mass-produced citizenry. Niggli not only allegorizes conflicts between families or villages but also between Mexican and American economic interests. When Monterrey becomes a "Texas suburb," the border zone suffers the cannibalizing progression of American political and economic interests; the seemingly quaint and "authentic" Mexican village and its inhabitants are transformed into mere commodities, fetish objects for consumption—the usual tourist kitsch:

In his silver-encrusted gray suit, with the silver-weighted gray sombrero beside him, he [Joaquín Castillo] looked like a travel poster painted to entice the tourist. He had the theatricality that was as false and yet as real as the theatricality of Mexico itself.

Outside the window, an Indito paused to admire the flowers. Here were two sides of Mexico's golden coin: the stolid earthen creature, and the quicksilver figure; the reality and the romance, the humility and the arrogance. Then the Indito walked on, and the picture dissolved into the pleasant view of distant mountains. (434–35)

Such touristic images, in Niggli's exposition, suggest the feminized and exoticized perception of Mexico as the fetish object of the neocolonial North American male gaze.

Within the modern economic context of transnational trafficking in goods and citizens, tourism becomes the neutral third term between the familiar and the alien, between self and other. As Bob Webster observes toward the end of the novel:

A passage in a travel book he had read returned to him: "Mexicans have a peculiar quality to patriotism. Other nations regard their country as sacred ground. . . . Not so the Mexican. To him his country is at once his mother and his mistress, his child and his wife. His country is a woman, and its symbol is a woman—the brown Virgin of Guadalupe." (486)

Niggli depicts Mexico as selling its image in tourist brochures that depict the country in exotic, feminine, and erotic terms. Furthermore, she displays an embellished and self-consciously fake "travel poster" image of a region that cannot hide the ambiguously composite—racially and historically layered—picture of Mexico in the 1920s.

Jameson suggests that we read the romance as a symbolic struggle between different socioeconomic groups during times of crises—such as the disappearance of a central authority and the subsequent chaos of "the war of all against all" or the move from older to newer modes of production. But Jameson moves beyond simple binaries by borrowing the conceptual frameworks of the uncanny and the misrecognition of the self as other from the psychoanalytic arsenal of repression and ego formation. The recognition of the hero's self within its villainous other, which exemplifies the simultaneous processes of misrecognition, repression, and ego formation in individual development, parallels the historical processes of forgetting and remembering that structure the development of national identity at a larger level. In romance narratives, according to Jameson, individual characters allegorically represent the mores and developmental conditions of social groups and historical epochs. While the political novel of the Mexican Revolution ignored the indigenous peoples of Mexico, and while the desperate situation of Indians in whose name the Revolution of 1910 was fought disappeared from public discourse in the ensuing struggles for political power, Niggli's romance returns the repressed history of Mexico's indigenous population to the country's "political conscious." Niggli gives voice to the Indians, as in the ancient ritual performed by Tía Magdalena.

Feminist critics reread the romance as an ideologically burdened and historically determined critical narrative form. When examining the narrative techniques of late nineteenth- or twentieth-century women writers of romance, both Rachel Blau DuPlessis and Susan Gillman read the genre of the romance narrative, much as Jameson does, as a "socially symbolic act, as the ideological—but formal and immanent—response to a historical dilemma."[7] DuPlessis defines the "marriage/death closure in the romance plot as a 'place' where ideology meets narrative and produces a meaning-laden figure of some sort" (19). DuPlessis suggests that twentieth-century women writers subvert the romance genre in order to interrogate "cultural conventions about male and female, romance and quest, hero and heroine, public and private, individual and collective" (ix). Similarly, Susan Gillman discusses the romance, and melodrama in particular, as the genre that "responds formally with varying imaginary resolutions to an array of social contradictions generated in the post-Reconstruction era by the conflicting demands of racial, sexual and national identities" (225). Defining the romance in a specific American historical period, Gillman understands the genre not only in terms of gender but also in terms of race; she calls romance the "nineteenth-century American race melodrama."

These interpretations of the romance genre as the expression of a historically situated ideologeme are useful in reading Niggli's hybrid text. Niggli appropriates the genre of the romance in order to historicize the Revolution and its aftermath, which she tells as a feminine romance plot of miscegenation within the modern political contexts of transnationalism and neocolonialism. While the historical imagination is preoccupied with separating the Revolution's heroes from its villains, Niggli's romance plot penetrates the surface structure of intrigue and politics and unearths historical and cultural layers and hidden genealogies in the Mexican-American borderlands. She breaks the narrative into distinct stories and replaces the single omniscient perspective with dispersed subjectivities which narrate in historical layers. The final product is a richly polyphonic and dialogic text, conveying the modern experience of being between borders and cultures in a flux of simultaneous developments.

Niggli's narrative solves the dilemma of the repetition and misrecognition of the self as other by invoking the uncanny, as the hostile other is reinserted into the familial—as familiar—but within a transnational context. Through the synecdochic allegory of an individual character taking on the characteristics of a whole region, Niggli makes visible the *Heimlich/Unheimlich*, the Freudian "uncanniness," of the Texas-Mexico borderlands. By giving three characters the same name, "Bob Webster," she confuses the familiar and the strange—the self with the other. The novel's historically determined but opaquely structured subplots of family romances and stories of miscegenation—the subsumed interconnected stories of the three families that make up Bob Webster's heritage—linger just below the seemingly transparent story of the Revolution's aftermath in the off-center locale of Hidalgo. Thus Niggli embeds the romance mode in her narrative of the Revolution's aftermath. The novel is not an obviously recognizable romance that ends with the heroine's or the hero's marriage or death at the end of the narrative. The heroes or heroines, such as Isabella Castillo or Tía Magdalena, are submerged under historical time and narrative layers. In Niggli's novel the conventional endings in death or marriage have already taken place before the story begins.

Bob Webster's genealogy is a replica of the sedimented history of Mexico: uncannily "Bob Webster" is also the name of the protagonist's father and half-brother. Webster is a Tejano *mestizo* whose mother is Mexican and whose father is from San Antonio, Texas. The father, also Bob Webster, rejects his illegitimate son: "Are you suggesting that I admit an Indian is a son of mine? Damn it, I'm a white man!" (Niggli 29). But family is also history. The secret of the son Bob Webster's connection to the Huachichil Indians is revealed through a letter his grandmother wrote just before her death but which does not reach its addressee until ten years later, the time of the narrative. It discloses that he is a descendent of the Castillos, the local Spanish colonial aristocratic family, and of Huachichil Indians. He is the great-grandson of Isabella Castillo, the eldest daughter and lawful heiress of the Castillos who was kidnapped by the Indian Mariano Menendez at her own brother's orders in the 1840s. Instead of killing herself as the Castillos claim, she marries her abductor. Their son is Daniel Menendez Castillo who later becomes the legendary bandit known on the frontier as *El Caballo Blanco*. The recovery of Webster's family romance is a clue to the history told as transnational borderlands romance.

Niggli also creates an uncanny return of the self as other—who immediately misrecognizes himself. She orchestrates an encounter between Bob Webster and his blond half-brother, also named Bob Webster, at a nightclub in Monterrey. The "blond Bob Webster" is the "father Bob Webster's" legitimate son meeting the "illegitimate *mestizo* Bob Webster." The meeting between the two brothers is a shocking mirroring of the self as other:

"I [the superintendent of the American-owned cement plant in Monterrey] asked for Bob Webster and with you there the waiter made a natural mistake. You shouldn't have such an ordinary name. Would you give the fellow I want a message for me? He's a blond, about your height, in a party with one woman and two other men. They're all from the States." . . . It had suddenly occurred to him why he had thought he recognized the blond American. We're brothers, he thought dazedly. Half brothers. It was myself I saw in him. Myself and . . . (466–67; final ellipsis in the text)

The intentionally confusing overuse of the name "Bob Webster"— the dearth of signifiers in relation to signifieds—suggests that clear demarcation between nations and cultures is hard to maintain in the border zone. Niggli excavates the repressed and sometimes foreclosed secrets of individual and national origins and emphatically connects the private and erotic domains with those of the public and the political. In a different context, Niggli comments, "Here is a microcosmic bit of Mexican history being played out in terms of family rather than of nation" (453). This quote reflects Niggli's preference to tell the story of the Revolution as romance and to foreground the microcosm of the family instead of the totality of the nation.

119 ~ *Josephina Niggli's* Mexican Village

Instead of simply rewriting the story from the perspectives of Mexican women from a single family, Niggli narrates the histories of three families, the Spanish Castillos, the American Websters, and the Indian Mexican Menendezes. In her subversive rewriting of the political novel, Niggli replaces the linear public plot with a polyphonic narrative of interpolated domestic romances that explore Webster's puzzling triple racial heritage. Through the use of multiple romance plots Niggli is able to demonstrate the cultural and racial complexities that make up Webster's, and ultimately Mexico's, history. In romantic liaisons between members of the three families, Niggli shows allegorically that under colonial and/or neocolonial rule nations and families forge hybrid, transnational and interracial, liaisons: "Here is a microcosmic bit of Mexican history being played out in terms of family rather than of nation" (452).

In order to examine the connection between the family and the nation, Doris Sommer's reading of the romance genre provides a helpful concept. Sommer's theory of the "national romance" focuses on the domestic sphere, in particular on the role of heterosexual desire within the project of nation-building. Sommer's theory of "coupling" the family and the nation supplements DuPlessis's reading of the romance as a "trope for the sex-gender system" and Gillman's notion of the "nineteenth-century race melodrama" that makes the racialized sex-gender system visible. In her work connecting the "erotics of politics" with the genre of the "national romance" Doris Sommer suggests that we read "national projects coupled with productive heterosexual desire" (2). For Sommer romances function as "new versions of historical narrative" which she explicitly identifies in the magical realism of Latin American literature (3). She writes:

By *romance* here I mean a cross between our contemporary use of the word as a love story and a nineteenth-century use that distinguished the genre as more boldly allegorical than the novel. The classic examples in Latin America are almost inevitably stories of star-crossed lovers who represent particular regions, races, parties, economic interests, and the like. Their passion for conjugal and sexual union spills over to a sentimental readership in a move that hopes to win partisan minds along with hearts. (5)

Sommer locates the erotics of politics in novels that allegorize "nonviolent consolidation during internecine conflicts" through plots concerning heterosexual love and marriage (6). She reads such plots as "wish-fulfilling projection[s] of national consolidation and growth, a goal rendered invisible" (7). Sommer argues that romance is the preferred historical and literary genre of the Americas.

Niggli appropriates the romance narrative to confuse the strict opposition between the political and the private domains. Her use of romance then utilizes both parts of Sommer's definition of the national romance: Niggli's narrative is both a familial "love story" and a national, historical "allegory." *Mexican Village* has several plots which center on conflicts between groups or communities, but which can only be resolved through erotic unions. For example, Niggli composes a variation on the story of the romantic union between Isabella Castillo and Mariano Menendez. Chapter 4, titled "The Street of the Hidden Water," functions as a parody of the Romeo and Juliet story where "tragedy" is recycled as "farce." A decade-long feud between two villages is resolved through marriage between a Hidalgo man and a girl from San Juan—but only after a failed attempt to settle the case with a public cockfight. After the wedding ceremony the two villages erase the symbolic chalk line between them and put an end to their bloody feud: "The priest lifted a handful of dust and sprinkled it over the white line that divided the two valleys. 'Tomorrow,' he said firmly, 'Don Serapio can blot out this line. There is no more need of it'" (219). Such acts of erasure of boundaries and borders characterize Niggli's novel as a whole. The allegorical marriage plot of heterosexual desire stands in for the political plot: Niggli opts for a "coupling ending" to the feud between the villages.

While I interpret Niggli's novel as the ideologically coded and discursively feminine "other" to the masculine Mexican political novel of the Revolution, critics usually read *Mexican Village* as a precursor to Chicano literature and Bob Webster's character as the prototype of Chicano subjectivity in the United States. They also comment on the authentic Mexicanism of the novel's representation of life in Hidalgo.[8] Some critics fault Niggli for not showing the damaging consequences of the Spanish past in her novel. For example, Héctor Calderón and José Saldívar place Niggli's novel as a historically important early Mexican American text, but they consider *Mexican Village* to be a "romantic, even quaint" view of "Spanish-Mexican experience," a novel which upholds "conventional Anglo-American views of their culture" (4).

Niggli's fictionalized Hidalgo is not merely the story of a traditional Mexican community; rather, *Mexican Village* is the narrative of the Mexican uncanny—a historically layered romance within the colonized, recolonized, industrialized, transnational, and culturally hybrid Mexican-American contact zone. José Saldívar calls the two-thousand-mile United States-Mexico border zone a "paradigm of crossings, intercultural exchanges, circulations, resistances, and negotiations as well as of militarized 'low-intensity' conflict" (ix). In examining the borderlands, Saldívar suggests that we focus on the alternative narrative of "the ethno-racialized cultures of displacement" in place of the "North's monopoly of cultural nationalism" (7). While Saldívar is mainly concerned with the theoretical reconceptualization of the borderlands within American cultural studies, his comments open the way to a re-reading of Niggli's novel as an ironic borderlands romance rather than a simple precursor to Chicano literature or a monologic Mexican nationalist narrative.[9]

The cultural hybridity and dialogism of border texts conceptually dislodges the neat cartographic demarcations of arbitrarily drawn political borders. These texts carve out a third zone, what Mary Louise Pratt calls the "contact zone" and José Davíd Saldívar the "*Transfrontera* contact zone" (14). Niggli's *Mexican Village*, set within the Mexican-American border zone at a time of coexisting "modes of production" or "moments of socioeconomic development" (Jameson 148), sheds light on how to rethink identity, culture, and nation in a modern imperialist context. Amy Kaplan has coined the term "borderlands" to better grasp the cultural, historical, and political complexity of such regions. She says, "the conceptual limits of the frontier, by displacing it with the site of the borderlands," links the "study of ethnicity and immigration inextricably to the study of international relations and empire" (16). Kaplan's understanding of the "borderlands" is particularly fruitful in connection with the genre of the romance.

Border writers facilitate the intercultural exchange between familiar and alien narrative practices through mistranslation and cultural mediation. As Emily Hicks suggests: "What makes border writing a world literature with a 'universal' appeal is its emphasis upon the multiplicity of languages within any single language; by choosing a strategy of translation rather than representation, border writers ultimately undermine the distinction between original and alien culture" (xxiii). Linguistically *Mexican Village* often reads like an English translation from the nonexistent Spanish original—like a "literal" mistranslation. Phrases such as "the Family Castillo," "frontier man," or the title of Guzmán's novel as "the shade of the commander" simulate Spanish diction by reproducing Spanish syntactical and idiomatic qualities. Each chapter begins with a literally translated Mexican proverb, for example: "Rivers rise in flood and destroy,/ Brooks water the land and sing" (2) or "He who eats with his nose, pays with his mouth" (64). As these examples suggest, Niggli's translations of Mexican proverbs do not always make sense in English. She does not clearly convey the message of the proverbs; instead, she translates the idiomatic phrases word by word. Thus her translation, while technically and literally accurate, has an alienating effect. Her mistranslations mirror and expose language as an uncanny alienating device: the familiar Mexican proverbs are reflected back to the English-speaking/reading audience of the novel as alien and unrecognizable.

Niggli often steps into the narrative by inserting intrusive glossary notes that are intended to aid the reader; they contain English translations and explanations of Spanish words and expressions. In one memorable glossary entry, Niggli draws attention to the problem of translation: in Chapter 2, "The Street of the Three Crosses," Webster calls his friends in Hidalgo his *compadres*, a word Niggli translates in her glossary as "Untranslatable. Literally, co-father. A term used between very intimate friends. The feminine is *comadre*" (91). The glossary gives a literal translation of the word instead of explaining its meaning in a particular context—it is thus a mistranslation that confuses more than it clarifies. Niggli's narrative technique of confusion or mistranslation—which contains both the original and its slightly "off" copy—parallels her gesture of appropriating the domestic and feminine genre of the romance within the culturally and politically confused locale of the borderlands.

Niggli's alienating narrative technique not only draws attention to such problematic "organic" units as the self, the family, the village, and the nation, and to the genre of the romance, but also to her own authorial position. She distances herself from academia and book learning through the somewhat humorous character of the Little Professor of the Hidalgo Boys' School who is afraid of his pupils. On a date with the mayor's homely daughter, Chela, the Little Professor describes the sunset in convoluted scientific language. He tells the "truth" of the sunset in terms of scientific facts, which the villagers mistranslate into fiction and fantasy:

> He cleared his throat, and from some filing card in his memory, stated in precise tones, "It merely means that the upper limb of the sun, because of a change in the earth's atmosphere causing the light rays to appear other than they are, sinks beneath the level of the visual horizon as caused by the diurnal revolution of the earth." ... No one believed these amazing tales, and he soon had a reputation for being as great a liar as Don Timotéo Gonzalez, the maker of cheese, but everyone liked him. (378–79)

Niggli writes the "truth" of the borderlands through the "lies" of romantic fiction. Instead of a factual account of the various assassinations that followed the Revolution, she focuses on domestic and romantic plots that make the borderlands their center. Niggli's dialogical romance exposes as untenable the rigid distinction between history and fiction, between private and public domains, and between the past and the present; she also erases the hierarchical divisions between geographical or political centers as artificially drawn and socially constructed. Niggli breaks up the linearity of the plot and interrupts the hierarchy of central and minor characters. The result is an archaeology of histories, none more dominant than another. Historical and personal events are only random artifacts from the shifting perspectives of different characters and geographical locations. History and fiction, dominant and minor motifs and characters, political hierarchies of the North and the South, and temporal hierarchies of past and present become random distinctions in Niggli's borderlands romance.

Furthermore, the layerings of space upon time, past upon present, culture upon culture, and languages upon each other can create paradoxical connections, such as the kinship the Tejano *mestizo* Bob Webster feels for his Irish American friend, Ned Kelley. In Niggli's borderlands romance Tejano *mestizo* subjectivity is coded as subordinate, similar to the Irish under English colonial rule. When his father rejects him, Webster understands racism in terms of the heightened sensitivity to difference in the border zone—whether between Mexico and the United States or between the Irish and the English:

His reception had cut into his pride, even though he knew that in Texas, that in all the border States, the prejudice against the border Indito is very strong—the Tejanos-, who are neither Mexican nor North American, who speak a patois rather than a language, who are in their way as illegitimate as Bob was in his.... Ned came from an immigrant Irish family which had come to the States after Ned's father was killed in one of the Rebellions. The two boys had worked their ways across the ocean on a cattle boat, and the warm odor of a barn still brought vivid recollections of that trip and Ned's pleasant voice telling tales of Irish heroism against oppression. Something in the stories fired Bob's imagination. He felt himself a spiritual brother to the black-browed heroes. (470)

As Niggli mistranslates the central into the marginal, she draws links between the Indito and the oppressed of other lands.

Intersecting voices and historical and cultural layers come together in the hybrid genre of the borderlands romance. Instead of focussing on a historical or political chronology, the text weaves together public and private domains through an intricate mapping of locales and subjects. Each chapter bears the name of a street, a plaza, or some other location in Hidalgo: for example, Chapter I "The Quarry—where a young man comes to the valley and meets a ghost," Chapter VI "The Plaza of the Viceroys—where a man makes candy, and a woman hates bulls," or Chapter IX "The Avenue of Illustrious Men—where an old maid finds an actor with a broken leg, and receives a school teacher's gift." While the locales in the chapter titles usually suggest historically significant persons and eras, the subtitles and the stories themselves refer to everyday and private events. Niggli elevates the seemingly insignificant and depoliticized realm of daily private life above the sphere of historically important events. Maurice Blanchot defines the everyday as the only access we have to history—to "moments of effervescence"—when everyday's privileged section, private life, transforms into a public existence (238). In Blanchot's radical rethinking of the everyday, the banality of private life becomes the site of spontaneous change or revolution without the danger—yet—of reifying, rationalizing, institutionalizing, and bureaucratizing social change. Decentering the historical story of the Revolution through everyday life in its aftermath, Niggli is able to project a more complex and fluid cross-section of the opposing players, interests, and cultures. Thus, she tells the story of the Revolution through the love interests and everyday squabbles of politically insignificant people in the heteroglossic and culturally hybrid region of the Mexican-American borderlands.

Rachel Blau DuPlessis rethinks the romance genre as a subversive narrative device or tool that female authors use to dismantle the sex-gender system. I would like to suggest that Niggli's novel performs a similarly subversive narrative act. Niggli rewrites the male narrative of the Mexican political novel within a feminine and domestic mode—as a romance. Yet the romance does not achieve a traditional ending. Instead of focusing on the male protagonist's heterosexual love interest, such as the Indito Candelaria or the mysterious Maria of the River Road, Niggli ends her novel *not* with death or marriage *but* with Webster's renewed ties to his male friends: "He said politely, 'Shall we go, cousin?' Joaquín's laughter was fresh and free. 'The word is *compadre*, or twin, or even brother, not cousin.' Bob, pleased with his private jest, said firmly, 'The word is cousin, I prefer it'"(491).

Webster has several ambivalent relationships with women throughout the novel. Candelaria and Maria of the River Road, to whom he is romantically tied at various points, play inconsequential roles compared to the men he considers to be his friends. Webster cultivates emotionally intimate friendships with several of the characters—such as Ned Kelley, Tommy Eaton the Harvard-educated and entrepreneurial war buddy from the States, the three Hidalgo men (Porfirio the carver of wood, Andrés Treviño the owner of goats, and Pepe Gonzalez who resolves the feud between two villages by marrying), and the two Spanish colonial aristocrats (Alejandro and Joaquin Castillo)—calling them all his *compadres*, a word Niggli translates in her glossary as "co-fathers" or "very intimate friends" (91). Niggli's version of writing romance "beyond the ending" takes forms of friendship as a promising model. The novel ends with the image of the two "cousins," Bob Webster and Joaquín Castillo, and the two Indian women, Candelaria and Tía Magdalena, walking out of Webster's house and out of the reader's vision:

They both grinned at her, linked arms, and walked—Bob, earth-solid and firm, Joaquín, air-light and arrogant—out of the patio.

The two women waited for a decent interval. Then they draped their shawls over their heads, and they, too went to the church.

The patio, with its tiled pool, its roses in bloom, and its trees in fruit and in flower, was quiet in the golden light. (491)

In this closing image Niggli mistranslates maleness into its feminine other, as the focus on the men disperses into images of pool, blooms, and fruit. The borders and boundaries—between the genre of the political novel and the genre of the romance, between the American North and the Mexican South, and between the precolonial past and the neocolonial present—slowly dissolve in the "golden light" of the afternoon sun.

What's a Nice Girl like You Doing in a Book like This?

HOMOEROTIC READING AND POPULAR ROMANCE

—Stephanie Burley

LOOKING FOR LOVE IN ALL THE WRONG PLACES

What could be more conventionally heterosexual (and less homoerotic for women) than the discourse of popular romance, a representational schema that takes as its first premise the erotic attractions of phallocentric heroes named Ben Penrod and Evan Mountjoy? The short answer: not much. But a more complicated approach to this question highlights the subterranean homoeroticism in the romance industry that has gone unnoticed in recent scholarship. Tania Modleski's groundbreaking study of popular romance, *Loving with a Vengeance: Mass-Produced Fantasies for Women* (1982), was one of the first academic texts to take seriously the cultural work done by this powerful genre in contemporary society. She examines the narrative formula of the typical Harlequin romance from a feminist perspective, highlighting the genre's patriarchal machinations.

In 1984, Janice Radway's ethnographic study of romance readers, *Reading the Romance: Women, Patriarchy, and Popular Literature,* found that women gain a sense of empowerment from the practice of reading romances despite the residual patriarchal ideology identified by Modleski. With the advent of cultural studies in the academy, popular romance is coming under more scrutiny than ever.[1] Yet most studies of romance to date take the heteronormative aspects of popular romance as given. My project here is to put pressure on the very core of the genre, to destabilize the heterosexual assumptions basic to our current understanding of popular romance. Thus, this paper rephrases questions of romantic heterosexuality in the Harlequin world: how can a women-authored industry produce erotic pleasure reading for women without becoming homoerotic? What narrative and discursive apparatuses prevent romance readers who profess a deep and abiding love of their favorite authors and fellow readers from seeing themselves as homoerotic subjects? Like Modleski and other theorists who study popular romance, my approach to the genre begins with my own experience as a habitual reader of romance fiction.[2]

AUTOBIOGRAPHY OF A HOMOSOCIAL READER

At the age of fourteen, I was introduced to paperback romances, an entire grocery bag of them, by my best friend, Dawn. I was spending the night at her house and we pawed through the jumbled stack of books with the excitement of untutored taste and discovery. I remember sitting up reading on the couch with her until three or four in the morning. In the coming years we talked about the heroes and heroines, the prettiest cover models, the relative advantages of shotgun weddings and abductions, the virtues of burnished auburn hair ... One night, Dawn looked up at me over *The Rake of Lancaster* or *The Rogue of Gloucester* and asked if I ever got a "funny feeling" when I was reading the "good parts." The moment of recognition was horrifying, almost gothic in the way it transformed me into an interrogated subject with a desperate secret. I understood perfectly well the erotic implications of the question and how answering honestly might jeopardize the status quo of our relationship: Was I sexually aroused? At that very moment? Had I ever masturbated to the fantasies portrayed in these books? Yes. Could I admit this to the girl in whose bed I was sleeping that night? No way. Despite the invitation to discuss details of my sexual responses to romance reading, I was unable to do so not just because such a conversation would require me to deal with difficult personal issues, but moreover because I was sure that if "nice girls" felt as I did when reading the sexually explicit climaxes of paperback romance (at that point I doubted that they did), they certainly did not discuss it. Rather than begin the process of owning up to my sexuality, I shrugged ambiguously and began another process, the one where Dawn and I politely continued to misrecognize the passion we felt for romance novels, and that I felt for her for years. We eventually zipped one another into our respective prom dresses and sent ourselves out into the world of heterosexual romance, a world that we came to understand largely in terms of the master narratives we were internalizing one paperback at a time.

I want to address here the way that female homoerotic desire permeates popular romance. It has long been my sense that homoeroticism is somehow trenched on the margins of the discourse of romance novels, both in its popular and its more scholarly venues. Queer theory, especially Eve Sedgwick's framework of homosocial desire, provides the critical apparatus and the vocabulary I will use to theorize how this genre of popular literature, in all its heterosexist machinations, continually threatens to exceed its foundational narrative trope, as it did for me all those years ago.[3] As a complement to Sedgwick's theory of the homosocial, I will employ a queer reading strategy that destabilizes the heterosexual assumptions of popular romance. I use the term "queer reading" both to denote an interpretive strategy that accounts for the multiple instabilities inherent in theorizing reading practices and to connote the fluidity of sexual fantasies that circulate around erotic texts, no matter how stable they appear to be on the surface. My queer reading strategy, like other oppositional readings, goes "against the grain" in order to defamiliarize some of the naturalized ideological investments that go unnoticed in "straight" readings. I do not want to suggest that the difference between queer and straight readings necessarily lies in the sexual identities of readers (whether these identities are self-professed, suppressed, or otherwise). I am not trying to *out* the legions of writers, fans, and critics who participate in this discourse, but rather to *point out* the importance of homoeroticism to the genre and the recuperative strategies that always seem to drag popular romance back to its heterosexual moorings.

Inherent in the female-centered erotic endeavor of popular romance is a homosocial apparatus that allows for, and even depends upon, homoerotic desire while simultaneously disguising, suppressing, or surmounting it. That is to say, when we find the heroines irresistible, love our favorite authors, and experience close personal relationships to our fellow readers of erotic literature, we are in fact engaged in a homoerotic practice. When we insist that we are all just friends, or are really just searching for infantile nurture from an idealized mother figure, we are disciplining homoeroticism into the homosocial; that is, we are misrecognizing how same-sex desire figures into our experience of reading romance. When we read romance against the grain, with an eye for the tension between our erotic investment in the heroines and our negotiations of the heterosexual heroes, we are engaged in a queer reading practice, one that destabilizes the foundations of the genre.[4]

I am not the first to attempt to liberate popular romance from its heterosexual prison. The 1990s have seen an increase in popular romances specifically addressed to a lesbian audience. These books "queer" the heterosexual assumptions of popular romance. Not unlike their straight counterparts, the typical heroines find one another by chance, overcome a set of social obstacles including predictable personal secrets, and live happily ever after. The most prominent publisher of lesbian beach reading is the Naiad Press, which puts out several contemporary romances each year and has also revived the classic torrid 1950s lesbian pulp of Ann Bannon. In this same vein, Mabel Maney's *Nancy Clue* parodies the story of Carolyn Keene's beloved girl-sleuth from a lesbian perspective. Nancy falls for the perky (and well dressed) nurse, Cherry Aimless, while solving mysteries with her gay chums, the Hardly Boys. These books literalize the homoerotic possibilities of popular fiction. I argue that the dynamic sparking the imagination of authors like Maney is already palpable in the Harlequin world.

The evidence I will present in support of the theory that homoeroticism plays a central part in the discourse of romance fiction is admittedly anecdotal. I chose reader comments, critical approaches, paratextual documents, and actual romance novels that lend themselves to the kind of oppositional reading strategy I propose. In most cases, it is relatively clear that the actors and images I study have no conscious homoerotic intention or homosexual affiliation. Nonetheless, the language and imagery of same-sex desire is readily available in the most mainstream books and magazines on the subject, suggesting that homoeroticism is more prevalent in popular romantic discourse than readers, writers, and academic theorists have heretofore acknowledged.

Because I am using Eve Sedgwick's concept of the homosocial in a way that she specifically cautions against, some clarification of how and why I think this critical framework applies to the case of romance fiction is in order. Sedgwick insists that there is an important difference between male and female homosocial discourse, namely that "female bonding" is more readily accepted and less dichotomously opposed to homosexuality in western culture than its more fraught male counterpart (2–3). Yet, several aspects of the discourse of popular romance make it prey to anxieties that ultimately require the homosocial as a defense against homosexuality. First, because its focus is explicitly erotic, popular romantic discourse requires strict boundaries in order to retain respectability and to differentiate it from "pornographic" literature. In other words, the genre necessarily employs various strategies to domesticate, or render familiar and nonthreatening, its erotic potential. Second, because it is created and consumed by women, boundaries are necessary to prevent women's desire from crossing into homoeroticism. Romance writers must rely on a series of disciplinary heteronormative literary conventions to write sexually exciting fiction for and about other women. Third, feminist critics have long observed popular romance's patriarchal dimensions, especially the way it functions as a compensatory narrative through which women reconcile themselves to their fears and anxieties about their place in a male-centered culture; romance allows women to fetishize this position, to conceive its erotic potential, and therefore to avoid radical politics of change. Yet, Radway and others have observed that patriarchal ideology has not been able to foreclose more liberating sexual and political effects of popular romance. Indeed, as Carol Thurston points out, romance reading has become a "revolutionary" site of women's sexual emancipation by allowing them to articulate fantasies of their own sexual agency. Thus, the patriarchal master narrative of romance—including its heteronormative tendencies—is articulated through a potentially disruptive discourse of female sexual empowerment. Thus, the homoerotic potential of otherwise harmless female bonding is even closer to the surface in popular romance than in other less explicitly erotic, less female-centered textual practices. If homoerotic counternarratives consistently threaten to disrupt the heterosexuality of popular romance, as I will attempt to show through my readings, then it should come as no surprise that a complex set of disciplinary codes similar to Sedgwick's homosocial are always already in place to prevent this kind of disruption.

A HOMOSOCIAL COUNTERNARRATIVE OF AUTHOR/READER DESIRE

It is not at all uncommon for readers to talk about their favorite romance authors and heroines in terms of love and physical pleasure. For example, Jayne Ann Krentz, a noted romance author in her own right, describes how reading an interview of fellow author Jill Smith "warmed me right down to my toes" and "left me with a lump in my throat."[5] Online chat rooms are filled with women who "love" Karen Robards, "get all warm and fuzzy" for Catharine Coulter's novels, and "have a deep, intimate, personal connection" to the heroines in Jo Beverley's historical romances. A romance fan from Manila writes that she "is desperate to know more about [author] Rosanne Kohake" (*Romantic Times*, Jan. '99, 24). Radway provides the following testimony from noted author LaVyrle Spencer:

[My first book] was written because of one very special lady, Kathleen Woodiwiss, whose book, *The Flame and the Flower*, possessed me to the point where I found I, too, wanted to write a book that would make ladies' hearts throb with anticipation ... I even got to the point where I told myself I wanted to do it for her, Kathleen, to give her a joyful reading experience like she's given me. (*Reading* 68)

Radway uses this statement as evidence of the appeal of romance to readers who become writers. But we can also see a counternarrative of female passion and the desire to create pleasure for women. Spencer, at least, imagines her project as one of reciprocal pleasure, with the ultimate goal of seducing other women as she has been seduced.

This intense love avoids its homoerotic potential primarily through the unstated normative idea that these women are all "just friends." Another strategy, employed primarily by academic critics analyzing the genre of romance, is to describe the pleasures of reading in terms of object-relations theory, so that the feelings of love and physical pleasure that women derive from these books are seen as replacements for the ideal nurturing love of a mother. According to this kind of reading, promoted by Radway and others, the hero is figuratively transformed into the nurturing mother who satisfies the infantile longings of readers. But this focus—for all it illuminates about the kinds of love that women want but do not get from men—distracts attention from the homoerotic possibilities inherent in reading and desiring women's fiction.

Chief among the "object-relations" theorists is Suzanne Juhasz, whose *Reading from the Heart* explores the act of reading romances written by women, both canonical and popular, through this framework. In her autobiographical prologue, "The Passionate Woman Reader and the Story of True Love," she describes the act of reading love stories as "an excitement and delight that make me feel vitally alive, both stirred and safe within the book, so the lack of this kind of reading makes me feel empty, incomplete, and lonely" (2). As she works in the "real world" she "needs to know [her romance] is there, waiting at home by my bed ... ready for me to go to when I want it" (2). She describes a complicated, uncannily familiar ritual of preparing to meet up with the female-authored love stories she enjoys so much: "I give myself the pleasure, now ... I take a bath (the book comes too). Then, cozy in robe and slippers, I curl up on the couch and get down to it" (3). In Juhasz's narrative of seeking and finding nurturing comforts in women's texts, we can see traces of a less infantile set of desires operating in her nightly encounters.

A homosocial counternarrative of Juhasz's self-described reading process reveals the latent sexual (and textually homoerotic) content hovering just beneath the surface. Riddled with the psychic drama of anticipation, preparation, and physical satisfaction, Juhasz's language signals the desires of an adult sexual subjectivity actively pursuing gratification through women's texts. Object-relations theory would have us believe that the intimate settings (bed, bath, couch) cast the reader back into the pre-Oedipal infantile imaginary where she reimagines the satisfactions of the mother's body, perhaps playing an endless game of *fort-da* with the maternal presences she rediscovers each night as she reads. But by resisting the tendency to infantilize women and their reading practices, we recover an equally plausible alternative. The act of reading is immanently *symbolic*, which is to say symptomatic of the reader's full membership in the adult world of language. Her organized pursuit of pleasure leads her to satisfy mature fantasies through the symbolic practice of textual engagement.[6] When we add the significant element that Juhasz is a woman seeking pleasure through the textual productions of other women, we have a homoerotic counternarrative. Juhasz's complex ritual of reading mirrors the discourse of American dating (rush home from work, soak in the tub, "get down to it" on the couch) in which the female text supplants Mr. Right. This reworking of the romantic reading scenario gives a more satisfactory account of the desire that conditions romance reading than the mother's love story of object-relations theory. Female readers experience complex, symbolic, erotic attraction to the authors and stories that provide sexual pleasure. This desire is, in fact, adult sexual desire that need not be displaced onto an idealized notion of a nurturing mother.

Juhasz does eventually address the homosexual potential of both object-relations theory and romance reading in her final chapter on lesbian romance fiction, only to dismiss it as another kind of narrative entirely. If what women really desire is female nurturing, why not dispense with the hero entirely? Juhasz responds: "[d]esire for a woman . . . [i]s this lesbian love? Not exactly, because lesbian love is not mother-infant love: it is love and sex between two adult women and therefore parallels rather than precedes heterosexual romance" (207). Thus, she discusses homosexual desire only in overtly lesbian stories like Isabel Miller's *Patience and Sarah*. This approach is troubling not only because it enforces a rigid homo/heterosexual dichotomy, but also because it theorizes adult sexuality out of the picture when it comes to women desiring the erotic pleasures of nonlesbian romance fiction written by women. The sexualized language that Juhasz and other readers use—the passion, the preparation, the proximity to the bed—signals adult desire. Object-relations theory infantilizes the desiring woman, disconnects her from adult sexuality, and replaces the homoerotic possibility with a safer, more heterosexual "family romance."

Even if women readers desire the romantic hero for his nurturing qualities, they also reveal less accountable desires for the heroine, the female author, and the female text itself. The homosocial framework helps us to recognize the queer potential of these multiple sites of same-sex identification and desire by alerting us to the complex mix of social forces that both facilitate same-sex desire and simultaneously disguise and deny it, insuring that this desire can pass underneath various homophobic radars. Structuring narratives of reading like Juhasz's along the homosocial continuum allows us to see the women whose toes curl up for their favorite authors not as infants, but rather as mature sexual subjects participating in a literary activity with a broad historical foundation and potentially homoerotic affiliations. This structure also lays bare some of the theoretical apparatus that persistently heterosexualizes the discourse of female fantasy.

(MIS)RECOGNIZING PHYSICAL PLEASURE

While object-relations theory prevents us from seeing romance readers as adult homoerotic subjects, a series of codes explicitly limiting the discussion of romance to the realm of the "heart" as opposed to the "body" keeps us from recognizing readers as sexual agents. Framed in the language of middle-class politeness, these codes construct romance reading as a sensual yet oddly disembodied act. Even when specific physical effects are described by readers, as in pounding hearts and stomachs full of butterflies, the tendency is to turn a demurring eye away from the narrative of embodied physical pleasure. Thus, while every issue of *Romantic Times*, every romance web site, every cover of every book is laden with sexual content, one important aspect of the sexual experience of reading romance, *masturbation*, is never mentioned overtly, except by critics of the genre who want to cast romance reading as an illicit, frivolous, or "dirty" activity.[7]

The avoidance of the sexual reading body in the Harlequin world promotes infantilizing narratives like the family romance. Yet, as in Juhasz's scenario of bedtime reading, traces of this little secret are visible just under the surface, once we are frank enough to look for them. For example, the readers in Radway's focus group describe their reading practices in terms of solitary escape and private pleasure. Reading romance creates a private space in these women's daily routines where they seek sensual fulfillment. Radway's Smithton readers, all habitual consumers of romance, "stressed the privacy of the act [of reading] and the fact that it enables them to focus their attention on a single object that can provide pleasure for themselves alone" (*Reading* 90).

Not surprisingly, this activity provoked feelings of "shame about their 'hedonist' behavior" for readers who then provided elaborate rationalizations for reading romance, including the explanation that the books they love teach them about history and foreign lands (*Reading* 90). The main objectors to this activity are the husbands, who resent the time and energy that reading consumes in their wives' lives. The Smithton women describe the covert strategies they have for dealing with this resentment, including neglecting housework in order to read when the husband is at work and being "delighted when he gets a business call in the evening because her husband's preoccupation with his caller permits her to go back to her book" (*Reading* 91). The tension between husbands and romance reading reflects a negotiation over the readers' erotic life. The claim that women are interested in romance for its history lessons may be partially true; yet Radway is quick to observe that it serves as a screen for the "sensual" fulfillment that these women desire. She is not willing to take the final step and ask her focus group what, *exactly*, they do when they are alone with their books, secreted away from their jealous husbands and family demands. Nonetheless the language of hedonism, shame, and guilt that these women use to describe their lives as romance readers at least suggests masturbation. The flowery vernacular of breathless, heart throbbing sensuality is a polite way to make this guilty practice more palatable; it is the socially acceptable discourse that allows words like "masturbation" to remain unspoken.

If theorists and fans avoid explicit discussion of women pleasing themselves as they read romances, ingenious marketers are overtly aware of this practice. In the backs of books and in the pages of romance magazines one can often find advertisements for a handy little invention called "The Book Mate." This device, designed to hold your book open while you are "traveling, vacationing, at work, *in bed*, studying, cooking, [or] eating," is tailor-made for the practice of masturbation. It "makes reading a pure pleasure!" specifically because it "leaves your hands free to do other things." Given the complex set of social codes that make it unacceptable for women to be forthright about masturbation, the suppression of this practice in romance reading is understandable. Romance readers, magazine editors, and publishing houses have long resisted the idea that the books they love and sell are pornographic.[8] They do not want to see them pulled off the shelves of local libraries, banned from supermarkets, and/or consigned to "adult" bookstores where nice girls rarely venture. Neither do I, although perhaps for some different reasons. I enjoy the ready availability of romance fiction, but I also want to resist the idea that the private physical pleasures that women derive from them are shameful. My aim in poking through the gauzy respectability that cloaks the romance industry is to dismantle some of the shame apparatus surrounding erotic engagement with reading in order to concretize the sexuality of romance discourse.[9] Reading against the heteronormative grain reveals a homoerotic counternarrative in which romance reading is a sexual-textual practice whereby adult women attain fulfillment at their own hands and through the pens of the female authors they love and admire.

138 ~ *Stephanie Burley*

DESIRING NAKED LADIES: HOMOEROTIC MARKETING STRATEGIES

Renarrativizing romance discourse as a story about adult women's sexual desire for the stories they tell one another helps to explain the appeal of the routine marketing strategies of the genre. For example, the suggestively titled *Naked Came the Ladies*, an anthology of short stories published a few years ago by thirteen of the "First Ladies of Romance," illustrates the prevalence of homoeroticism in romance discourse. Its *Romantic Times* write-up consists of a full-page article detailing the madcap adventures of the authors and a smaller advertisement, both of them stunning in their representations of homosocial desire. In the article the authors, speaking univocally as "The Naked Ladies," describe how they abducted a male editor (whom they happened to pass as they cruised around San Diego in their limo) and pitched their book to him. They fondly recount to their uneasy captive (and to the audience of *RT*) how they came to write their book:

> "We were at the mineral hot spring—lazing in the water—our critique group, you know. Anyway, we were naked."
> He gulped. We went on.
> *"We got high on champagne. Started comparing notes on love and life— revealed our most intimate fantasies*—our not-so-true confessions. Sort of *took romance and eroticism to their bawdy limits."*
> The man squirmed. He looked flushed.[10]

On one level, this narrative is one of heterosexual temptation, appealing to the male editor by evoking a scene of unbridled passion. But there is no mistaking the homoerotic bait dangling on this hook. In fact, the "squirming" editor seems to sense that this is no place for him. He is terrified and finally jumps out of the car "before it had stopped rolling." So we are left with the image of the "Naked Ladies" trolling down the road in search of their erotic limit. The fantasy of the authors' naked bodies is further supported by the cluster of publicity head-shots that frames the text. Thirteen exuberant faces with varying degrees of air-brushing smile at readers and pull them into the bawdy scenario. Of course, the authors are not literally naked, but the text that proclaims "We're the 'Naked Ladies' and we're proud" figuratively undresses them before readers' eyes.

Twenty or so *RT* pages later, a smaller advertisement for *Naked Came* features eleven naked Lilliputian women reveling on the bare chest of a Gulliver-sized man. The homoerotic implications of this image are striking. The bodies of the women are far more exposed and enticing than the giant-man's; and the reiteration of their nudity, by virtue of their numbers and the provocative positions they assume, makes them the focal attraction of the image. Their tiny stature does not suggest disenfranchisement because the women are engaged in the active work of tying up the hero. Instead, their size makes them objects of erotic fascination: in the same way that one leans closer to a whispering speaker, one's eyes rove over the tiny bombshell bodies in search of exciting erotic details.

The intended audience for the *Naked Came* image makes the homoerotic potential impossible to ignore. If this ad appeared in a men's magazine, we could dismiss this potential as a male fantasy, as in "what man wouldn't want to be tied up and pawed over by beautiful naked dolls?" But the readership of *Romantic Times*, like that of romance fiction in general, is overwhelmingly female, evoking at least three different possibilities for reader identification in this image, all of them homoerotic. We may identify with the naked women, standing atop the hero with our arms thrown up in triumphant abandon. In this case, the largeness of the passive male body transforms him into mere landscape and pushes him to the margins of the erotic scene. Like the editor who was captured in the "Naked Ladies'" limo, he is an erotic toy rather than an active participant in their project. If anyone in this picture is likely to have sex, it is the gorgeous two- and threesomes of women intoxicated by communal s/m pleasure. The excitement and the intense athletic activity of this image center on the women, who may be imagined amid sounds of conspiratorial laughter, joint physical effort, and female pleasure.

Or perhaps we identify with the hero. His passive position and long hair may effeminize him enough for us to imagine ourselves in his lucky shoes. His large euphoric face draws us in and makes us envy him for the pleasure written there. In this case, the question becomes one of same-sex fantasy: "what woman doesn't want to be tied up and pawed over by beautiful naked women?"—especially on Valentine's Day.

In a third possibility, we stand outside the scenario as voyeurs, unable to imagine ourselves anywhere in the context of this scene or unable to choose between the active women and the passive man. Even this position asks viewers to revel in the pleasures that all of the figures take from the image of domination. The ad wants us to desire the fantasy of women working together to subdue The Man. The "Naked Ladies" want it, Gulliver enjoys it, and we (are supposed to) take pleasure from viewing it. Our gaze and the pleasure we get from the nudity and the action implicate us in sadomasochism, leaving no innocent space unclaimed by the erotic appeal of female nudity.

Marketing campaigns like that used for *Naked Came the Ladies* rely heavily on the suggestive appeal of homoerotic imagery. But they also depend on the safety of romance discourse (the pages of fan magazines, chat rooms, and web sites) for the indulgence of these ludic same-sex female fantasies. Thus, fans, authors, and editors have constructed a discursive space in which homoerotic potential is present, yet suppressed by a series of heteronormative master narratives: the Naked Ladies and their readers are "just friends"; the jittery editor and oversized man are the primary attractions and legitimating heterosexual cues; the women are able to participate in erotic activities without becoming seduced by each other. These master narratives continually discipline the potentially homoerotic content of romance discourse so that participants can have it both ways: they can avail themselves of the homosocial pleasures of same-sex fantasy in a way that does not actually disrupt the heterosexual assumptions of popular romance.

HOMOEROTIC REFLECTIONS: LOOKING AT THE HEROINE, LOOKING AT OURSELVES

Just as these paratextual documents play with same-sex desire, the text of many contemporary romances encourages readers to experiment with various modes of female-centered erotic pleasure through the complex process of reader-heroine identification. Radway's readers consistently claim that being able to "relate" to heroines is a primary component of an "ideal" love story; reader comments in romance magazines and on websites support this assumption. Women want to feel intensely connected to romance heroines, and if the heroine is silly, unbelievable, or the victim of too much violence, readers are less likely to engage with her in a satisfying way. Maureen, one of Radway's readers, describes this process and how it can go wrong:

> I resent characters in books that are absolutely too naive to be believable, because that way I feel the reader is—the writer is putting me down. So I will be offended.... That's why I avoid these books that are so depressing ["failed" as opposed to "ideal" romances]. All these terrible things that happen to the heroine are happening to me.... (*Reading* 159)

Maureen's identification with the heroines is almost seamless, as if the fictional characters are her doubles or imaginary stand-ins. As Sedgwick observes, the effect of doubling creates desire through the "slipperiness of identity" (105). To identify with one's double, especially out of longing for the double's power, is ultimately to desire the double itself. Yet, the ideology of individuality, the asymtotic space between the desiring subject and its double which is never entirely closed over, means that the identification is never fully complete and the desire operates continuously; one yearns for ever closer identification with the double.

Given the overtly erotic language used to describe the way women experience romance reading and the intense level of reader-heroine identification, a similar homosocial dynamic can be seen at work. Readers who inhabit the heroine's body dwell on the pleasures they find there. The language of Maureen's description suggests that, more than anything, readers are invested in the pleasure of their heroines. The female power of these narratives is the attractiveness of the heroine, wherein lies her mysterious ability to subdue the recalcitrant rake. When the boundary between the subject and object of desire dissolves, as Sedgwick sees happening between "doubled" male characters in gothic novels, *identification with* the doubled object of desire is inextricably linked to *desire for* that double. For romance readers, this imaginary doubling allows both a fantasy appropriation of the heroine's powerful attractiveness and a fantasy enjoyment of another woman's body as attractive. Readers can revel in her seduction *and* be seduced by her.

The process of desiring the heroine is also supported by the standard narrative details of romance novels. In general, these texts spend a great deal of energy describing the heroine's body, especially in sexual settings, ostensibly to foster close reader identification: readers have to know what kind of body they inhabit as they read. Yet readers are also encouraged to revel in the beauty of the heroine, to consume it in erotic detail. On one level, readers like Maureen identify with the heroine's body. But since this process is never entirely complete, readers also occupy an extratextual space in which they are voyeurs gazing with pleasure on the heroine's body; the heroine is a mirror image, a spectacle of identification. Sometimes, the erotic fascination of heroine as mirror image is explicitly thematized in the text, as it is in *Nobody's Angel*, one of my favorite historical romances. In the final scene of the novel, the heroine, Susannah, catches a glimpse of herself in a mirror. She is both subject and object of the seductive erotic gaze:

> [the hero] turned her to face the mirror more fully. Then, standing behind her, he began to unfasten her dress. Susannah could only watch, mesmerized, as he stripped her garments from her item by item, until finally she was naked. She felt like the worst kind of voyeur as she stared at herself in the glass. . . . (Robards 369)

At first, Susannah is mortified by this kind of specular eroticism. The hero coaxes, "'No, don't look away,' when she would have done just that." "Unable to help herself," the heroine continues to watch her naked image:

> Her mouth went dry as she gazed at her own body as though it belonged to someone else, gazed at the full white globes of her breasts tipped by nipples the color of brown sugar and engorged with wanting, gazed at her tapering rib cage and flaring hips and shadowy navel and the sable nest of hair between her thighs . . . suddenly a wild hot ache spiraled to life inside her and she moaned. The sound that emerged from between her lips also seemed to come from the wanton in the glass, and watching even as she experienced such pleasure was the most erotic sensation in the world. . . . (Robards 369–70)

In a literal process of mirror identification, Susannah is captivated by the spectacle of her own body in the throes of passion. The reader can experience the homoerotic attraction of this scene on at least two levels. As we embody Susannah, we are, like her, seduced by the reflection in the mirror. The text guides our eyes over contours that provoke "the most erotic sensation in the world" specifically because they are those of the mirror image. As readers, we experience the attractiveness of the heroine's "real" body, which can be imagined as a mirror image of our own. While the mirroring effect is usually less explicit, the possibility that we can identify with but never become the heroine means that the heroine's body is always available for our voyeuristic pleasure. Wanting to be her verges upon wanting *her*.

The homoerotics of this scenario are recuperated within a homosocial framework, as Susannah feels like "the worst kind of voyeur" and "would have" looked away from her own image if not encouraged by the hero. As readers, we might be tempted to think of ourselves as voyeurs too, were it not for the presence and approval of the hero. Susannah's shyness at what is coded as a potentially naughty self-pleasuring activity allows the reader still to consider the heroine, and herself, as a "nice girl," one who waits for the male stamp of approval before indulging in the attraction of the female body. Furthermore, the presence of the hero insists that this is a heterosexual scenario. Thus, we can imagine the reader, the hero, and the heroine occupying points on the homosocial triangle. Our potentially homoerotic desire for the heroine is mediated through, and heterosexually legitimized (i.e. rendered homosocial) by the presence of the hero.

THE HEROIC NEGOTIATIONS OF QUEER READERS

Recent trends in the romance industry facilitate even more potential queer reading practices. Until the mid-1990s, publishers required stories to be told exclusively from the heroine's point of view. This presumably kept the hero's motives cloaked in mystery and allowed readers to participate in their unraveling. Now, we increasingly read from the hero's perspective, as in Kristen Hannah's historical romance, *The Enchantment*, approximately half of the story is told through the hero's voice. In this book, Larence sees the heroine Emmaline change from a "coldly beautiful . . . marble statue" into a "flesh-and-blood woman of incredible loveliness" (216). At points in the text where we see the heroine through his eyes, our identification shifts, and we become seduced by the heroine in yet another way.[11]

Tania Modleski recounts in *Old Wives' Tales* (1998) how such changes in perspective have led to homoerotic dynamics. In a chapter titled "My Life as a Romance Reader," she describes how her conditioning as a self-professed romance addict was "so massively structured as heterosexual that the switch in erotic attachment from male to female seemed drastic and perilous" (*Tales* 34). But upon reading more recent romances where the hero's point of view is included, she finds herself "identifying with the lover of woman as well as the woman herself and vicariously experiencing the touch, taste, and smell of a woman's body" (*Tales* 64). She even goes so far as to "illustrate how easily the novels lend themselves to cross-gender readings" by citing a sex scene from one of her favorite popular romances—a scene in which heterosexual penetration is momentarily set aside (*Tales* 64). Because this scene is written from the hero's point of view, Modleski asserts, the reader can "change the names and the masculine pronouns and you have . . . lesbian sex" (*Tales* 64). Even here, traces of homosocial recuperation remain to discipline Modleski's reading: the hero's name, "Whip," suggests his masculine phallic power. He glories in the fact that "the virgin widow was his—whatever he wanted, however he wanted it" (*Tales* 64). Yet a queer reading such as Modleski's highlights the instability of this heterosexual iconography in spite of the hero's ludicrously phallic name and his objectification of the "virgin widow."

The shift in perspective that Modleski finds so compelling is one of several potentially queer innovations in the genre. The conventional dynamics of gender in romance novels have undergone a significant change since the 1970s, arguably because of the influence of feminism on mass culture. *The Enchantment* provides another interesting example, for Larence is a member of the newest breed of male romance protagonists: the Virgin Hero. Incredible as it may seem given historical/literary codes of sexuality, romances with Virgin Heroes have become one of the most popular subgenres in the industry and the subject of a special feature in the 1999 Valentine's issue of *Romantic Times*. On the *RT* website "theme spotlight," readers can look up books specifically about Virgin Heroes.[12]

In *The Enchantment*, Emmaline is the experienced sexual aggressor, eager to introduce Larence to the world of adult sexuality. In the consummation scene, Larence lies paralyzed with a naiveté rivaling the most pristine heroine's. As Emmaline stands naked before him in invitation, he asks her one ridiculous question after another to hide his anxiety. When she answers, "No, Larence. I want you," he spirals into deeper panic: "Uncertainty and confusion consumed him. What did she mean? Certainly not that she wanted to—" (Hannah 281). The language of hesitation, sexual insecurity, and curiosity standard for the heroines of yesteryear is now spoken by the hero. For a readership used to inhabiting the virginal character and experiencing the pleasures of innocent seduction, Larence seems a more likely candidate for reader identification than other "voiced" heroes, like "Whip." When we identify with Larence, we get the chance to be seduced by the heroine, to feel the power of her erotic gaze.

The final change in popular romance discourse that I want to discuss signals a more radical, and therefore more titillating and perhaps even queerer shift in the genre: the standard romance fantasy of reforming the recalcitrant rake through love is increasingly represented in terms of female-dominant s/m imagery. As if sex without penetration and virgin heroes weren't enough to confuse the usual iconography of female passivity/male dominance, now plots and book covers literalize female aggression. For example, the cover of *Nobody's Angel* features the heroine towering over the hero, who has been sold to her as an indentured servant, with a whip raised to strike him. He is off-balance, his arms held up to ward off her blows. Still more striking is Dara Joy's recent fantasy/romance, *Mine to Take*, a similar captive/captor story. Rather than a heroine in the grasp of a male figure, the cover shows instead a naked man with his hands chained over his head. The fully clothed heroine approaches him with a suggestively angled set of keys threateningly pointed towards his exposed body. The sexualized whips, chains, and keys, all clearly linked with both sadomasochism and phallic representation in the popular imagination, suggest a momentary destabilization of the hero's power. Deployed on the cover as a primary means of evoking reader desire, these images suggest a fantasy of phallic appropriation in which the male is now transformed into a passive object.

The process of objectification alongside the trend towards an increasing interiority of voiced heroes highlights the representational malleability that both allows for and disciplines queer readings of popular romance. On the one hand, these images show the instability of conventional codes of masculinity. Cover models like the famous Fabio exemplify a kind of vacuous hypermasculinity that can take on a variety of meanings, from dominant to submissive, predatory to virginal. On the other hand, the image of the hero—and the heterosexuality he symbolizes—is the necessary presence that keeps the romance genre inside the boundaries it threatens to exceed.

The examples I have chosen highlight the same-sex language, imagery, and desire circulating within popular romance discourse and the homosocial disciplinary apparatuses that only (but always) obscure homoerotic potential. However blurred sexual boundaries may have become, and regardless of spunky whip-wielding heroines and cowering heroes, every popular romance eventually ends in a celebration of heterosexual union. But what kind of heterosexuality is this? Popular romance represents itself as a heterosexual discourse, but one rife with sexually suggestive language describing readers' desire for their favored authors, whose invitation to a complex dynamics of identification brings the reader ever closer to fetishized heroic female bodies. Trends in popular romance signal a move towards queerer economies of representation, especially with respect to the "typical" hero. The replacement of 1970s-style bodice-rippers with virginal men and sexually experienced women (a replacement that occurred in response to readers' preferences) suggests a taste for more fluid erotic affiliations in women's popular culture. The homosocial discipline of popular romance manages to rein in its inherent homoerotic implications in order to present a would-be-coherent ideology of heterosexuality that is, like its masculine poster-boy Fabio, open to and erotically dependent upon its homoerotic fungibility.

Desire and the Marketplace

A READING OF KATHLEEN WOODIWISS'S *THE FLAME AND THE FLOWER*

—Charles H. Hinnant

Fredric Jameson's influential definition of genre as a social contract between "any writer and a specific reading public" has given rise to numerous studies of the ways literary production has been shaped by social, economic, and technological factors such as the histories of printing, publishing, and the reading public (160; see also Barthes 89–90). As a part of this enterprise, Janice Radway (1991) has shown how an audience for romance began to redefine itself in the early 1970s and to be redefined by the marketing strategies of American publishers who introduced a whole host of new authors and subgenres to an avidly receptive reading public. In the space of a generation, the publishing industry as a whole was transformed by the emergence of new houses and lines catering to a discrete but mass audience. In Radway's survey of the reading practices of forty-two diverse women from the midwestern community of Smithton, we come to understand the process by which these readers were initially confronted by an emerging set of undirected variations that opened up a multiplicity of possibilities, then actively made a choice, a decision that selected one particular set of narrative patterns and eventually rejected others. Beginning with Kathleen E. Woodiwiss's seminal *The Flame and the Flower* (1972), an unsolicited manuscript that became a surprising bestseller and then a model for other authors, Radway shows how a relatively brief interval of limited experimentation was brought to an end by culturally determined preferences and calculated marketing decisions that prepared the ground for an era of relative stability and homogeneity.[1] Like other mass-market genres, contemporary paperback romance novels are distinguished from mainstream fiction by their formulaic tropes: settings, contexts, dialogue, characters, and even plots are subject to innumerable permutations and variations, while core conventions remain unchanged.

The explosive growth and norming processes of this new market deserve the kind of attention Radway has given it, but by itself her analysis does not give any indication of the economic ideology embodied in this newly reformulated genre. Given the scope of the publishing phenomenon and given the awareness of authors, editors, readers, and critics of this phenomenon, it would be surprising indeed if at least a few contemporary romance novels did not contain traces of the values guiding this vast marketing enterprise. In an analysis of Woodiwiss's *The Flame and the Flower*, I propose to show that contemporary romance embodies a distinctive point of view, one that departs in significant ways from longstanding assumptions about the character of modern liberal market ideology.

According to the conventional argument, the contemporary American economy is driven by desire rather than by need but this desire is embodied in the figure of an implicitly masculine and autonomous subject, rationally pursuing his economic (and libidinal) self-interest in an open marketplace governed by the dual imperatives of scarcity and competition. Yet in spite of the advantages of such a bold and rugged, not to say ruthless, individualism in stimulating innovation and destroying customary constraints on enterprise, it seems that—moral considerations aside—individualism imposes important limitations on one's capacity to grow, by restraining intersocial exchange. What the contemporary genre of romance adds to this model of a rational and theoretically self-sufficient desire is the narrative of an external agent that reinvigorates, supplements, and vastly heightens this desire. In romance, this agent is embodied in the figure of "woman," a young and spirited heroine whose beauty and vulnerability proves capable of attracting the most obdurate and driven hero. When Jayne Anne Krentz describes the basic trajectory of contemporary romance novels as the "taming" of the alpha male by the heroine (112), she is describing a process, I contend, in which traditional masculine economic ideals of self-sufficiency, rationality, and rugged individualism are modified, if not overthrown, by a new commitment to the civilizing and feminizing virtues of sociability, empathy, and interdependence.

It is in this context that a careful study of *The Flame and the Flower* becomes relevant to more general theoretical issues. Even though contemporary romance novels have become the subject of rigorous feminist critique, it deserves to be emphasized that texts like *The Flame and the Flower* can be shown to correspond—at virtually every point—to a certain strain of feminist criticism of mainstream economics. Paula England describes the model of human nature embedded in neoclassical economics as "separative" because "it presumes that humans are autonomous, impervious to social influences and lack sufficient emotional connection to each other to make empathy possible" (Ferber and Nelson 37). Ann L. Jennings notes that "the term 'economic man' is an artifact originating in nineteenth-century cultural interpretations, which conflated man with dynamic market activity and woman with unchanging familial roles" (Ferber and Nelson 122). And in "Reading Neoclassical Economics: Toward an Erotic Economy of Sharing," Susan L. Feiner speculates as to whether a shift from "*homoeconomicus*" to "*heteroeconomicus*" might not be possible (Kuiper and Sap 163). In a very real sense, a novel like *The Flame and the Flower* seeks to flesh out the imaginative dimensions of such a possibility. The historical differentiation between masculine rationality and feminine affectivity has helped to shape the narrative responses of authors who make the domestication of the alpha male the basic trajectory of their narratives. The most striking fact about such narratives is the extent to which they also seek to dismantle the modern economic stereotype of a ruggedly self-sufficient, implicitly masculine, identity.

In spite of her vulnerability, the figure of the heroine, I argue, is meant to be understood as a progressive force in modern commercial society, one that openly questions central assumptions about modern capitalism.[2] In contemporary romance, this force is associated as much with desire, passion, and imagination as with the rational imperatives of accumulation and profit maximization. It can be seen in rudimentary form in *The Flame and the Flower*, a historical romance that is set in the Napoleonic period, an era of burgeoning commercial affluence yet one that flourished, as Ellen Meiksins Wood puts it, "before the real transformation of production and the labour force by industrial capitalism was very well advanced" (85). Within this world, the heroine is an imperiled figure, for her access to private autonomy and public life is restricted through limitations imposed upon a woman's legal rights to ownership. We can put this most clearly in Marxist terminology (though it is widely accepted). Heather Simmons, the orphaned heroine of *The Flame and the Flower*, occupies a marginal position in which she has no direct access to the means of her own reproduction as a human being. It follows that when her labor is appropriated by others, it is done so by what Marx called "extra-economic means"—that is by the overt coercion exercised, for example, by her tyrannical and sadistic Aunt Fanny. As Heather's guardian, Aunt Fanny is a particularly vociferous advocate for the structures of power and exploitation associated with a declining feudal patriarchy. Financially and socially impoverished herself, Aunt Fanny enforces upon her unprotected female charge an especially virulent species of Calvinism, characterized by rigorous asceticism, abject self-loathing, relinquishment of individuality, and the acceptance of socioeconomic deprivation as divinely ordained. Protestantism is here entirely an instrument in the service not of capitalism, but of social control, a rationalization for the economy of a hereditary and feudalized social structure. Indeed the patriarchs have disappeared from this decadent patriarchalist household: Heather's father, Richard Simmons, is dead and her uncle, John Summers, has become a pathetic broken man.

Given this precapitalist context, it is not surprising that the heroine becomes a tempting target of the lust and vanity of whose who would attempt to exploit her for their own private ends. The exemplary figure of such corruption in *The Flame and the Flower* as in many other romances—the epitome of vice, deceit, and sexual repulsiveness—is the tyrant-villain, here played by William Court, the brother and willing ally of Aunt Fanny. A shopkeeper who is also the partner of Lady Cabot, the mistress of a house of prostitution, Court lures Heather from her dreary life in the country to London under the pretext of placing her in a finishing school. In contrast to the entrepreneurial values of the hero, whose wealth arises from the innovative aspects of large-scale enterprise, Court's economic strategies are those of the petty trader, based on narrow speculation and short-run opportunism. Lacking a broader vision, Court is unable to actively search out and create new sources of wealth; he can only grasp occasions as they fitfully arise and is thus unable to comprehend the potential embodied in the figure of the heroine. Pursuing his interests in narrowly precapitalist terms, he seeks to seize her body by force, so that he can satisfy his own private needs and make a small killing, not seek to expand his limited enterprise.

This trajectory of the tyrant-villain's lust will be familiar to readers of eighteenth-century novels of rape and seduction: it represents the self-consuming nature of his passion, a desire that would burn up the very qualities in the object that incited it in the first place. In a sense, one might characterize the passion of the tyrant-villain as a predatory auto-sexuality that is marked by an exclusion of the other. This exclusion invites us to approach the tyrant-villain's passion as an inefficient utilization of the heroine's resources. Seeking to use her as object for his own immediate gratification, he will quickly grow weary of his prey, thus foregoing the potentially lucrative form of activity that might arise from her full productive (and reproductive) development of her talents, a development that would be inseparable from her ability to enjoy real freedom. Court reveals his limited expectations in telling Heather, "When I tire of you I shall allow you to join Lady Cabot's lovely group. You'll not find boredom there. And in time perhaps I'll even let you wed some rich soul who fancies you" (21).

The Flame and the Flower differs from older novels of seduction, however, in that it presents a narrative, not of her rescue by a masculine hero, but of a justifiable Lockean self-defense and rebellion—embodied in Heather's apparent murder of Court—against an oppressive despotism. If the heroine symbolizes the natural right of individuals to an independent and secure possession of their own property, including the property of their bodies, the tyrant-villain symbolizes a sinister, historically backward mode of appropriation. He is a figure of historical regression whose attempt to deny the heroine her natural right to life and liberty would drag her back into the swamps of feudal despotism and sexual servitude. A symbol of all that is diseased and hateful about this world is provided by Court's repulsive assistant, Thomas Hint, a murderous opportunist who later reveals to Heather that he has actually carried out what she mistakenly believed she had accomplished—the slaying of Court. His subsequent rape and murder of two other women embodies in concentrated, virulent form the unscrupulous tactics of the petty trader. From the standpoint of an emergent liberal market ideology, the sexual exploitation of women does provide opportunities for profit in an outmoded system where economic prospects are marginal, moral considerations entirely absent, and the scope of trading highly circumscribed; but at the cost of adopting an essentially carpe diem attitude toward commerce.

Perhaps the most notable single aspect of the novel's portrayal of Court as a petty shopkeeper, especially when compared to the far-flung mercantile activities of the hero, is his close alliance with a decadent nobility. Court's customers consist mainly of those who are wealthy enough to be able to afford the luxury fabrics he sells in his shop. His aim is not so much to create or stimulate a new market for these fabrics or for the young women he presumably provides for Lady Cabot's establishment; rather it is to make the most out of his opportunities to sell to a preestablished clientele. The pattern for the entire market is consequently given directly by the shopkeeper's avarice in catering to the whims and desires of an idle and profligate aristocracy.

The traditional plot of female virtue in distress highlights the vulnerability of a figure whose unique position is that she can serve, in Marxist terms, as both use value and exchange value in this highly traditional market. In addition to his demand for a body for exchange, the tyrant-villain also seeks an object of immediate gratification. Indeed it is her seeming availability, above and beyond any exchange value she might have, that makes Heather so eagerly sought after. Thus of the two thieves who later seek to abduct her from the bedroom she is sharing with her newly wedded husband, Brandon Birmingham, at the inn, she observes that "if they had been successful in taking her she would have been used many times by both of them before she'd have been presented to the Duke" (139). Brandon rejects the offer of the thieves to buy Heather from him in terms that are at once patriarchalist and Lockean: "This girl is *my* wife and carries *my* child. She belongs to *me*, and what is *mine*, I *keep!*" (140). At the same time, Brandon fails to recognize that Heather is not the possession of the autonomous, rational male property owner of Lockean theory but the rightful owner of her own body. It should not be surprising, therefore, that he also fails to comprehend the extent to which she has already become an object of impassioned, irrational, and libidinal desire. The calculated, cynical opportunity presented by the two thieves threatens not only the demise of the patriarch's desire for offspring but also the destruction of his sense of self, deeply invested at it is already in the bonds of a growing mutual desire which the thieves would have shattered.

Although Brandon's defense of Heather appears Lockean and patriarchalist, he uses his male status early in the novel to attain his own private libidinal gratification, every bit as much as William Court and the two thieves seek to do. Indeed if it were not for the presence of these tyrant-villains, the very idea of the hero would become threatened and the difference through which he acquires his superior moral status would break down. Brandon's unquestioning assumption that masculine privilege is his natural right surfaces most visibly in the way he initially forces himself upon Heather, whom he views as "a small tempting flower from the woods" (27). And, in truth, even his later marriage to the now-pregnant heroine, imposed upon Brandon by her aristocratic uncle, Lord Hampton, is still framed within the same system of feudalized coercion as the earlier episodes of seduction and rape. Brandon may be compelled to do the right thing, but he is nonetheless brought to marry Heather by the same means exercised by seducers and thieves as by landlords, employing their superior force, their privileged access to physical, military, judicial, and political power. Within such a context, the heroine still functions as exchange value—as the ideological product of material and symbolic exchanges between men.

Here, then, is the difference between a precapitalist and a capitalist ethos. The latter has nothing to do with the forcible extraction of wealth from others and everything to do with socioeconomic activities that take place without direct coercion. Individuals have both the right and the power to formulate their own plans and projects. Needs and desires are private: the individual (and household) are sovereign, constituting a personal sphere which must remain free from the interference of external figures who might seek to impose their own ends. For romance, the tyrant-villain is the figure that most obviously threatens this sphere; but patriarchalism—usually exemplified in the residual ideology of the hero—can also endanger individual sovereignty. It is in this sense that contemporary romance can be said to embrace a reinvigorated liberal market ideology: it is about freedom of choice in the form of a personal liberty that extends to women as well as men and about the accountability of public forces to private interests.

Yet it is also about social dynamism and progress; by insisting that institutions be directly accountable to individual desires, contemporary romance promotes initiative, enterprise, imagination, and the exuberant entrepreneurial energy that are taken to be the hallmarks of contemporary American capitalism. Brandon initially belongs to that class of merchant-adventurers which was the chief impetus behind the prosperity of colonial America. As Brandon tells Heather, long-distance trade between America and England united former enemies into a single commercial network and also provided him with the profit of a turn-around carrying trade: "I am a man of business. I sell my cotton and goods to the English for a profit. They sell me what my people will buy for more profit. I never hold grudges if I think it will interfere with the business of making money. Besides, I do a service for my country in bringing back things that are not yet obtainable" (136). Brandon's objective is not merely to stabilize and regularize ties with his commercial partners but also to capitalize trade. As he tells his mates,

Jamie Boniface and Tory MacTavish, about the goal of his last voyage, "Jeff and I both invested heavily in the cargo.... I'd like to see our money doubled. If we make it back in time it will be" (206). In contrast to this kind of entrepreneurial dynamism, the city of Charleston is depicted as having what Clifford Geertz termed a bazaar economy—i.e., one in which the total flow of commerce is fragmented into unrelated person-to-person transactions: "There were buyers and sellers and a great multitude of neither who yet sought to trim some small profit from the great sums of money that changed hands during the day" (426).[3] Although such an economy has the advantage of being able to mobilize large numbers of people on marginal or near-marginal levels of subsistence, it has the disadvantage of turning even wealthy buyers and sellers away from an interest in expanding markets and toward immediate gains and short-run killings. Upon his return to Harthaven, Brandon recognizes that progress toward more advanced patterns of economic activity can only take the form of a movement from a feudal, aristocratic slave economy to a modern capitalist economy based on free choice. Just as workers depend upon the market to freely sell their labor as a commodity, capitalists depend upon it to purchase labor that would be more productive than if it were coerced. Brandon explicitly recognizes this when he discusses his plans to purchase a timber mill with his younger brother, Jeff: "If the slaves were taken out and wages given for good workers, we could make it pay" (295).

It is in the central part of the novel, which is concerned, like so many other contemporary historical romances, with life after the ceremony at the altar, that the heroine begins to fulfill her role as a participant in this capitalist system. The comedic narrative of marital discord (and sexual frustration) enables her to fulfill this function by taking the by-now somewhat antiquated courtship plot as its model: like would-be suitors, initially troubled spouses must undergo a repetition of internal tests and external obstacles before freely discovering their mutual affection at the narrative's end. It is noteworthy that this long process of mutual discovery dovetails at every point in the narrative with an account, first of Brandon's highly profitable activities as a merchant-adventurer, then as an "improving" landowner, and finally as the restorer of the derelict lumber mill.

In the novel's plot, morever, the strategic use of striking juxtapositions, complementary episodes, climactic moments, and devices of parallelism help to sustain our belief in an analogously ordered system governing both private passion and public prosperity. And in *The Flame and the Flower*, as in a multitude of contemporary romance novels, the imposition of such an analogy functions specifically to support the reconceptualization of personal life in individualist terms: the happy ending of the marriage plot as well as its opposite, the failure of the tyrant-villains to gain their ends, point to romantic marriage as the desire and rightful goal of a reformulated capitalist ethos, even though Heather Birmingham, in contrast to a host of later heroines, does not become directly involved in commercial activities herself.[4]

Like other historical romances, *The Flame and the Flower* complicates this formula by taking over and colonizing certain aspects of a rival genre, the male romance of adventure. At the opposite end of the spectrum from the older courtship plot, the adventure romance constructs a homosocial family or team with strong affective, though hierarchical, ties among men. In a manner that anticipates many other historical romances, *The Flame and the Flower* disrupts this construction by thrusting the heroine into the established routine of Brandon's commercial sailing vessel *Fleetwood* during their long voyage from London to his home in Charleston, South Carolina. Even though newly married, she still gives rise to a certain tension because men as sailors, fighters, drinkers, and casual wenchers are encouraged to remain independent yet are vulnerable to the male sexual longing and jealousy produced by the mere presence of a woman in their midst. Her disruptive impact is comically illustrated by her early and relatively easy escape from *Fleetwood*. Of this escape, Brandon later tells her that his cabin boy and manservant George "was quite embarrassed when he found that you had tricked him. The fact that a mere wisp of femininity had made him quake before an empty gun injured his pride" (134). By means of this dislocating narrative principle, and its destabilizing effect on the ship's relationships, roles and structure, the text appropriates the male adventure romance for its own ends, calling into question easy assumptions about the ramifications of this genre for a liberal market ideology.

It is much more difficult to make a similar case for the heterosocial world into which Heather enters when she arrives with Brandon at his estate, Harthaven, outside of Charleston. It is not simply that this world figures in *The Flame and the Flower* as a sort of kinship support system, standing for all the stabilizing tendencies that were lacking in Aunt Fanny's household, William Court's shop, and on board Brandon's sailing vessel, *Fleetwood*. What is more important is that Heather, like the heroines of the great romances of the eighteenth and nineteenth centuries, finds in the country-house ethos her ideal of the good life. Yet in the instance of Heather Simmons, this process of identification is left notably incomplete. In addition to being alienated from Harthaven by her poverty, compromised marriage, and secret past, Heather spurns a subordinate position as inadequate to her desire for personal self-fulfillment. Woodiwiss in fact rejects the traditional aristocratic role of the country house; in *The Flame and the Flower*, Harthaven has ceased almost altogether to exist in a manorial atmosphere. What Austen for instance had defined as a feudal system—and which she had imaged in the country estate—had been a vision of order, continuity, and hierarchy; it was the ideal of hospitality and community. Woodiwiss, on the other hand, has modernized the image of stability by infusing it with elements of a capitalist system. Moreover, the country house is no longer the embodiment of an aristocratic ideology. Traditional preoccupations like conspicuous expenditure, inheritance, and strategic marital alliances are exposed as shabby and decadent. Indeed, with the arrival of the hero and heroine, Harthaven becomes the locus of a newly energized entrepreneurial system. Whatever her real situation—which is made clear by her anxieties about money and status—Heather is just what this system apparently needs in order to become transformed into a thriving commercial economy.

It is within such a context that we should be wary of drawing a sharp line between romantic love and marriage as ideal categories characterized by opposed pairs such as disinterest/interest or innocence/experience (see, for example, Cohn, 21). Such contrasts obscure both the libidinal dynamics linking the central characters and the contrast between calculating self-interest and passionate desire which is my focus here. Instead, I argue that in contemporary romance there is a continuity or 'fit' between romantic desire and the passions driving a new feminized market economy. If there are instances of disinterested passion to be found in *The Flame and the Flower*, they are embodied in the hopeless love of the pathetic, rejected rivals, Brandon's manservant George, Henry Whiteside, and Sybil Scott. Heather Simmons, by contrast, is no romantic innocent; if at first she seems inordinately passive, accepting without question the arranged marriage that Lord Hampton has planned for her, she later turns into an energetic woman, determined to establish a place at Harthaven: "My first night here and yet I feel an odd, delicious oneness with this land. It's so immense, so vast beyond my wildest dreams, a great wide space to let my heart run free, and never again know the mean toil of a drudge" (267). Heather's interest in involving herself in the affairs of the country house increases in proportion to her desire and respect for her husband. Contemporary romance, the text implies, is as void of disinterested notions of romantic love as are the novels of Jane Austen.

In affirming the complex ambiguity of the heroine's attitude toward love and marriage, the text simultaneously implicates the hierarchy of male and female roles that too often transforms love relations into a battle for mastery and possession. The figure of the heroine exists partly through negative counterpoint in *The Flame and the Flower:* Brandon's former fiancée, Louisa Wells, exemplifies the limitations of conventionally constructed identities rooted in aristocratic traditions of privilege and power. Louisa's doomed assertiveness quickly grows into a monomaniacal desire to possess and use others; in seeking to reclaim Brandon for herself, she accepts the terms of aggression and intrigue still valued by a partially feudalized society. Yet her artful blandishments and calculated affronts are consistently called into question by her aristocratic habits of promiscuity, debt, and exorbitant consumption; she hatches her comically ill-conceived schemes not merely to keep Brandon but to maintain her threatened status, wealth, and power: "Now, since Louisa had been left alone by the death of her parents a few years back, her land was being neglected and misused. Louisa was badly in debt. She had spent the fortune her father had left her and had sold all but a few of her slaves to keep up her high standard of living which had become only a front now" (32). In this connection, one might argue that the significance of Louisa's example resides in the threat that her femininity poses to the novel's emergent liberal ideology. The antithesis of the rational utility maximizer and rugged masculine individualist is the figure of the consumer as dupe—as a passive slave to desires, whims, and impulses; in conventional market ideology this figure is usually coded as feminine.

But such a stringently negative interpretation simply excludes by definition the alternative conception of womanhood embodied in the figure of the heroine. Although Heather, like Louisa, is preoccupied throughout the narrative with clothing and appearance, she is introduced into the world of consumer fashion, represented by Madame Fontaineau's shop, by her impeccably well-tailored husband. It is through this pattern of mediated consumption that the hero constructs woman as desirable object; the implication is that the production of the heroine as feminine icon falls within the register of masculine power and that this production will replace distinctions based on class with distinctions based on beauty and the fashion system. Yet it is not entirely surprising to discover that Brandon's remaking of Heather into a repository of masculine desire is a public as well as a private act and thus can evoke sexual jealousy and rivalry as well as personal delectation.

The episode in Madame Fountaineau's shop exemplifies the mediated way in which a fascination with dress is presented in *The Flame and the Flower*. Heather's obvious delight in the shops of London is explicitly related to her recollection of "her childhood pleasure of going with her father to these same shops" (163). There is thus no automatic, natural female appetite for luxury goods. It would be misleading to contend that *The Flame and the Flower* promotes a culture of consumption, a materialistic culture based on money, concerned with "having" rather than "being." On the contrary, it rejects the claim that desires are insatiable and attributes the moral pathology associated with this claim to the rival figure and identifies it with casual promiscuity. What is being contrasted in Woodiwiss's reworking of the venerable Rowena–Rebecca opposition is Louisa Wells's capacity to destroy wealth with Heather's similar power to participate actively in the production of wealth. At the level of plot alone, the significance of the former is suggested by Louisa's sale of her ancestral lands to Brandon. This transfer points to the demise of a once-dominant social order—aristocratic feudalism—and implies the opening of an ideological space which allows for the reconceptualization of womanhood in terms of a liberal market ideology. Hence in contrast to her compulsive and wasteful rival, the heroine shows little interest in maximizing short-term gains or in purchasing more than she actually needs.

Just as there is no valorization of exorbitant consumption in *The Flame and the Flower*, so there is no justification of ascetic production and accumulation, no defense of a naturalized *homo economicus*. Commerce and agriculture, insofar as they can be pursued profitably, presuppose a mean between the Puritan orientation toward extreme thrift, savings, and the future and an aristocratic ethos of spending and credit. Given the hero's initial appearance as a merchant adventurer "with the look of a pirate about him" (26), however, one might be forgiven for assuming that he neglects the feminine ethos of hospitality and caring and embodies an exclusionary definition of capitalism instead. This view of capitalism hinges on the conviction that the ideology of liberal individualism understands itself as a social form grounded in the imperatives of relentless accumulation and profit maximization and thus no longer requires the virtues of liberality, sociality, and sentimentality. *The Flame and the Flower* challenges this assumption. Brandon exemplifies the vigorous, self-interested pursuit of wealth but ultimately comes to embody this endeavor in conjunction with a commitment to a certain degree of generosity and altruism. This commitment is apparent in his changing attitude toward Heather. In fact, her desirability as an object of love and as a repository of value for Brandon increases in proportion to his ability to imagine her as independent not only of the scheme by which their marriage was arranged but of all socioeconomic exchange. For him, she is exempt from the temptations facing others in his social world, a freedom seen in the fact that she has "never succumbed to selling herself or openly pleading for sustenance" (425). This comment reveals Brandon's growing awareness of Heather's strong sense of her own rights, her indignation at injustice, and the willingness to rebel that had liberated her from the clutches of William Court.

Brandon's generosity and altruism become evident not only in the gifts he lavishes on Heather but also in the money he gives to Aunt Fanny in order to be free of any subsequent claims she might make on Heather and their child (395–96). These qualities are perhaps most obvious, however, in his recruitment of the unemployed and depressed Jeremiah Webster to be the manager of his newly purchased timber mill, his rehabilitation of Webster and his impoverished family, and his personal supervision of the cleaning by his own family of the house that he has rented to the Jeffersons. These economic activities are basically social and cultural. The managerial relation between Brandon and Webster is an unequal one, inappropriate for family and friends. Nevertheless, the tie is a social one and far from crudely exploitative. It is mediated by the generous assistance that Brandon and his family provide to the astonished and bewildered Jeffersons.

This collective yet interested approach to economic activities, and in fact to entrepreneurship and innovation as such, bears a resemblance to what was characterized in the eighteenth century as "*doux* commerce" (Hirschman 58–63).[5] This is the notion of commerce as a civilizing process that polishes the manners, tames violence and unreason, and promotes peaceful intercourse between individuals, groups, and nations. But *doux* commerce also functions as a broader metaphor for the social and personal: for the free exchange not only of goods and services but also of ideas, sentiments, and even libidinal pleasures. The growing passion of the hero and heroine represents the mutual attraction of this kind of uncompelled libidinal exchange. The climactic sexual episode in the novel (391–94) generalizes this kind of erotic transaction and represents its generalization—in contrast to their unsatisfactory initial sexual encounter (26–33)—as broadly desirable. Heather exemplifies this eroticization of self-interest—the feminization of virtue in the marketplace—when she engages in barter with the peddler, Mr Bates, trading the beige gown she wore on the night she first met her husband for the piece of green velvet with which she makes him a new coat (274–75).

The spread of sexuality across the narrative of contemporary romance novels occurs, firstly, because sexuality becomes a central focus of *doux commerce* (in the specific sense that the central protagonists reproduce social relations through sexual exchanges) and in the sense that other foci become less important (e.g. good manners and conventional sexual propriety); and, secondly, because the values associated with sexuality acquire a prestige that is seen as permeating all areas of life. This kind of passion is the antithesis of the auto-sexuality embodied by the villain-tyrant in feudal-aristocratic narratives of rape and seduction. The latter is characterized as an indifference to the other, whereas genuine passion, as a purely subjective activity, is inscribed within an intersubjective space (be it that of dialogue, dissent, or erotic exchange). Such a subjectivity, even if it does not go through the detour of acceptance by the other, must come to terms with the traces of its difference from itself. Yet this intrusion of difference does not seem to disrupt the relation between the two selves but rather seeks to seal it in the permanence of shared desire.

The degree to which *The Flame and the Flower* incorporates such erotic sympathies is nowhere more evident than in the change that takes place in the figure of the hero during the course of the narrative. As his younger brother, Jeff, tells Heather, "before he met you, he believed he could control his emotions and felt very self-assured. Having never sampled honest love, he obviously finds himself at a loss and cannot cope with the emotions you inspire" (380–81). Here romantic love brings more than a challenge to an ancient homosocial tradition of masculine self-mastery. Within the context of the novel, it also creates a climate in which the modification of the masculine economic ideals of rational self-interest and rugged individualism by the civilizing and feminizing virtues of passion, imagination, sentimentality, and interdependence come to seem plausible. In the narrative, this transformation is reinforced by Brandon's decision to give up his earlier career as a merchant-adventurer in order to return to Harthaven. Such an ethos is also responsible for idealizing the archetype of the owner-laborer relationship reproduced in Brandon's reclamation of Jeremiah Webster. The profits that the mill begins to yield

(366) are meant to testify to the benefits of an enterprise that rests on the trust and group loyalty wholly lacking in an ego-centered economy.

This union of reason and emotion is a precarious one and is repeatedly threatened by the violence unleashed upon the body of the heroine by the tyrant-villain's lust. Like Amelia, the heroine of Henry Fielding's last novel, the heroine of contemporary historical romance is often subject to multiple assaults upon her body, in most cases saved by the last-minute intervention of the hero. Yet the passions aroused by these assaults can also become a paradoxical source of strength. To imagine the heroine as victim of rape or seduction is to make the threat of bodily assault into an impetus for the passions that fuel the new liberalized market economy. The tyrant-villain is not simply a holdover from an earlier social order; he also becomes the origin of passions that transform the feminized intervention into the new market society into a more potentially subversive public articulation than might otherwise emerge. This may be why contemporary romance is so closely related to the romantic suspense novel or "pure" suspense novel with just a touch of romance. In these tough-minded, often violent character-driven fictions, the fears aroused by sexual pathology are likely to become paramount while the desires associated with romance recede into the background. The small group of authors who started writing paperback category romances and then shifted to suspense novels have not necessarily abandoned the premises of their earlier works. On the contrary, they have continued to embrace an overall vision of the harmfulness of a predatory auto-sexuality and a commitment to demystifying the economic ideology that might sanction it.

Roland Barthes argued that the ideology informing the marketing strategies that produced the classic novel is "represented *en abyme* in the narrative" (89). This view of buyer-seller relationships is justified in this case by the way in which the vast circuit of authors, would-be authors, editors, admiring critics, and avid readers of romances have come to represent themselves as an extended family with shared interests and common desires. Within this family—much as within the Birmingham family in *The Flame and the Flower*—the identification of capitalism with an impersonal self-regulating marketplace is replaced by the realignment of capitalism with a social order in which economic exchanges are coextensive with the personal relations between individuals. The last section of a romance makes a significant contribution to this ethos, for it usually contains not only an excerpt from the author's next romance, a brief advertisement listing bestsellers and an address from which they can be ordered directly, but also and most importantly, a brief note by or about the author, frequently accompanied by a portrait-photograph. A point of imaginative induction into the narrative, the convention of the personal note and photograph are a device by which the distance between author and reader, seller and buyer, can be narrowed; it implies that their shared interests and concerns belong to a different level of imaginative intensity, affection, and intimacy than relations between the authors and readers of more conventional books.[6]

It seems apparent, in fact, that the distinction between the economic sphere and the sentimental sphere, so familiar to us in the modern world, is precisely what the genre of romance seeks to contest. We might say that romance fiction represents the vision of a capitalism transformed from within, indeed purged of its more brutal features. It is out of this ideological commitment that romance seeks to overcome the longstanding Aristotelian opposition between production for use (the household) and production for exchange (commerce). For Aristotle, the former (the *oikos*) is associated with the aristocratic values of leisure, hospitality, and the contemplative life, the latter (*chremisthos*) with the plebeian exploitation of others and an unnatural desire for gain. Within romance, these antithetical domains—long ago recoded as feminine and masculine—are integrated through the love plot into a tertium quid that seeks to overcome the limitations of both. The idea of economic change then transforms the image of a capitalism where everyone seeks to better his or her own lot into the image of a progressive or dynamic system that leads to a higher level of welfare for the community as a whole.

A Story of Her Weaving

THE SELF-AUTHORING HEROINES OF GEORGETTE HEYER'S REGENCY ROMANCE

—*Karin E. Westman*

> *Literary reputations rise and fall, but Georgette Heyer's has yet to get past the first hurdle of knee-jerk critical disdain. . . . It's time she was resurrected from the genre cleansing that despatched the historical romance to the bottom of the literary pit.*
> —Rosemary Goring

> *Talk about my humour if you must talk about me at all!*
> —Georgette Heyer, *to her editor*

An institution for several generations of readers in America, Australia, New Zealand, and particularly the U.K., popular romance novelist Georgette Heyer (1902–1974) is a British cultural icon few will admit to having read in their teens, let alone in the decades that follow. Though "despatched," as Goring notes, to "the bottom of the literary pit" for the genre she chose, Georgette Heyer deserves to be resurrected. Of her many contributions to twentieth-century British literary culture, one stands out: Heyer offers a fascinating perspective on the relationship between history and romance, choosing to invest the women of her Regency romances with the possibilities of self-authorship and a concomitant control over their worlds. Combining masculine speech with masculine knowledge, Heyer's Regency heroines can make story into history, thereby altering the expected narratives of their lives.

For the Regency heroines, "authoring" one's own history depends on knowing the rules of patriarchal society, particularly knowing how to deal in three currencies of that society: money, sex, and wit. The heroines of Heyer's modern and contemporary romances, four novels suppressed by Heyer soon after their publication in the 1920s, differ greatly, highlighting the scope of power accorded to the Regency romance heroines. The heroines of the "moderns," excepting the title character of *Helen*, falter in the knowledge and verbal skill needed to revise the social script, and they particularly lack control over an important currency: knowledge of sex. Their failures suggest that, for Heyer, successful revisions to the expected narratives of women's lives come more easily within the past of the Regency than within the present of readers' lives. Without knowledge of male sexual desire and fluency in the language of masculine power, the heroines of the "moderns" cannot write themselves into the happiness and shared humor that characterizes the relationship between Regency hero and heroine.

Before reading Heyer's heroines, we should note the vexed position Heyer and her romances hold within literary history—how her work balances between the "literary pit" of romance and a higher canonical shelf. Though she is the author of 56 novels and one collection of stories, Heyer is hardly received through the literary establishment's front door. Instead, thanks to her phenomenal success as the mother of Regency romance, Heyer typically enters literary conversations as Jane Austen "lite"—a "literary bubble bath," as romance novelist Elizabeth Mansfield remarks.[1] Though Heyer published only one romance novel, *Powder and Patch* (1923), with the infamous Mills and Boon (subsequently moving to Heinemann and Bodley Head), many presume that all of her romances follow the house stereotype.[2] By contrast, Heyer's mysteries often place her in the more respectable company of Dame Agatha Christie and Dorothy Sayers, while in a few circles Heyer is elevated to the role of historian for *An Infamous Army* (1937), an historical romance used to teach Wellington's strategy at Waterloo to public school boys (Hodge 168).

The historical detail of *An Infamous Army* is hardly unique within the body of Heyer's work. Though presumed only "escapist" romance, Heyer's novels rely on realistic layers of rich historical detail culled from old turnpike records, slang dictionaries, and Regency biographies and memoirs. Visitors to Heyer's home reported the "impressive library of about one thousand historical books among which she sat to write," including her own notebooks on Regency life and culture indexed "under such headings as *Boots and Shoes, Beauty, Colours, Dresses and Hats, Household, Prices*" (Raine).[3] The recognition Heyer received for *An Infamous Army*, however, never carried over to her other novels, despite their historical detail. The lack of critical acclaim illustrates and replicates traditional criteria for cultural worth: when the subject is love and war, Heyer's efforts are publicly valued as "history," but when the subject is love and marriage, her efforts are relegated to the realm of the popular.

Her Regency romances, however, made Heyer a household name and continue to grant her lasting narrative power within contemporary culture. She is remembered each year on the *Times* and *Independent* "Anniversaries" page of births and deaths alongside other prominent cultural and political figures of British history, attesting to her eminence within British culture.[4] Her romance novels have enjoyed enviable sales since their initial publication,[5] with several titles currently in new print runs in both the U.S. and the U.K., and they have also appeared on the radio, on the stage, and in contemporary novels.[6] The cultural status of her works, by contrast, remains under debate: when a reviewer aligns Heyer with other "bodice ripper" romance writers, there is sure to be a letter to the editor correcting the mistake.[7] Heyer is as likely to be named in the company of popular authors ("Harold Robbins, Georgette Heyer or Sidney Sheldon," writes Tan Ling Ai for Malaysia's *New Straits Times*) as in the company of women writers of literature ("Georgette Heyer, Jane Austen and George Eliot," writes Philip Howard for *The Times*). Heyer's presence on the cultural landscape, high or low, is not even limited to the literary: her name is frequently invoked to conjure for the general reader the Regency period as a whole. Whether the topic is a new study of eighteenth-century history (Mandler), the slave trade in Britain (Gregory), or the latest trend in fashion (Alexander), the mention of "Georgette Heyer" guarantees that readers have in mind the leisured upper-class social world of Regency England that Heyer created. Such recurring cultural significations, dwelling apart from the novels and the author herself, suggest that the Heyer narrative holds considerable sway over the British cultural imagination.

Although Heyer's substantial if slippery narrative power persists, few critics have addressed the place of Heyer's historical romances within literary history, exploring neither her innovative narrative structure nor her extensive readership.[8] One exception is Helen Hughes, who persuasively argues in her study of *The Historical Romance* (1993) that Heyer's novels are best seen as not merely initiating a much-imitated Regency genre, but as a crucial link between earlier "cloak and dagger" romances of Stanley Weyman and Rafael Sabatini and the "bodice-rippers" of the 1970s (10). For Hughes, the initial popularity of Heyer's novels, from roughly 1920 to 1970, suggests that the narratives they contain resonated with an increasingly female audience, who struggled to reconcile new strides in social welfare with established perceptions of women's role in society (11, 17, 133–4).[9] Josef Hurtubise's essay "A Consideration of Her Period Influences" (1998) focuses on Heyer's relationship to an established canon of literature, offering an insightful analysis of the relationship between Heyer's romances and the works of Samuel Richardson, Sir Walter Scott, Fanny Burney, Charlotte Smith, the Baroness Orczy, Richard Sheridan, and Oscar Wilde, as well as the oft-cited Jane Austen. Whereas Hurtubise divides Heyer's historical romances into three overlapping categories (romance, intrigue adventure, and comedy of manners), the critics E. R. Glass and A. Mineo in their essay "Georgette Heyer and the Uses of the Regency" (1984, 1986) offer a less nuanced, more structuralist, and ultimately more conservative reading of Heyer's development of the genre, "tracing her progress from the picaresque tale" to "the novel of manners," "from action to psychology" (285). A recurring theme in these three critical appraisals of Heyer's work, though, is her link to the comedy of manners—a connection worthy of further analysis, given the power granted to words and speech within Heyer's novels.

In Heyer's Regency romances, as in the world of Oscar Wilde's comedies, saying something makes it so: speech becomes act, story becomes history, so long as one can persuade one's audience to believe it could or should be so. Heyer's most extended foray into this performative narrative mode occurs in *The Talisman Ring* (1936), a romance set in 1793. Although the novel's setting precedes the Regency period (1811–1820), the novel itself appears in 1936, just after Heyer initiates her long line of Regency romances with the publication of *Regency Buck* in 1935. In *The Talisman Ring*, not only does Heyer play with the conventions of gothic romance much as Austen does in *Northanger Abbey*, but she also provides us with a metatextual commentary on the romance form by having her characters debate the narrative they enact for each others' and the readers' pleasure.

When the banished and dashing Ludovic returns to claim his right as the tenth Baron Lavenham and must flush out the double-timing Basil, cousin to both Ludovic and the more sober Sir Tristram Shield, Heyer's characters search for stories to enact against Basil as well as to explain the events they experience by his hand. Their situation frequently leaves them jockeying for authority over the developing narrative:

> Miss Thane interposed placably. "Don't argue with him, Eustacie. It's my belief he's in a high fever."
>
> [Ludovic] grinned at her. "I am," he agreed. "But my head's remarkably clear for all that."
>
> "Well, if it's clear enough to grapple with the details of this story of yours, tell us what became of the groom's horse," said Miss Thane.
>
> "The smugglers' killed it," offered Eustacie.
>
> Ludovic shook his head. "No, that won't do. No corpse. Damn the horse, it's a nuisance! Oh, I have it! When I was shot the brute threw me, and made off home."
>
> "Maddened by fright," nodded Miss Thane. "Well, I'm glad to have that point settled. I feel I can now face any number of Excisemen." (70)

Since the novel's narrative revolves around the characters' desire to develop the best "story" to tell a given audience or to explain a series of events, all the characters—and not just the young and romantic Eustacie[10]—engage in imaginative story-telling with the aim to persuade, as well as to enact the stories they have composed.

Through the young heroine Eustacie and the older heroine Sarah Thane, Heyer offers a pointed commentary on a woman's role as author and actor. Frustrated that "just because one is female one should never be allowed to have any adventures" (46), Eustacie is ready to create the adventure she desires—a sentiment shared by the quiet and wiser Sarah Thane, who is more than willing to join a romance-in-progress when she comes upon Eustacie binding up the wounds of the bleeding Ludovic. Sarah observes, "I see I've thrust myself into an adventure," quickly reassuring Eustacie, "My dear ma'am, I have been looking for adventure all my life!" (57–8). Dispensing with the traditional gendering of authorial control and heroic action, Heyer places both men and women as the tellers and performers of the novel's tales: Eustacie can command Sir Tristam to listen and act because "I have made a plot" (98), even if later she must castigate Sir Tristram for usurping her narrative: "'Well!' Eustacie turned quite pink with indignation. 'It is too bad! This is *our* adventure, and he has left us without a word, and, in fact, is trying to take it away from us!'" to which Sarah Thane replies, "Men!" (223). By allowing the indignant Eustacie and amused Sarah to proffer commentary on—and by the end of the novel revise—the quality of Sir Tristram's and Ludovic's narratives and authorial skill (81), Heyer suggests that women, as well as men, can author a story and choose the history they would like to enact.

The characters in *The Talisman Ring* set the stage for the self-determining heroines of the Regencies,[11] heroines who shape their lives by revising existing narratives and manipulating the narrative expectations of their social "audiences," and who do so to garner maximum freedom and satisfaction for themselves as well as others. The Regency heroines nearly always succeed in their endeavors and on their own terms; for them, the ability to "author" one's own story or history depends on knowing the rules of patriarchal society and deftly exercising masculine knowledge of money, sex, and wit. Even though Heyer's Regency heroines may not *have* money or sex—though most do have wit—the heroines have knowledge of how men use these social currencies to succeed. As a result, Heyer's Regency heroines are able to "write" their own histories, as well as others', by revising as much as possible the patriarchally scripted lives they are expected to live, rescripting their lines in the "author's" voice.[12]

Some Regency heroines, of course, are more successful authors than others, since with age and experience comes skill. Roughly three degrees of narrative control are illustrated by Heyer's Regency heroines: first, there is the young heroine recently launched into fashionable society (the *ton*) who is just learning the power her words could have, represented by the Honorable Phoebe Marlow of *Sylvester* (1957); next, the young but more experienced heroine who can shape history to her own ends even if she lacks personal knowledge of physical desire and love, represented by Frederica Merrivale of *Frederica* (1965) and Sophy Stanton-Lacy of *The Grand Sophy* (1950); and lastly, the older heroine closing on thirty and therefore "on the shelf" who can exercise the greatest control through her knowledge of the "ways of the world"—verbal, fiscal, or sexual—, represented by Lady Serena Carlow of *Bath Tangle* (1955) and Annis Wychwood of *Lady of Quality* (1972). Looking at each of these representative heroines[13] in turn, we can evaluate their success at self-authorship and the degree of narrative control each enacts, noting not only the skill of the older heroines but the difficulties faced by the younger, since the younger heroines' mistakes also define what constitutes success.

First, the heroine recently launched into society, just learning the power of words: Phoebe Marlow, the young heroine of *Sylvester, or the Wicked Uncle* (1957), best illustrates the ingenue who attempts authorship in the face of masculine authority and privilege, only to have her narrative taken out of her control. While all of Heyer's young heroines must learn how to use language if they wish to control the narrative of their lives, Phoebe's difficulties include the written as well as the spoken word. Escaping an arranged marriage for an impromptu second season in London at the same moment her gothic satire of London high society, *The Lost Heir*, is being published anonymously, Phoebe hopes to write herself into a happy domesticity with her former governess. Her plans are upset when she discovers that she has accidentally made Sylvester, the most eligible and powerful bachelor as well as the man her parents wish her to marry, into the "Wicked Uncle" of the novel's subtitle. Who else could Phoebe's creation, "Count Ugolino," be but Sylvester, with *those* eyebrows, and an uncle as well (131)? To Phoebe's horror, the accidental *roman a clef* enjoys wonderful sales, coming on the heels of Lady Catherine Lamb's *Glenarvon* (49);[14] still worse, Phoebe's published words take on a life of their own as each member of the *ton* offers a "translation" of the novel's sharply drawn characters and begs to speak with Phoebe, on the sly, about a reading of who is who. At first enthralled by "a story of her weaving" (168), Phoebe despairs of ever unweaving its threads.

Phoebe's skill in caricature, particularly her choice of sinister eyebrows for her devilish hero, nearly undoes her reputation: Sylvester's pride prevents him from laughing at her spot-on portraiture, and Phoebe wounds his pride further by abandoning him on the ballroom floor after he taunts her for her published portrait. Though in the end she is able to redeem Sylvester's good opinion through her care of his nephew, her social standing is saved by three older women who shape the social script to her advantage. Sylvester's mother, *a grand dame* who is herself an authoress, places her powerful social voice behind Phoebe (315, 323). Sylvester's cousin Georgiana advises Phoebe's grandmother to take Phoebe to Paris, while she puts about a counternarrative to the current gossip, trumping another's speech by her close relation to Sylvester:

"You know that no one can be more valuable than I in this affair, because I am Sylvester's cousin, and what I say of him will be believed rather than what Ianthe says. I shall set it about that that scene last night is the outcome of a quarrel which began before Sylvester went away to Change: what could be more likely? *And*," said Georgiana, in a voice of profound wisdom, "I shall tell it all in the *strictest* confidence! To one person, or perhaps two, just to make sure of the story's spreading." (222)

The Dowager wonders whether "anyone will believe Phoebe didn't write that book," but Georgiana responds, "They must be *made* to" (222). Her response marks the combination of will and tactical knowledge of public speech Phoebe currently lacks but might attain. The novel ends with

Phoebe promising not to bring Count Ugolino back to life in a sequel and "abandon[ing] (for the time being at all events) any further attempt to bring [Sylvester] to a sense of his iniquity" (332). The parenthetical qualification suggests that Sylvester's mother may prophesy correctly when she thinks "there would be some lively fights if he married Phoebe" (321): clever with the written word, Phoebe may soon learn to be as clever with speech.

To be published, then, to have one's words taken and fixed in print, can be a strike against successful social authorship; by contrast, a limber script, a quick wit, and knowledge of the more seamy sides[15] of Regency society allow more experienced heroines like Frederica Merrivale and Sophy Stanton-Lacy of the novels *Frederica* (1965) and *The Grand Sophy* (1950) to get what they want and be who they choose. These two "managing" females—one through candor and one through blithe strength of will—succeed in rescripting their lives and the lives of those around them thanks to their fluency with the language of men.

Frederica's experience managing her father's estate and keeping her three brothers in line provides her with a worldly perspective and language that belie her youthful appearance. Setting herself up as chaperon to her younger sister Charis, twenty-four-year-old Frederica tells Alverstoke that she finds "it very agreeable to be an old maid, and rid of tiresome restrictions!" (161–2), wishing she had thought to set herself up as a widow so there would be no doubt about her independent standing. The bored and wealthy Alverstoke is drawn to the otherwise average-looking Frederica because she is "perfectly composed" (33) and speaks with "disarming candor" (148) within moments of their first meeting. In Heyer's Regency world, to speak with "candor" means to speak in a masculine voice that prefers masculine slang to "polite" conversation, as Frederica's first speeches to Alverstoke indicate: Frederica admits to making a "bumblebath" of her request for his assistance (34) and a "shocking mull of it" (36), asks for confirmation that Alverstoke must be therefore be "an out-and-out cock of the game" if he is so improper (37), and retorts that she is hardly so "ramshackle" as to come to London with her younger sister without a nominal chaperon (40). Conversant in slang from her years caring for her brothers, Frederica has a ready vocabulary at hand. Although Alverstoke later teases her for allowing such "cant expressions on the lips of delicately nurtured females" (146), Frederica gets his joke—yet another sign of her ability to converse with men and garner respect and favor.

Frederica's humor and her willingness to deploy it attract and maintain Alverstoke's interest in her family's cause, allowing her to shape, with Alverstoke's financial and social support, the family's success during the London season. Increasingly aware of the effect humor has on Alverstoke, she uses it to her advantage, speaking frankly and responding in jest to his comments (55–6), knowing he will do the same. Sure of his love of the comic from the moment when she foists ownership of the large and blundering family dog Lufra onto his shoulders after a run-in with some cows, a cowman, and others in Green Park (78–84), she remains a "diverting" source of amusement for Alverstoke. Though she often wishes to "come to cuffs" with him when he presumes he knows the best for her, she prudently holds back, since he could withdraw his patronage (85). Their laughing relationship is briefly complicated as they gradually develop deeper feelings for each other, tempering the candor and free exchange which have made their friendship a success. When Alverstoke alters the terms of their relationship by kissing her hand, Frederica worries about the change which must result (170). Any doubts the two have, however, are put aside, as Frederica assures herself of Alverstoke's regard for her family and for her, and he of her regard for him. Shared laughter reminds the heretofore bored Alverstoke of his pleasure in her company and his love of her: "Only for an instant did she look puzzled; as he watched the laughter spring into her eyes he reflected that she had never yet daunted him by asking, fatally, 'What do you *mean*?'" (214). The novel ends as they share a joke about the next series of exploits to issue from Frederica's youngest brother, Felix (351).

The well-traveled and well-heeled Sophy Stanton-Lacy is even more fluent with the masculine language of power than Frederica. Though only twenty years old, Sophy has, according to her father Sir Horace, been "out for years"— "Never anything else really" (3), he adds to his sister, who will oversee Sophy's stay in London. Raised by her diplomat father during his campaigns around the world, Sophy's experiences in the world of men stand her in very good stead: she has been "acting hostess" for her father for several years (19) and managing his household and parties since she was seventeen (60); she also understands finance, shocking her aunt by doing her own banking while her father is abroad (60). Further, Sophy sets up her own stables, much to the dismay of her more proper cousin and the novel's hero, Charles Rivenhall (62–4, 95–7). Declaring to one of Charles's friends that she "was born without any nerves at all" and "almost no sensibility" (99–100), Sophy therefore manifests few typically feminine qualities: like Frederica, she relies on "disconcerting frankness" (40) rather than good looks to achieve her desired ends. She can also shoot a pistol with great skill, much to the chagrin—and ultimate pleasure—of Charles Rivenhall, who admires her pluck as well as her weapon (225–6). "The Grand Sophy," as the soldiers call her, indeed gains her name from her commanding and enchanting character as much as her height (36, 84).

Aghast to discover that her relatives have "fallen . . . into a shocking state of melancholy" and that the women of the household could "permit" Charles to "grow into such a tyrant" (46), Sophy sets out to revise the narrative of their lives. Thanks to her experiences abroad and in the company of men, Sophy has a veritable arsenal of tones and phrases to deploy according to the occasion, from the speech of legal and illegal business practices to schoolboy slang. A better older brother to young Hubert Rivenhall than Charles (222), Sophy recognizes that Hubert is beset by troubles, having seen similar expressions on the faces of young officers (58); offering her assistance in such a way that he does not lose face, she soon discovers that he has fallen into the hands of a moneylender. Acting without Hubert's knowledge, she sells a pair of diamond earrings; she then visits the moneylender herself, a gun tucked into her muff, where she shows a most "unwomanly knowledge of the law" (207) as well as great rhetorical control in her retrieval of the family ring Hubert pledged. Most importantly, Sophy understands the masculine code of honor: unlike the ever-truthful Eugenia Wraxton, Charles's bethrothed, Sophy does not tattle. She keeps her word with Hubert until he confesses the incident to

Charles (230). Sophy's "frank, open manners" certainly appeal to Charles, as does her ability to have "enjoyed [a] joke just as he had known she would" (284), but it is Sophy's unwillingness to "betray a confidence" (230) that makes Charles realize he cannot possibly marry the insufferable Eugenia Wraxton.

An expert author for her young years, capable of revising scripts even as they play out, Sophie manages to match everyone up with an appropriate partner by the novel's end in a comic *tour-de-force* climax. Appropriately quoting Wellington as she plans her strategy—"Surprise is the essence of attack" (267–8)—Sophy never doubts her plan, even though it entails lying to several people, diverting them outside London to her father's country manor, and shooting someone in the arm. The comic resolution of Sophy's plot also concludes the novel itself—an ending kept from the reader until Sophy's script is played out, granting Sophy a degree of authorial control beyond the realm of the characters alone. "[D]ragged irresistibly to the door" by Charles on the last page, Sophy still calls out suggestions to the remaining members of her assembled group, happily surprised that Charles should love her. For the moment Sophy may go "meekly" (347) to the stables, as the last line reads, but the novel as a whole reveals that Charles will indeed, as he says to Eugenia Wraxton, be "shocked, maddened, and stunned" by Sophy, "but not disappointed" (344) by his choice of wife.

Attuned though they are to the masculine world, Frederica and Sophy still have a youth that works against their narrative authority; older heroines Lady Serena Carlow from *Bath Tangle* (1955) and Annis Wychwood from *Lady of Quality* (1972) can better execute revisions because they have moved more about the "world's" stage, acquiring a range of personal experiences as well as observations.[16] Both mistress and master of their respective homes and families, Serena and Annis must nonetheless wrestle with those who would displace their authority because they are women. Both are up to the task.

Like Sophy, Lady Serena Carlow has lived in her father's political world, and she is quick to argue her opinion, though not always with Sophy's rhetorical persuasion. Setting up house with her young stepmother Fanny after her father's death, Serena at twenty-five (5) chafes under her new and decidedly feminine existence. Not only is she restricted from her considerable wealth by her father's will until she marries, but Serena must relinquish the reins of the estate she ably ran for her father from a young age (6). Since "it was natural for her to command" (34), a quality her father admired and encouraged, the transition is difficult. Her most serious loss is "the companionship of someone with wits to match her own" (37). Serena yearns for some discussion of current political events—even debate with her aunt Lady Theresa, whose opinions she opposes, would be welcome, as would a fight with her childhood friend and former fiancé Ivo Rotherham (59). For a while Serena plays the role expected of her by a patriarchal society demanding subservience; she even believes she loves an old suitor, Hector Kirby, who idealizes her character. Yet Serena cannot maintain her role in this narrative. In the end, she alters the script, embracing instead the political world embodied by Rotherham. She marries him as a political partner, not a subservient wife, as they mutually agree to "do better" this time (285).

Serena's knowledge of politics is indispensable to the place she occupied within the masculine world when her father was alive, and it secures her a place within that world when she realizes she must return. Yet Serena's firsthand knowledge of sexual desire, signaled by her "racy fashion" of speech, also plays a crucial role in her return. Her sexual knowledge, together with her knowledge of politics, grants her insight and power within the narrative of her life. Criticized by her new fiancé Hector Kirby for reading the scandalous *Glenarvon* (a book sent to her by Rotherham for her enjoyment and described by Serena herself as "rather warm"), Serena questions both Kirby's need to censor her reading and his right to do so:

"How can you be so absurd, Hector? Do you believe me to be an innocent Calantha? Rotherham knows better!"

"*What*?" he demanded sharply.

"No, no pray—!" Fanny interposed, in an imploring tone. "Major Kirby, you quite mistake—Serena, consider what you say, dearest! Indeed, your vivacity carries you too far!"

"Very likely! But it will be well if Hector learns not to place the worst construction upon what I say!" Serena retorted, her colour considerably heightened.

He said quickly: "I beg you pardon! I did not mean—Good God, how could I possibly—? If you were not an innocent Calantha, as you put it—now, don't eat me!—I am persuaded you would feel as strongly as I do the impropriety of anyone's sending you such a book to read! Throw it away, and let us forget it! You cannot like to see your friends libelled, surely!"

"Now, this goes beyond the bounds of what may be tolerated!" declared Serena, between vexation and amusement. "*My* friends? The Melbourne House set! Do you take me for a *Whig*? Oh, I was never so insulted! I don't know what you deserve I should do to you!" (127–8)

Sex and politics meet in *Glenarvon*, precipitating their convergence in this exchange between Serena and Kirby. Their argument highlights several important points about Serena's knowledge of sex and the view of sexual knowledge that Heyer's novel endorses by endorsing Serena: that women of Serena's age and class know about and allude to sexual desire in their speech; that it would be hypocritical to believe otherwise; that Rotherham is a better man than Kirby because he realizes these facts; and that a misreading of political allegiance is even more damning than a misreading of a woman's virtue. Lashing out against Kirby's worldview, which would restrict her free movement, Serena establishes her independence by association with the world of her father and Rotherham.

Serena's understanding of sexual dynamics is vindicated when Rotherham proposes to the young and pretty Emily Latham and Emily retreats to Bath soon after spending time at his estate. Only Serena correctly interprets Emily's retreat as a sign, not of Rotherham's waning love or Emily's fear of his well-known temper, but of Emily's response to his ardor:

"I have every reason to believe, dear Fanny, that he loves her *a corps perdu*," she said, in a dry voice. "Unless I much mistake the matter, it is the violence of his passion which has put her in a fright, not his withering tongue! Of that she stands in awe merely. . . . For a man of experience, Rotherham has handled her very ill. If I did not suspect that he has realized it already, I should be strongly tempted to tell him so." (188–9)

Fanny is "quite scandalized" by Serena's analysis, especially when Serena adds, "He's impatient, but I never knew him to be so on the box or in the saddle. I own, I am astonished that a man with such fine, light hands could have blundered so!" (189). Equating sexual desire with animal instincts, thereby naturalizing those desires, Serena establishes sexual knowledge as another necessary tool in negotiating one's independence as a woman in upper-class patriarchal society.

Annis Wychwood in *Lady of Quality* is perhaps the most interesting of all the heroines examined here, since she enacts a narrative role typically reserved for older men in Heyer's novels: like Alverstoke or Sylvester, Annis takes charge of a young woman making her appearance in society. Annis does so in part because she wishes to help, but mostly because, like the heroes, she is "bored" (8, 104). Her older married brother and the companion he has chosen for her are both quite shocked by her decision, but Annis, at twenty-nine (60), has maturity, money, wit, knowledge of sexual desire, and therefore power: she can choose to write herself into the role of "hero," if she wishes. When Annis desires "a life of her own" (4), she has sufficient money to escape the domestic role of "spinster aunt" (125). Her brother reproaches her for her lack of familial duty, but Annis recalls the fate of a "Miss Vernham, who is only valued for the help she gives her sister, and can be depended on to look after the children.... She can't escape, because she hadn't a penny to fly with. But I have a great many pennies, and I *did* escape!" (125). Annis's desire to avoid the confinements of women's social roles encourages her to help the young Lucy Carleton with her entrance into the social world. Believing "experience" (40) to be the most valuable quality for success, Annis establishes Lucy in Bath so that she may learn the ways of the world there before her first Season in London.

Though Annis's brother criticizes her for expressing herself with "such an unfeminine want of refinement" and declares "levity" to be her "besetting sin" (49), Annis's self-acknowledged "unruly tongue" (21) attracts the attention of Lucy's uncle, Oliver Carleton. Recognizing a kindred desire for independence in her, Carleton is as much a friend, advisor, and confidant as a lover. Like other successful heroines, Annis is conversant in masculine speech and slang, and she appreciates Carleton assuming she will understand his (173). Annis and Carleton also speak easily and bluntly about sexual mores, both dismissing false notions of propriety when they do not apply (78, 80, 240), although aware of the need to protect those like Lucy who may not yet have the experience to evaluate their circumstances. In her last Regency romance, Heyer offers her readers a vision of marriage as companionship, a union which does not require ceding independence (175–6, 237), thanks to a heroine who can conduct herself as a hero.[17]

Given the degree of authorial control the Regency heroines have over their lives, reading about the heroines of Heyer's suppressed "moderns" comes as a shock. Faltering in the knowledge and verbal skill needed to revise social scripts, the heroines of *Instead of the Thorn* (1923), *Helen* (1928), *Pastel* (1929), and *Barren Corn* (1930) are restricted to the historical moment of the 1920s and *lack* control over their lives, particularly their relationships with men. The narrative in these four modern novels grants the heroines few options in a world where sex alone, rather than wit coupled with sexual and fiscal knowledge, might accord women any control over their lives. Perhaps the saddest situation is Laura's in *Barren Corn* (1930): she enters a cross-class marriage held together only by sexual desire, bereft of the cultural resources of Heyer's Regency heroines, particularly their wit—hers is indeed the antiromance narrative. Heyer suggests, I think, that in a post-Freudian culture young women cannot maximize the liberating benefits of the romance plot or vary the expected ending when men and women are governed by "instincts and impulses" (*Pastel* 260). Knowledge of wit and money can temper these forces but never trump them. Knowledge of sex is therefore a crucial coin of the twentieth-century realm, but such knowledge restricts the heroines' happiness.

Take for example the heroine from *Instead of the Thorn* (1923), who is born Elizabeth but soon renamed "Elizabeth Anne" by her perceptive and renegade godfather Mr. Hengist, who sees all too clearly the debilitating influence Elizabeth's Aunt Anne and her Victorian ways have upon the growing girl. Ignorant about money and politics, she is also ignorant about personal relationships and physical desire. Discussing Stephen, whom she will marry, with one of her friends, Elizabeth "longed for courage to confess ignorance and beg enlightenment" about the dynamics of relationships, "[b]ut years of training stood in her way, and the implanted belief that knowledge was wrong" (64). Though a lifelong bachelor, Mr. Hengist tries to convince her Aunt to tell Elizabeth about the sexual act of the wedding night—for Stephen's sake, if not Elizabeth's—but Anne refuses to do so, claiming that Mr. Hengist is "making mountains out of molehills" (97). He is not, of course, given Elizabeth's confused experiences that night and in the nights and days that follow.

Entering marriage completely unprepared for the realities of male sexual desire, Elizabeth also lacks the words to communicate her confusion and initial fear and disgust; only further experience and time on her own bring her calm and enlightenment. Thinking in retrospect that her Aunt was "cruel and wicked" to allow her to marry without some knowledge, Elizabeth decides one needs to learn from someone who has had "experience" (224). The motherly Mrs. Gabriel provides that knowledge for Elizabeth late in the novel, instructing Elizabeth that she must "be unselfish," so she can "fit in" to the selfishness of men, adding: "I'm not saying that if we could start all over again we wouldn't have things different, but seeing as how they are as they are, we've made the best of 'em, and we've learned to fit in as quickly as possible" (275). Successful relationships in *Instead of the Thorn* depend on acquired knowledge of an unchanging dynamic within men's and women's relationships and an ability to capitulate to that dynamic: offered no option but to "fit in" if she desires happiness through marriage, Elizabeth returns to her husband and learns to adjust to his desire for her and, slowly, to speak hers for him.

Like Elizabeth in *Instead of the Thorn*, Frances, the heroine of *Pastel* (1929), must create her history through the narrative provided by her patriarchal society. Frances has also "enjoyed the doubtful privilege of a careful upbringing" (103); even her sense of humor and her knowledge of Dr. Marie Stopes's best-selling books on sexual relations in marriage cannot counter her lack of personal experience (137). Frances willingly marries the solid and dependable Norman, but there is regret in Frances's view of her life as a married woman: "I don't really want to think that all our instincts and impulses are governed by our biggest and most natural job in life. Only I'm afraid it may be so, and to have children will always be the main thing for us, our real fulfillment," concluding: "And, speaking as a woman, I do think it's nicer and much more comfy when men run the show, and we just run the men" (260). *Pastel* repeatedly emphasizes how unchanging "physiological reasons"(260, 261) stipulate that women "weren't made to rule" but "made to be ruled" by men (258), in turn preventing women like Frances from imagining alternative narratives. Frances is hardly encouraged to revise the expected social script when her male friends lament that they live in "an Age of Women" that tends "towards the effete,"[18] "modern thought-stunts," and "enthusiasm over half baked ideas" (257) and when her female friends agree with that opinion. Instead, Frances chooses to find happiness through the "instincts and impulses" she now knows through childbirth, willing to "run" the man in her life rather than the "show" itself—a poor compromise of power, in comparison to the heroines of the Regency romances.

Only the heroine of *Helen* (1928) has some control over her world, tenuous though that control may be given the war and the shoals of sexual desire in the first decades of the twentieth century. Unlike the other heroines of the "moderns," Helen Marchant has money as well as skills with spoken and written language because of her time in her father's world, even becoming a published writer. She also knows about sex: her father chose not to keep her in ignorance, and she gained further experience volunteering at home during the First World War. In many ways, Helen is the twentieth-century twin of Serena from *Bath Tangle*, if also somewhat more tragic: adoring her father and adored by him, Helen suffers the same kind of grief as Serena does after her father dies, unable to speak of her emotion, even to those who care for her. As Serena returns to Rotherham, Helen marries Richard, who has known her since childhood and known her father. Richard can thus understand Helen's masculine independence, her desire for a career as a writer, and her reticence. Helen is also like Serena in her recognition of sexual desire, understanding its pull as a pleasurable if dangerous impulse and not the sign of love (286).

Unlike the other two heroines of the "moderns," Elizabeth and Frances, Helen is capable, and for a time willing, to go around with a variety of suitors, setting the terms for her engagement with the social world. Helen also decides when to call a halt to her social life so she can write (292), suggesting that she can negotiate those "instincts and impulses" which trouble Frances in *Pastel*. Believing Richard stands "for love, and for friendship, and for security," Helen foresees a way to exist within a world she cannot always control (328).

Heyer's decision to suppress her four modern novels is significant, I think, to understanding her preference for the Regency period in British history and the type of world she creates within the pages of those historical romances. The heroines of the modern romances go reluctantly into the marriage plot, burdened by the determining "instincts and impulses" of the body and for the most part unable to rescript their lives in the face of those forces. Except for Helen, the heroines of the "moderns" do not control the narratives of their lives as the heroines of the Regency romances do. Without knowledge and negotiation of sexual desire, a fluency with the language of masculine power, and the perception that they can successfully initiate another story, these modern heroines cannot write themselves into the degree of happiness and humor characteristic of the Regency heroines' lives. The realism of the modern romances also provides little opportunity to show life other than it appears to be, fixing these heroines to their historical moment. The "Age of Women" may be "wrong," "turning everything upside down," as one character remarks in *Pastel*, but he concludes, "I don't say we can rectify it" (257). To write a modern romance whose heroine determines her history would require Heyer to move away from realism, further towards the fantasy of romance.

The very realism that stifles the female characters of the modern novels, however, liberates those of the Regency romances. Constrained though they may be by restrictions of their time, the Regency heroines revive the freedom and self-determinism embodied by a select few women of the late eighteenth century, such as Georgiana, the Duchess of Devonshire, whose private letters, public canvassing of votes, and influential social gatherings swayed many personal and political decisions.[19] What was possible for only a few women in Regency history becomes accessible to Heyer's many heroines within the pages of Regency romance. These romances indeed offer what A. S. Byatt calls an "honourable escape" (1969): an escape into a world where women can revise the social script of Regency history according to their desires and, perhaps, offer some ideas to their twentieth-century audiences as well.

The Race, Gender, Romance Connection

A BLACK FEMINIST READING OF AFRICAN AMERICAN WOMEN'S HISTORICAL ROMANCES

—*Rita B. Dandridge*

In contemporary literary studies, black women's historical romances have been grossly ignored. Whether the romance element in these novels discourages critics' interest or whether the historical romance is, as George Dekker would have us believe, swollen with "specimens deformed by... racism [and] sexism," the fact remains that African American women's historical romances have an unexamined relevance to African American women's literature and the historical romance genre (4). These romances often portray black women's activism against a racist and sexist national environment and opposition to patriarchal structures embedded in traditional black male-female relationships. I argue that three African American romance writers—Beverly Jenkins[1] in *Indigo*, Shirley Hailstock[2] in *Clara's Promise*, and Roberta Gayle[3] in *Sunshine and Shadows*—attempt to recreate nineteenth-century history from a feminist point of view. Their heroines fight for self-determination in romantic relationships with black men who, equally oppressed by race, claim domination of black women as their right. Choosing to set romances in the nineteenth century, at crucial, defining moments in African American history, these authors highlight invigorating calls to action and empowerment, but also consider the limitations reflected in heterosexual romance.

While romance fiction may seem to avoid the political realm entirely, black women's historical romances take strong political positions. As Barbara Smith argues, "A Black feminist approach to literature that embodies a realization that the politics of sex as well as the politics of race ... are crucially interlocking factors in the works of black women writers is an absolute necessity" (25). Beverly Jenkins's *Indigo*, for instance, politicizes race and gender by centering Hester Wyatt in the Abolitionist Movement. A staunch opponent of slavery, Hester fights against institutions that disenfranchise her people and demean black women as lascivious beings, appealing to "the widespread controlling image that African American women are sexually promiscuous, potential prostitutes" (Collins 174). Her activism opposes white slave hunters and black male abolitionists harboring sexist beliefs about black women. *Indigo* explores racism and sexism as "crucially interlocking [political] factors" in black women's oppression and resistance in culture and in romance.

While nineteenth-century African American women insisted on their identities as "true women" in the model prevalent in dominant culture—chaste, pious, passive, and gentle—they also recognized the need for activity, passion, and force in struggles to end slavery and to gain full citizenship. In 1832, Maria Stewart, considered "one of the first black feminists," delivered "An Address Delivered before the Afric-American Female Intelligence Society of America" in which she argued that "It is useless for us any longer to sit with our hands folded, reproaching the whites; for that will never elevate us. Possess the spirit of independence ... Possess the spirit of men, bold and enterprising, fearless and undaunted" (53). This message encapsulates a crucial issue for black women in the nineteenth century: the qualities perceived as necessary for significant change in relations between the sexes and races are gendered male. Stewart's call to action and plea for independence resonated throughout the nineteenth century as black women began to assume public positions as abolitionists (Harriet

Tubman), teachers (Anna Julia Cooper), preachers (Jarena Lee), doctors (Rebecca Lee), and journalists (Mary Shadd Cary). Their empowerment comes as a result of their various strategies to strengthen the "weak" position they were assumed to hold in their interactions with "strong" men.

Shirley Hailstock's *Clara's Promise* embraces this stimulating period in black women's history by dramatizing Clara Winslow's negotiations of the double imperative to serve others and to empower herself. Maintaining a "bold and enterprising" spirit through personal hardship, Clara travels from Virginia to Wyoming to take her first teaching position. She manifests traits common to the black woman activist described by Clenora Hudson-Weems: she strives for wholeness and self-definition while remaining family-centered, working with males in the freedom struggle, and demanding respect and recognition.[4] In the romances, we often find these characteristics embedded in an Afrocentric ethos.[5]

Black women writers interpret black women's activism within an African-centered helping tradition which, in the romances, begins during slavery and continues through Reconstruction, when the American government failed to eliminate the inestimable misery in black people's lives. Central to this African-centered culture is "a collective psychological space" which separates African Americans from white oppression and enables them "to generate a sense of worth, dignity, affiliation, and mutual support" (Parham 14). In Roberta Gayle's *Sunshine and Shadows*, the Afrocentric cultural practice of caring for children, one's own and those of others, creates the psychological space separating the protagonist Roses Jordan and her adopted family of Ute Indians from white prejudice. In *Sunshine and Shadows*, as in most historical romances by black women, Roses Jordan involves herself in meaningful work at the historic site of activism, which becomes the site of romance.

At this site, the interests of black women, black uplift, and black patriarchy intersect and clash. Before the war, free black men imitated the gender hierarchy found in white relationships. This discriminatory paradigm prevailed and caused conflict within black male-female relationships at a time when black people were fighting to abolish slavery. As black patriarchy struggled to maintain its footing, it regarded black women's emerging roles as threats to black male positions in the community. Despite the argument of Benjamin Quarles, a noted African American historian, that "black women were the first women in America to sit down with their men around political matters," some black men who rose to public positions in the nineteenth century chastised the black woman for or interfered with her performance of public roles (178).[6]

The white power structure contributed to the patriarchal privilege of the black man after the Emancipation Proclamation. The Freedman's Bureau, for instance, listed the black male as the head of the household and made him responsible for signing labor contracts for his entire family. This leadership position was endorsed in the public sphere, as black males became mayors of all-black towns, members of military units (the Buffalo soldiers), and delegates to black conventions. Their authoritative positions contributed to and even complemented their sexist notions about woman's "place" in the home and in the community. In black women's historical romances, black men often seek to impose a prescriptive code of ethics concerning black womanhood.

The patriarchal structure of black male-female relationships is evident in Shirley Hailstock's *Clara's Promise*, in which Clara Winslow contends with the authoritative Luke Evans. Considered the less important of the two, Clara is challenged by Luke's macho exercise of patriarchal privilege. Luke vows to never marry, but makes public advances toward Clara. Pervasive sexism threatens Clara's career and her efforts to empower herself and others, but she works with Luke in the struggle against white oppression.

Black women's historical romances explore discordant and complicated interconnections between racism, sexism, and romance. They confirm the historic difficulty that black women and men have had in establishing viable romantic relationships. In a slaveholding white society, romance was demolished by indecent slave masters who disregarded slave marriages, and white men violated black women after the Emancipation Proclamation.[7] In Beverly Jenkins's *Indigo*, Hester Wyatt is a product of a racial history that exploited and destroyed romance. Her father, a free black man, sold himself into slavery to be near his slave wife, only to have her sold away from him. Her parents' romance colors Hester's view of marriage. She tells the hero,

"'I don't wish to marry for love. I don't need misery in my life'" (82). The white man's greed and perception of black women as sexually available are continuous threats to romance (for the bounty hunter, Shoe, intends to rape and re-enslave Hester), while the hero's sexism and patriarchal assumptions pose threats from the other side. In these romances, black women negotiate for self-definition within the romance, their African American communities, and the nation at large.

Looking closely at these historical romances written by African American women—Beverly Jenkins's *Indigo*, Shirley Hailstock's *Clara's Promise*, and Roberta Gayle's *Sunshine and Shadows*—I will explore the ways in which romance both ameliorates and intensifies the dilemmas of black women seeking to establish personal autonomy and an active place in culture. Choosing a historical moment when black women were forcefully claiming power *and* attempting to fulfill the female roles traditionally valued in American culture, Jenkins, Hailstock, and Gayle construct romances that validate black women's activism.

BEVERLY JENKINS'S *INDIGO*: ROMANCE WITH/IN THE ABOLITIONIST MOVEMENT

Indigo (1996) vividly dramatizes the Abolitionist Movement as the historic setting which calls black women to action. Set in Whittaker, Michigan, in 1858, during the final stages of the antislavery movement, the novel represents the heroic exploits of Hester Wyatt, a free black antislavery agent for social change. An Underground Railway conductor who does not wait for whites to hand over freedom, Hester fights for the liberty of her people.

Mobilizing her efforts in the face of the Fugitive Slave Law and the Dred Scot Decision, Hester is a fictional representative of those black antislavery agents who commenced the crusade of conscience against slavery. Working for an order that "originated" with successful black male Underground Railroad conductors (Jenkins 44), Hester houses runaway slaves in the passageways of the large Michigan home bequeathed to her by her abolitionist aunt, and belongs to the Detroit Ladies Abolition Circle. She supports the

Free Produce Movement, refusing to buy goods such as cotton, rice, and sugar produced by slaves, and a black vigilante group modeled after the New York Committee of Vigilance which David Ruggles, a black man, founded in 1835. Hester's "bold and enterprising" actions, conducted both in "ladies" work and in more covert, male-oriented realms, are counterbalanced by the fact that she is limited to low paying gender work. She offers piano lessons to children, sells apples, and writes antislavery tracts. Tedious, time-consuming, and restrictive, her work seems an added oppression, but she turns her situation to her own advantage and to the benefit of others.

Hester's covert involvement in the antislavery movement differs considerably from the typical pattern of white involvement. Having been a slave, Hester bears marks that, if discovered, could return her to slavery. As a child laborer on an indigo plantation in South Carolina, her hands and feet were permanently stained by blue dye. Indigo dye becomes a trope of disfigurement reinforcing the theme of racial dehumanization, and it is the identifying factor that could return Hester, now a free woman, to slavery. She tells Galen, the hero, "'I was once told my hands would brand me a slave for the remainder of my years'" (28).

As a free yet "branded" black woman, Hester struggles against double threats based in race and gender. Feminist historian Evelyn Higginbotham writes, "In societies where racial demarcation is endemic to their sociocultural fabric and heritage—to their laws and economy, to their institutionalized structures and discourses, and to their epistemologies and everyday customs—gender identity is inextricably linked to and even determined by racial identity" (254). Hester's race exposes her to exploitation and ultimately determines her gender poverty; she is a product of the racialized history that has always regarded black women as sexually available. Menaced by rapacious white slave hunters who attempt to gang rape her and remand her to slavery, Hester holds them at bay with a revolver and debunks the myth of the constitutionally "lascivious" black woman. To Hester's thinking, white men "believe the awful myths about the women of the race ... myths that slanderously labeled Black women as voracious in pursuit of the vices of the flesh and willing to accommodate anyone to satisfy their carnal cravings" (203).

Hester uses trickery to mask her subversive actions, while projecting a nonthreatening and ladylike demeanor. She carries a concealed revolver and hides her indigo-stained hands. She boldly impersonates Fanny Blackburn, a neighbor, and frees her when slave catchers intend to send Fanny back South. Hester's disguises enable her and her fugitives to pass through white legal barriers such as the Fugitive Slave Law and the Dred Scot Decision. Overall, trickery as a cultural ploy assaults white patriarchal domination by enabling the triumph of "the weak" over "the strong." Trickery maximizes Hester's effectiveness at the philanthropic site.

Her effectiveness as a caregiver and activist for her race is both underlined and endangered through the dynamic of romantic love, introduced when Hester nurses the seriously wounded Galen Vashon, alias Black Daniel, a wealthy Louisiana resident. As philanthropy becomes romance, black patriarchy threatens Hester's efforts on behalf of her race. Galen's presence as a successful conductor on the Underground Railroad makes the house a target for the white bounty hunter, Shoe. Searching Hester's home, he hopes to find Black Daniel hidden so that he can put Hester on the auction block, too. Further, Galen's insistence on proceeding with his abolitionist endeavors before his healing is complete undermines Hester's attempts to help him. His dark moods, gruff tone, and refusal to take orders clearly manifest his masculine assertiveness over Hester even when he needs her most. Commenting that Hester's healing ointment "smells female," he forces a distinction in the work that black men and black women perform for the abolitionist cause. They confer briefly as equals about the community's traitor who has informed Shoe of his whereabouts, but Galen clearly represents the strong black male who regards his public role as more important than Hester's.

Hester's struggles against slavery's dehumanization complicate the romance as much as Galen's exercise of patriarchal privilege. Hester's racial identity and even her indigo-stained hands and feet determine how she responds as a black female. Fearing the abuse of her sexuality, Hester minimizes her own attractiveness; she buys no cotton for new gowns and wears her rough Quaker clothing and worn calico dresses as a Free Producer supporter. Yet her actions and feistiness produce a sexuality that attracts Galen.

As in the typical romance formula, the hero's promiscuity clashes with the heroine's determination to retain her virginity until she finds love. Galen's insistence that "a combative woman is usually a passionate woman" gives Hester all the more reason to withhold her emotions. The struggle escalates, and Hester refuses to become part of Galen's menagerie. Unlike the "vapid, perfumed bits of fluff and calculating predators masquerading as virgins" that Galen has known, Hester is a self-determined, intelligent woman and a virgin scented with vanilla extract. Her refusal to give in to Galen's demands enables her to gain his respect, as she has also earned respect in the community she serves.

Hester's eventual acceptance of Galen's genuine interest reduces the discord between the two. She accepts the gown he buys for her and meets his abolitionist friends, who help her attain greater eminence in the abolitionist movement. She maintains her self-identity as a strong abolitionist even as she invests emotional energy in the romance with Galen. After withholding the sexual act for months in order to "bring the dragon [Galen] to his knees," Hester visits Galen's home to consummate their relationship. Her participation in Galen's "prolonged, erotic tribute" seals a caring relationship (233) and their bond energizes a chivalric sentiment in Galen, who eloquently defends her in church against the town's gossip. He tells the church, "'There are rumors that Hester Wyatt is my whore. You are wrong. It is my wife I wish her to be'" (246). No longer fearing what the future holds for their relationship, Hester accepts Galen's marriage proposal and rejoices in the goodness of his own commitments to the Abolition movement. Her noble purpose and her romantic fulfillment complete each other.

SHIRLEY HAILSTOCK'S *CLARA'S PROMISE*: LOVE AND THE BLACK WOMAN'S CALL TO EDUCATE

Hailstock's *Clara's Promise* (1995) is set at the end of the nineteenth century, in an era when women fought vigorously for education. Black women joined the nationwide struggle of women who challenged the notion that only men had a right to higher education. Black women had a special interest in this struggle. Educationally disenfranchised before slavery and discriminated against after the Emancipation Proclamation, black women aimed for their race to overcome a formidable ignorance: ninety-five percent of blacks were illiterate during Reconstruction, and in the 1880s fewer than one-third of Southern black children received a free education (Morris 85, Sterling 377). Anna Julia Cooper, a black feminist who was born into slavery, believed that eradicating ignorance was an essential reason for educating black women, who would then be better able to perform the duties of wife and mother. In her essay "The Higher Education of Women," Cooper endorses black women's education for two reasons: first, "both the [woman and the man] are needed to be worked into the training of children"; second, "intellectual development, with the self-reliance and the capacity for earning a livelihood which it gives, renders woman less dependent on the marriage relationship for physical support... Neither is she compelled to look to sexual love as the one sensation capable of giving tone and relish, movement and vim to the life she needs" (Lemert 78, 82). Cooper advocates education both in order to foster black women's independence from the lure of romance and to enhance their performance in the roles of wife and mother, where they may contribute to racial uplift.

Clara Winslow, the Southern protagonist of *Clara's Promise*, demonstrates her desire to be less dependent on the marriage relationship and her wish to be educated. The daughter of a physician who marries her at fifteen years old to Wade Pierce, an older Virginia farmer, Clara's drive to improve herself educationally stems from the gender oppression she encounters in her marriage. Wife to Wade and stepmother to his four children (two left by his deceased wife and two by his sister), Clara finds herself overburdened by her husband's demands. Clara's drive toward self-realization leads to conflict with her husband, who expects services from her. Wade permits her to attend Teacher's College in Washington, D.C. on the condition that she completes her chores, but he refuses to spare her a farm animal for the ten-mile passage to and from school. Her husband exercises control over her and uses her as a scapegoat to gain leverage amid the racial tensions between himself and the largely white community.

Clara's desire for self-actualization leads her to revolt against Wade and to refuse the functions he has forced on her. Having lived as a dependent woman in her father's house and then in Wade's, she realizes that "she wanted her own space" (35). She severs her relationship with Wade and vows, "This [is my] life" (36). She takes a job as teacher in Waymon Valley, Montana, in 1899 and abrogates her marriage promise "to love, honor, and obey" (314). While Clara initially violates principles of family loyalty which are basic to African American culture, she gains a necessary self-sufficiency that will enable her return to productive participation in the African American community.

Her flight "to a secret life in the open spaces" of Montana offers Clara a means to self-definition through racial and gender uplift (87). Working in a race-prejudiced area where her students are not expected to succeed because "Indians and Negroes don't go to college," Clara encourages a Native American girl to attend school and expands the limited curriculum for Negroes to include piano lessons and the blues (181). Clara removes the sexist barrier in sports, allowing her female students to play baseball with the boys. Challenging the school's discriminative policies, Clara helps her students to develop good self-images at an institution historically guilty of race and gender objectification.

But Clara still faces society's objectification of her as a woman. The community expects women teachers to be of "good" character and to demonstrate "goodness" by remaining unmarried, pious, and chaste. Passing as unmarried, she must not be seen with men, nor can she develop a relationship with any male without risking her reputation. For Clara, these strictures complicate the connection between career and romance, for she is attracted to Luke Evans, the town's widower and builder. A patriarchal figure, Luke has followed his father to this untamed territory from race-torn Illinois. For Luke, "Life was hard enough," but losing his wife Peg was even more difficult (25–26). Mixed grief over Peg's death and a desire to make his own career central, advancing as a black man in the town, shape Luke's inconsistent disposition toward Clara. Determined that he does not need a wife, Luke nevertheless expresses interest in Clara, whom he goads into committing an infraction when he kisses her in public. His inconstancy in the romance, aggravated by the patriarchal position he holds in the community, jeopardizes Clara's reputation and her job. Town gossips, men and women, black and white, convene to discuss the night Clara spent in the mountains with Luke after he found her caught in a storm. Believing that Clara has behaved improperly with Luke, the community offers her two undesirable options: she can either give up her job or have Luke declare for her so that "They can get married in the spring" (301). Losing her job would send her back to Wade, but accepting Luke's declaration would make her a bigamist. The town's patriarchal regulation encloses a woman in marriage, where her husband defines and controls her identity. The Waymon Valley community replays the same restrictive script as the rural Virginia town where Clara was forced at fifteen into a marriage she did not consummate with Wade, a man whom she did not love.

Their romantic involvement clarifies and resolves the tensions between Luke's temptation to view Clara as a sexual object and Clara's desire to experience sex in the context of a loving relationship. Clara initiates the sexual act when she sees that Luke cares enough about her to search for her in a driving storm, emphatically telling him, "'Make love to me'" (220). Her initial hesitancy identifies her as a virgin, but Clara decides that "she didn't care about her job or what anyone would think, only the sensations that ran through her. Tonight might be her last night with Luke, and she wouldn't give it up because of petty gossip" (280). Clara's refusal to be limited by the community's moral codes and her determination to follow her own intuitions strengthens her as a woman. Her self-affirmation is tested when she becomes trapped between Wade's sudden appearance in the Valley and Luke's sudden decision to declare for her. Annulling one marriage and planning another, Clara finds a sense of feminine wholeness: her sense of Luke's attachment to her is fully confirmed. Far from being a sexual object to him, she is desired for both mind and body, and her commitment to racial and gender uplift not only earns Luke's respect but promises to make them equals in partnership.

Clara's mental and moral commitments are validated by Luke and by the town as the novel ends. Her teaching post is restored, and she carries on the Afrocentric tradition of sharing which critic Jacqueline Jones explains emphasizes "group cooperation... rather than... the accumulation of goods" (100). As an agent for ethnic advancement, Clara voluntarily assumes responsibility for Wade's four children when he dies suddenly. Just as Wade cared for his sons and the daughters of his dead sister, Clara cares for his children. To Clara's thinking, "the children could go to school and maybe do something more than grow up and work the same land their father had and his father before him" (329). Clara's choice to accept this responsibility as "mother" briefly jeopardizes her romance with Luke, who argues that the children should "go to a relative or to the woman Wade was going to marry" (330). Clara understands that Luke's selfishness derives more from his grief over the deaths of his wife and infant son than from avoidance of the folk tradition of cooperative child-nurturance. Ultimately, Clara's self-direction and patience with Luke firmly seal the romance between them and join them in marriage as caretakers of the four orphans. As an educated woman, Clara provides good training for the children at the same time that she overcomes gender dependence and racial disenfranchisement. In this sense, Clara finds power in the convergence between a traditional romance role and a less traditional feminist role as an independent, working, self-actualized, educated black woman who is committed to improving the lot of her race and her gender.

ROBERTA GAYLE'S *SUNSHINE AND SHADOWS*: ROMANTIC SERVICE

Sunshine and Shadows (1995) illuminates a history of race prejudice shared by the Uncompahgre Ute and the black Americans who sought refuge with the tribe after Emancipation. Set during the expansion of the American West (1850–1889), the novel engages discourses of self-determination embedded in the myth of the frontier in ways that focus its assumptions about race and gender. Moreover, the novel exposes the government's complicity in racist practices carried out by white settlers who fought the Ute and by white terrorists who drove Southern blacks westward. The government's failure to come to the aid of the Ute, a peaceful tribe inhabiting Colorado, Utah, and Nevada, made them victims of white settlers who viewed the Ute and other Plains Indians as barriers to their expanding mining, frontier, and transportation networks. The American government herded the Colorado Ute to a permanent mountain reservation in Utah in 1868, and the tribe ceded its land to the United States (Billington 572). Corralled into a small area, the Ute, who used to roam the Plains for buffalo, now had little water and food. They were restricted to the reservation and denied the right to litigate.

During the same period in American history, blacks who had been freed by the Emancipation Proclamation were terrorized by Southern whites who regarded blacks as interlopers. Failing to come to the aid of blacks, the government instead restricted them to second-class citizenship through black codes and segregation polices. Bringing the histories of Native and African Americans together, Roberta Gayle creates a protagonist, Roses Jordan, whose black parents escaped white terrorism in the South by fleeing to the West. Finding that Spanish townships and white settlers in the West had no use for educated black house servants, they sought refuge with the Ute. As a five year old, Roses had watched U.S. Army soldiers raze the Ute mountain camp and herd the tribe and her family to a desert reservation in Utah. She and her family did not qualify for food at the Indian Agency and less than a year later, her parents died of malnutrition. Roses identifies with the Ute rather than with the whites of Cedar Valley, Colorado, where she has gone to train to become a veterinarian.

In this historical moment of prejudice, racial persecution leads to the intersection of Roses's life with that of Tobias (Tobe) Hunter, the hero. Their lives converge on a dirt road where Roses collects flowers for her medicine and where Tobe accidentally runs over her as he flees from Kansas after having been accused of killing a white woman. Roses's acceptance as one of the few blacks in Cedar Valley and Tobe's incarceration for "attacking her" speaks to whites' historical accommodation of a few individual blacks while rejecting the masses of what they perceive as "brute Negroes." The relative positioning of blacks demanded by white racism is metaphorically rendered in the novel's title: "sunshine" (acceptance and primacy) and "shadows" (rejection and second-class status).

Racism is inextricably linked to sexism, which impacts Roses in similar ways to other protagonists of African American historical romance. The white town regards black women's sexuality as excessive and dangerous, and they attempt to control Roses's potential sexual identity by dictating her choice of a mate and pressuring her toward marriage. Because of her race, Roses is expected to bond with Tobe, a black man, despite his negative first impression on the town. Yet, some townsmen fantasize that she should make herself available to do the white man's sexual bidding. Roses's rebellion against these sexist speculations casting her as the willing concubine to lascivious white men or slavish partner to a strange black man speaks not only to her self-determination as a black woman, but also to her desire for a compatible mate of her own choosing. She considers Tobe "as backwards about the People [Ute] as any one she has met" because he refers to them as savages, and she wants the town folk "to realize how ridiculous it is to think that because we're both colored we're a perfect match" (73). Identifying what she does not want, Roses defines herself through her right to desire and choose.

A hard worker, Roses wants to become a veterinarian so that she may return to the Ute reservation and assist the people she considers her family. Entering a male-dominated profession, she cares for animals in Cedar Valley. She works odd jobs, saves her money, acquires domestic skills, and collects tools, leather, skins, and books for her return to Uintah Valley.[8] Her public run-in with Cedar Valley's racist white minister and the sexist gossip about her and Tobe hasten her departure from the town. Seeming to "possess the spirit of men, bold and enterprising" that Maria Stewart advocated in 1832, Roses creates the space needed to separate herself from racism and sexism in Cedar Valley, while she also displays the traditional feminine qualities of service and empathy.

Roses's activism stems from her sense of indebtedness; she wants to repay the Ute for sheltering her family in their tribulations during Reconstruction. As dislocated and oppressed minorities in white America, the Ute and blacks share similar histories and some cultural similarities. In areas such as herbal medicine, respecting nature, and caring for children, Roses's beliefs correspond with theirs. Knowing about these similarities is one way that Roses attempts to clarify who she is and "where she belong[s]" (228). But her return to the Ute illuminates a problem with her sense of identity. Believing all along that she could live with the Ute and become one of them, she is overwhelmed by the lack of change that has occurred at the camp since her departure. The Ute have little money, inadequate food and water, and no options. The Indian Agency has failed them miserably by sending rotten food, settling them on unproductive land, and restricting them to the reservation. Sympathizing with the tribe's plight, Roses buys what food she can, but their misery forces her to reevaluate her reasons for returning to them: "she felt there was more to being 'home,' then [sic] just coming to this place" (304–05). She struggles with a sense of dislocation from this former home, now so grim and hopeless it is just a "place."

Through Roses's experiences, readers are offered a revision of American history. Native Americans and blacks had meaningful interactions, but institutionalized racism (the Indian Agency, the Freedmen's Bureau) deprived the groups of any productive interdependence. The whites' fenced-in land blocking off the Ute Pass in the foothills serves as a spatial metaphor separating the perishing Ute from their thriving oppressors and from others who might come to their aid. The separation between the Ute and the whites hinders Roses's work as a veterinarian and joins her with Tobe in the struggle against racism.

Black patriarchy, which Tobe represents, also challenges Roses's uplift efforts with the Ute. Tobe's active, forceful pursuit of Roses to the Ute camp bonds them as lovers, and his flight from the law as an alleged murderer forces Roses to understand that Tobe needs her, perhaps more personally than the Ute. Tobe's self-affirmation in the relationship orients him to follow the path of other black men (Nat Love, Deadwood Dick, and George Washington, founder of Centralia in the Washington territory) who migrated West, took advantage of opportunities, and did not answer to anyone. Tobe wants more than the "chance at a good life, a fresh start" that Roses suggests (305). He wants the safety and comfort of a black township where "the sheriff, the town council, even the mayor is colored" (305).

The relationship between Roses and Tobe underscores the discordant interconnections between racism, sexism, and romance. This discord is evident in both of their families: the American government destroyed the marriages of both their parents. Roses's mother died of malnutrition soon after the government relocated Roses's family and the Ute to the reservation, and Tobe's father died in the Civil War. Racism remains a continuous threat to both partners, as Roses is under constant surveillance by whites and Tobe is wanted for killing a white prostitute. Reared by a mother who became a prostitute after her husband's death, Tobe, in Roses's view, defines love as sex; for her, loving someone means having a committed sexuality in which "you're willing to sacrifice everything for them, that you did what was necessary to protect them" (309). The distinction between appetite (Tobe) and the kind of love which critic Hubert Benoit refers to as "willing the good of" (Roses) eventually gives Roses power in the romance.

Roses's success in her relationship with Tobe derives from her ability to combine strengths that transcend gender (vision, commitment, and the ability to voice her opinions) with a vulnerability which marks her as the traditional woman. Telling Tobe "'we're never going to get anywhere if we spend all day in bed'" (306), Roses directs Tobe's focus away from short-term pleasures to long-term issues and commitments. As Benoit argues, "When man *feels* sexual desire, he feels it as an invitation, not to impartial participation in the cosmos, but to the affirmation of himself" (75). Roses invites Tobe to affirm himself in moral rather than physical terms when she initiates proceedings to clear him of the murder so that he can affirm his self-respect. Diverting his energy to a good cause, Roses prepares him to take a position of honor in the community, wherever he settles; she realizes that once he is free of the moral taint of a murder accusation, he can take on social and racial goals. She is not motivated by selfish desires, whether reward or marriage; instead, her primary aim is achieving growth for Tobe and thereby acting out her own identity. According to her creator Roberta Gayle, her "strength comes as a result of her vulnerability ... [because] as women, we are built on our weakness" (Gayle, interview with Dandridge). Vulnerable because she has come to care for Tobe, she converts this potential weakness into strengths for both of them.

Roberta Gayle, Shirley Hailstock, and Beverly Jenkins set their novels in historical periods when African Americans were actively writing their own history. In this time of tremendous possibility for and resistance to change, black women stood at the nexus of competing and conflicting discourses about public and private roles for African Americans. Depicting heroines working with/in discourses of race and gender to construct romantic lives as fulfilled women and public lives as agents for ethnic advancement, these authors position romance as both the reflection and the end of activism.

Notes

"Introduction: Reading Romance, Reading History," by Susan Strehle and Mary Paniccia Carden

1. Harlequin's claim about its readership appeared in a 1980 publicity release called "Facts about Harlequin," which Radway discusses (19–45).
2. For discussion of the changes in romance production and of sub-genres of romance, see Fallon (51–64).
3. See Carol Thurston for a similar argument.
4. See Snitow (1979) and Modleski (1982). For other critical discussions of popular romance, see Mussell (1984), Fallon (1984), Cohn (1988), and Krentz (1992).
5. For a related reading of the romance as family wish-fulfillment, see Juhasz.
6. An intriguing reversal of this dynamic, where the revolt is pictured on the surface and acquiescence buried beneath, appears in Wyatt's reading of *Jane Eyre* in *Reconstructing Desire* (1990): "on the level of lucid and compelling rhetoric, Brontë advocates feminist ideals, arguing against patriarchal institutions that confine and warp women's energies and for an open field for women's ambitions; yet underneath flows unchecked a passionate desire for that most restrictive of all female spaces, the bubble of bliss promised by romantic love" (39).
7. See also Rabine, who argues that "romantic love has held at its heart an intense contradiction," providing "one of the few accepted outlets through which women can express their anger and revolt at their situation in a patriarchal order. On the other hand, it idealizes and eroticizes women's powerlessness and lack of freedom" (viii).
8. Pearce and Wisker's introduction to *Fatal Attractions* (1998) places romance in the context of queer theory. Work on romance in the context of alternative sexual practices and of gay and lesbian sexualities appears in Pearce and Wisker and in Pearce and Stacey, *Romance Revisited* (1995).

"Making Love, Making History: (Anti) Romance in Alice McDermott's *At Weddings and Wakes* and *Charming Billy*," by Mary Paniccia Carden

1. This is not to deny other dynamics of love, desire, and sexuality, but to acknowledge and explore heterosexuality as a force that structures culture and that everyone must reckon with.
2. People who choose not to choose spouses and those who choose spouses of the same sex have found themselves in violation of both consent and descent relations. Viewing

heterosexual union as epistemology raises the obvious question of its relation to non-heterosexual union, a question I do not have space to address. For discussion of this issue, see Roof, de Lauretis, and Butler.

3. According to Hasia Diner, emigrants "who left Ireland in the decade after the Famine came from the poorer classes" and tended to migrate "in family units rather than as single men" (90). These penniless immigrants settled mostly in American cities. In New York City, where by 1880 one third of the population "stemmed from Irish parentage" (93), Irish immigrants "entered lunatic asylums, charity hospitals, prisons, and almshouses more than any other group. They had the city's highest rates of ... diseases that accompany hunger, poverty, and congestion" (99–100). Irish immigrants "were blasted from the politicians' stump, in the columns of the city's press, and on the pages of popular pulp fiction, which screamed about the Irish threat to American liberty" (100).

4. McCaffrey notes that in "1870, 72 percent of the American Irish were concentrated in seven urban, industrial states" (67). And New York City, where McDermott's novels are set, was often described as "America's 'most Irish city'" (Diner 87).

5. Throughout, Billy articulates romantic faith in terms of religious faith. Refusing to reconcile himself to Eva's death, he insists that "saying that death is just ... an ordinary part of life" essentially "makes a mockery of the Crucifixion ... Anyone saying that is saying Our Lord's coming was to no avail" (204). If death "doesn't trouble us, the injustice of it, then we don't need heaven or hell ... It might as well be a lie" (204).

6. The conventions of heterosexual romance plot function as both metanarrative—which controls other stories—and micronarrative—which teaches about specific expectations in specific contexts. The editors of *Memory, Narrative and Identity* note that "we 'remember' not only things that have actually happened to us personally, but also, and perhaps even more importantly, we 'remember' events, language, actions, attitudes, and values that are aspects of our membership in groups" (17).

7. This ambivalence is reflected in the novels' narrative structures. McDermott's narrators function almost entirely as listeners and tellers of romantic stories: Dennis Lynch's daughter provides only a vague outline of her own story and the now-adult Dailey children have no textual function beyond their re-telling of sad stories. These "stealth narrators" (Cooper 13) reflect the simultaneous presence and absence of romance, a dynamic which destabilizes its foundational authority while also maintaining its privilege as locus of historical, cultural, and individual yearning.

8. According to DuPlessis, "writing beyond the ending means the transgressive invention of narrative strategies" which "express critical dissent from dominant narrative. Writing beyond the ending ... produces a narrative that denies or reconstructs seductive patterns of feeling that are culturally mandated, internally policed, hegemonically poised" (5). She views writing beyond the ending as a "consistent project that unites" many twentieth-century women writers (4).

"History and the End of Romance: Danticat's *The Farming of Bones*," by Susan Strehle

1. My translation. Danticat writes in her "Acknowledgments" that "President Sténio Vincent's letter ... was found among the papers of Sumner Welles in the Franklin Delano Roosevelt Library by Ambassador Bernardo Vega" (312).

2. The novel refers to the death of Trujillo in May 1961, "in a monsoon of bullets as he was being driven out of the capital city on a highway named after him" (267). The Generalissimo's death makes possible Amabelle's return to the Dominican Republic. She makes this visit, and the novel ends, in an unidentified October, the month of the massacre.

3. Massé's "premise is that what characters in [Gothic] novels represent . . . is the cultural, psychoanalytic, and fictional expectation that they *should* be masochistic if they are 'normal' women" (2).

4. Danticat notes that this book was published in the United States as well as in the Dominican Republic (312).

5. Among the other sources credited by Danticat, Hicks uses a similar genealogical approach. His book concludes with a lengthy list of Dominicans, many of them highly ranking politicians and military men, who were murdered by Trujillo.

6. See Diederich and Hicks; both of these sources are acknowledged by Danticat.

7. Diederich, p. 71. *In the Time of the Butterflies* is Julia Alvarez's narrative of the sisters' lives and death. Danticat acknowledges help from Alvarez.

8. See Olsen, p. 12.

"Stopping Traffic: Spectacles of Romance and Race in *The Last of the Mohicans*," by Janet Dean

1. Richard White notes that French traders often married native women to gain safety, trading status, and property. Such alliances were encouraged by the government.

2. Eve Kosofsky Sedgwick's *Between Men* also uses the exchange of women paradigm as "a sensitive register . . . for delineating relationships of power and meaning" (27). But it, too, raises questions about how the triangle can be distorted when these relationships involve not just gender, sexuality, and class, but also race. Susan Fraiman analyzes the erotic triangle schema deployed by Sedgwick in several contemporary scenarios and concludes that women's position "between" has implications for political and racial domination—for male relationships characterized not by attraction, but by violence (67–84). Like Fraiman, I want to suggest that there is more going on "between men" than homosocial desire.

3. Another analysis of the centrality of spectacle and the gaze in Cooper's work may be found in Bergland (87–96).

4. For a useful review of scholarship on the white patriarchal gaze, see Smith (169). Her important study of nineteenth-century visual culture, with its demonstration of the mapping of racial and gendered essences on the body, corresponds to my reading of Natty's faith in "plain" signs.

5. For a discussion of the removal of Cora's veil at the end of the novel in the context of her mixed race, see Cagidemetrio (39–42).

6. Many Cooper critics have difficulty explaining the heroine's race. One tendency has been to underplay Cora's mixed race by characterizing her as one of several racially or sexually "mixed" characters in the novel; see, for example, Slotkin (89). Such inclusion fails to account for Cora's uniqueness as an example of *physical* race blending. A second tendency has been to pass over the issue of Cora's race altogether. For instance, in her otherwise excellent essay, Romero limits her discussion of Cora's race to a footnote (401). Finally, some critics comment on the importance of Cora's mixed race and yet seem occasionally duped by her passing. Tompkins, who theorizes that Cooper's text is preoccupied with categories of

race that Cora's mixed heritage problematizes, also argues that the final confrontation between Magua and Cora "admits of no compromise because Magua is a red man and *Cora is white*: there is no choice to be made between the wigwam and the knife of le Subtil because the Anglo-Saxon tradition of *racial purity* would not permit it" (109, emphasis added).

"What 'Race' Is the Sheik? Rereading a Desert Romance," by Susan L. Blake

I would like to thank the Obermann Center for Advanced Studies at the University of Iowa for material and intellectual support during the research and writing of this essay and Teresa Mangum for sensitive reading and stimulating conversation.

1. For further discussion of the cultural impact of the film and the Sheik phenomenon in general, see Melman 89–93. Melman's biographical information about Hull in the same section, however, contains errors. In the absence of information in standard reference sources, it is worth summarizing what can be learned about Hull from public records. She was born Edith Maude Henderson in 1880, married Percy Winstanley Hull, a gentleman farmer and consulting engineer, in 1899, and died in 1947. She had one daughter, Cecil Winstanley, who accompanied her on the Algerian tour she recounts in *Camping in the Sahara*, 1926. The frequently repeated assertion that Hull had not visited the North African sites of her novels before writing *The Sheik* implies that she knew nothing of them. We do not know when the several previous trips she mentions in *Camping in the Sahara* took place, but the thoughtfulness of that narrative and the reference in it to her first visit to Algeria as a child (48) suggest long interest in and familiarity with North Africa and Arab culture.

2. In his biography of Rudolph Valentino, Irving Shulman reports that when the novel was released in the United States, the British Embassy in Washington issued a statement that "no proper white lady would have anything to do with a 'wog', even an educated one" and quotes producer Walter Wanger's assertion that Paramount initially turned down his proposal to film *The Sheik* because "a love story between a white woman and an Arab was considered too radical" (160–61). Although most reviewers of both the novel and the film characterized the story in such general terms as "racy" and "a shocker," in this context such terms may be euphemisms for miscegenation as well as sado-masochistic gender relations.

3. For a summary of British dealings with the Hashemite Arabs before and after the war, see Marlowe 20–23. For the beginnings of the legend of Lawrence of Arabia, see Hodson 11–12.

4. Callaway makes this point, 32; Rich 55–56 and Strobel 5–7 provide historical evidence of it. In *Allegories of Empire*, Sharpe examines the relationship between fear of interracial rape and rebellion in Indian colonial literature.

5. Blunt 11; Brantlinger, quoting and characterizing Burton, 159–60.

"Behind the Mask of Coquetry: The Trickster Narrative in *Miss Numè of Japan: A Japanese-American Romance*," by Huining Ouyang

I thank Susan Strehle and Mary Paniccia Carden for their helpful comments on earlier versions of this essay. I am also grateful to Leonard N. Neufeldt, who guided me at all stages of my dissertation, "(Re)presenting Interracial Sexuality: Race, Sex, and Discursive Strategies in Sui Sin Far and Onoto Watanna" (Diss. Purdue U, 1998), on which this essay is based.

1. According to Wilkinson, Loti has been credited with creating the "novel of exotic romance," also known as the "colonial novel" or "the novel of desertion" (113, 115). Set in far-away Asian countries, such as Turkey, Tahiti, and Japan, Loti's novels follow the same plot. A young white naval officer falls in love with and sometimes marries a young native woman. When he leaves her behind at the end of his sojourn, she commits suicide or dies of a broken heart (114).

2. As Wilkinson notes, derived from *musume* (daughter in Japanese), the word mousmé was adopted by the French language due to Loti's usage and acquired the meaning of "young lady" or "pretty prostitute" (115).

3. For other studies of the linkage between nation and desire, see Young, Parker, et al., and Stoler.

4. For further discussions of Western colonial expansion in Asia in the late nineteenth century, see chapters 7–9 of Thomson, Stanley, and Perry. Also see chapter 1 of Chan and chapter 11 of Takaki.

5. For more on Watanna's self-fashioning, see Ling, *Between Worlds*; Ling, "Creating One's Self"; and Matsukawa.

6. See the "Japanese" designs of Loti's *Madame Chrysanthème*, Long's *Miss Cherry Blossom of Tokyo* and *Madame Butterfly*, and especially Holland's *My Japanese Wife*, whose miniature size underscores the author's exoticization of Japan as an "idealized doll's-house land" (2).

7. For more details of Watanna's rivalry with Long/Belasco, see Oishi xxii–xxiii.

8. Gates suggests that "the obscuring of apparent meaning" is the defining characteristic of black rhetoric. The poetry of the Monkey tales, for instance, exemplifies the language of trickery (53).

"Romancing the Borderlands: Josephina Niggli's *Mexican Village*," by Rita Keresztesi

I would like to thank Ronald Schleifer and Susan Strehle for their thoughtful comments on earlier versions of this essay.

1. Niggli's book was later adapted, with Norman Foster, into a rather melodramatic and musically "enhanced" movie titled *Sombrero* for Metro-Goldwyn-Meyer (1953).

2. See Eberly.

3. For a more detailed description of Niggli's life and literary career, see Dvorkin, Eberly and Stone.

4. See Paredes in Baker. For the first book-length study of Chicano literary history, see Tatum.

5. Williams uses the terms "residual" and "emergent" to describe alternative and oppositional forms of culture on 40–41.

6. After serving in the Mexican Revolution as a colonel under Pancho Villa, Guzmán spent two decades in exile, first in the United States and then in Spain. Originally published in Spain, Guzmán's novel went through several revisions before it was published in Mexico. Julio Brancho adapted Guzmán's novel for the screen, but *La sombra del caudillo* (1960), the single most censored film in Mexican history, was not released until 1990.

7. See Jameson 139 (quoted in Gillman, 224).

8. See Herrera-Sobek, xvi–xxxi and Paredes, in *MELUS*, in Baker, and in Elliott.

9. Bakhtin's theory of dialogism could also be read as a cultural and aesthetic theory of border-crossings. In "Content, Material, and Form in Verbal Art," Bakhtin addresses borders and boundaries; see especially 274. For an extended discussion of Baktin's text, see Schleifer.

"What's a Nice Girl like You Doing in a Book like This? Homoerotic Reading and Popular Romance Fiction," by Stephanie Burley

1. For example, *Paradoxa: Studies in World Literary Genres* published a special double issue in 1997 devoted exclusively to popular romance. The articles are written by fans, romance authors, and career academics (and some who are a mix of the three); like Radway, they look past the obvious patriarchal aspects of romance to explore how it becomes a liberating site of pleasure for women readers.

2. Theoretical approaches to romance now have an established tradition (one owing a debt to feminist revisions in scholarly practice) of incorporating personal experience with academic scrutiny. Many of the most influential romance theorists, including Modleski, Juhasz, and the contributors to *Paradoxa*, foreground their own experience as romance fans in their efforts to articulate the dense dynamics that surround the act of reading. Unlike more traditional literary discourse, romance studies privileges the knowing reader over the detached, supposedly objective observer.

3. In using queer theory as the interpretive lens for this project, I depart from romance scholars who rely on psychoanalytic models. Radway, Modleski, and several others base their theories on Freudian or Lacanian models conceptualizing romantic desire as a response to a fundamental psychic "lack," caused either by the process of early childhood individuation that compels adults to continually seek the lost parent (as in Freud), or (following Lacan) by the "loss of plenitude and agency associated with the 'Imaginary' phase of infant development" (Pearce and Wisker 3). While I do not want to dismiss these important ways of understanding romance, I will argue below that psychoanalytic theories have led us to overlook important queer aspects of romance/reader dynamics.

4. For other examples of "queering" mass culture, see Creekmur and Doty. My project does not assume a queer readership, but focuses on the queer aspects of the genre itself. I share with Creekmur and Doty the notion that the term "queer" helps to destabilize sexual hierarchies and the belief that the pleasures of pop culture are open to a wide range of queer interpretations.

5. Other letters in this May 1999 issue of *Romantic Times* come from readers who "can't wait" to get to the next convention to meet up with their friends, whom they "love," "adore," and "miss" (9, 32–33).

6. Unconscious infantile fantasies may be part of the reading process, but I believe that the infantile fantasy narrative has overdetermined the way we view female readers. It keeps them children, thus obfuscating any analysis of the adult sexual pleasures operating in the act of romance reading.

7. Walter Kendrick's rant against romance as "escapist, masturbatory [and] exploitative" is a typical negative characterization of female pleasure (quoted in Radway 1999, 397).

8. Early feminist critics of romance like Ann Barr Snitow pointed out the resemblance of romance books to forms of pornography geared towards men.

9. Feminist critics might argue that because romance plots are rooted in heteronormative and phallocentric models, the sexual fantasies generated by them would necessarily

re-inscribe female passivity and powerlessness. However, readers suggest that they experience romance reading as an empowering imaginative activity that resists patriarchal (and, I would argue, heteronormative) machinations.

10. The highlighted portions of this excerpt—which contain, not coincidentally, the most overtly erotic language in the article—appear in large print in the center of the ad.

11. Radway (1999) observes that romances "[offer] not only different visions of female sexuality but different subject positions for their readers to take up and to try on— that is, different ways of inhabiting a feminine self now no longer constructed as the object of another's gaze. The romance is straining ... to remap gender divisions, or, more accurately, to rethink the construction of masculinity and femininity, since the two basic categories are always retained and seen as necessarily related" (412).

12. The themes listed on the *RT* site are arranged alphabetically according to a number of intriguing and sometimes hilarious categories, including old standards like "amnesia," "cowboys," and "doctor/nurse," and less conventional ones like "bad girls" and "disguised as a man."

"Desire and the Marketplace: A Reading of Kathleen Woodiwiss's *The Flame and the Flower*," by Charles H. Hinnant

1. For a survey of changing tastes in romance, from the early twentieth century to the mid-eighties, see Thurston (33–90); on the proliferation of subgenres in the nineties, see Mussell (3–14).

2. This argument is not in contradiction to that of Jan Cohn (1984), which traces the lineage of the contemporary heroine back to the tradition of Austen and Bronte in which the disempowered female protagonist appears as the emblem of an upwardly mobile—and socially implausible—quest for power, status, and economic security. But I do hold that contemporary romance fiction is much more than a conservative genre "that places sexuality squarely in the service of love, love in the service of marriage, marriage in the service of status quo economic relations between the sexes" (174). For discussions which argue that romance is used by an unresconstructed capitalism to maintain the patriarchal domination of one gender over the other, see Dubino and Ebert.

3. On the difference between a bazaar economy and modern forms of capitalism, see Geertz (28–81). I am indebted throughout this part of the essay to Geertz's formulation of this distinction.

4. For surveys of the newly-emergent subgenre of the contemporary career-oriented romance, see Rabine and Thurston (91–112).

5. J. G. A. Pocock notes that "economic man as conquering hero is a fantasy of nineteenth-century industrialisation... His eighteenth-century predecessor was seen as on the whole a feminised, even an effeminate being, still wrestling with his own passions and hysterias and with interior and exterior forces let loose by his own fantasies and appetites" (114).

6. The studio portrait, characteristic of romance authors, affords a studied contrast to the more naturalistic portrait-photographs of mainstream authors who are presented as dwelling in their own private space of creative genius rather than looking out at the reader directly.

"A Story of Her Weaving: The Self-Authoring Heroines of Georgette Heyer's Regency Romance," by Karin E. Westman

1. Cavendish describes Heyer's novels in the *Chicago Sunday Tribune* "as something of a literary bubble bath wherein her readers so inclined may take a delightful and frothy dip" ("Biographical Information").

2. For an informed discussion of Mills and Boon, see Dixon.

3. Those who have seen Heyer's Regency notebooks remark upon their detail and organization: "Her notes for all of them survive, written in her neat longhand and carefully bound together with green ribbon.... She said herself that she had covered every one of the many contemporary sources for the Battle of Waterloo ... and the notes are there to confirm this, meticulously cross-referenced. Complete with their own bibliographies, the notes for each book are illustrated with careful sketches of uniforms and hand-drawn maps" (Hodge 51).

4. The centenary of Heyer's birth in 2002 has prompted proof of her continued popularity; see, for instance, Fenton.

5. During her life, Heyer's novels "topped the best-seller lists in hardback, outselling Graham Greene" (Jardine). Glass and Mineo note that according to a 1984 report in *The Times*, "suburban libraries often [lend] from four to six copies a day" and sales average "400 a month" (283). In the 1988–89 report from the Public Lending Right office, Heyer is one of the top ten most borrowed authors (O'Brien).

6. In 1995, the BBC ran at least two of Heyer's romances as part of a series titled "Romance" (Bernard; Reynolds). At the Lifeline Theatre in Chicago, Christina Calvit has adapted three Heyers for the stage (Houlihan). In contemporary novels, for example, Heyer's romances make appearances in A. S. Byatt's *The Virgin in the Garden* and *Still Life*; the heroine of Barker's *Hens Dancing* bears the name of one of Heyer's heroines, Venetia, and her narrative records frequent readings of Heyer's romances.

7. In her letter to the *Sunday Telegraph*, O'Connor writes, "Jenny McCartney was wrong to describe Georgette Heyer as a writer of bodice rippers (Focus, April 23). No Heyer heroine ever gets her bodice ripped. Her heroines are witty, intelligent, strong-minded, resourceful women, all of them far more interesting characters than silly, self-obsessed Bridget Jones, or any of the tiresome women who stalk the pages of the novels nominated for the dreadful Orange Prize for women writers."

8. For the full discussion of Heyer's work to date, see Fahnestock-Thomas. Along with many reviews, this collection reprints most published and a few previously unpublished critical analyses of Heyer's writing.

9. Bell ably develops Hughes's line of analysis in her essay.

10. Eustacie is certainly the most "romantic" of the characters, naive in her embrace of all narratives which could bring excitement. However, Eustacie is no Arabella from Lennox's *The Female Quixote* or Catherine from Austen's *Northanger Abbey*. Eminently "practical" in her romantic calculations (89), however, she recognizes the difference between tale and truth while still seeing the possibilities for a story within the everyday.

11. Heyer wrote 38 historical romances, 26 of which were set during the Regency (1811–20).

12. I therefore take issue with Glass and Mineo: while they believe "Heyer's heroines are doomed to a relative capitulation by the mandatory happy ending, as their usual liveliness and enterprise stays within the limits of marriageable convention" (286), I place less emphasis

on the ending and more on the "*confrontation transactionelle*" or "negotiated resolution" which Glass and Mineo too readily dismiss. My argument advocates for the heroines' rhetorical attempts to work within the patriarchal system for the best narrative possible, given the "mandatory happy ending."

13. I've selected these heroines as representative of the range of Heyer's Regency romance heroines. The heroines of the remaining twenty-one Regency romances would fall into one of the three categories noted above.

14. In addition to Lamb, the scandal created by Phoebe's anonymous *roman a clef* also has echoes of the Duchess of Devonshire's autobiographical novel *The Sylph*, published anonymously in 1778 (Forman 60).

15. My reading departs from A. S. Byatt's, which attributes "a certain unworldly innocence" to Heyer's heroines (237). By contrast, I argue that just such a "worldly" knowledge is a key to success.

16. The heroine missing from this discussion is Venetia Lanyon of *Venetia* (1958), one of Heyer's favorite books (Hodge 152) and the most literary of her romances.

17. Annis's role illustrates how Heyer's romances meet the criteria for romance novels today, according to the arguments put forward by both Dixon and Krentz. As Phillips states, the heroine "always wins" (Krentz 56).

18. Heyer's distaste for the "effete" culture of the 1920s may explain her preference for the Regency period, when the knowledge of money, sex, and wit, the adherence to standards of honor and fair play, were valued by upper-class society.

19. See Forman's prize-winning biography, especially chapters 8, 9, 17, and 23. Forman argues for a re-evaluation of women's roles in public life at the end of the eighteenth century, noting that nineteenth-century descendants often blithely "blanked out" written evidence of women's work (348).

"The Race, Gender, Romance Connection: A Black Feminist Reading of African American Women's Historical Romances," by Rita B. Dandridge

1. Beverly Jenkins (née Hunter), an African American from Detroit, Michigan, and lay preacher, writes under her married name. She gained from her mother an appreciation of history, especially of the black experience which was virtually ignored in textbooks in the public schools that she attended. Lamenting the fact that few people knew anything about black history between the end of slavery and the civil rights movement, Jenkins says, "History books have a tendency to say we didn't exist.... It's always black folks came to America, black folks were slaves, black folks were freed in 1865. Then we disappeared. History picks us up again rioting in Watts in 1975. But what happened for those 100 years?" Jenkins answers this question in her historical romances, for which she does extensive research. Her primary focus in these novels is how black women forged public careers and achieved self-expression despite race and gender prejudice. Jenkins's seven historical novels to date are *Night Song* (1994), *Vivid* (1995), *Indigo* (1996), *Topaz* (1997), *Through the Storm* (1998), *The Taming of Jessie Rose* (1999), and *Always and Forever* (2000). See Decker.

2. Shirley Hailstock (her pen name, maiden name, and current name) is an African American from Columbia, South Carolina, who teaches in New Jersey. She has published only one historical novel, *Clara's Promise* (1995), which won the Utah Romance Writers

Heart of the West Award. Primarily a writer of women's fiction, Hailstock offers advice about writing ethnic, especially African American, historical romances. She suggests that writers include background, traditions, taboos, methods of speech and expression, descriptions of physical attributes, occupations, and setting. She believes that "books written by African American ... women [using these characteristics] will bring a new perspective to the genre." Hailstock's works include *Whispers of Love* (1994), *White Diamonds* (1996), *Legacy* (1997), and *More than Gold* (2000). See Hailstock's webpage: http://www.geocities.com/Paris/Bistrp/6812 (Hailstock interview with Dandridge, 7 Dec. 2000).

3. Roberta Gayle, pen name for Roberta Gayle Cohen, is a New York City resident. The daughter of an African American woman and a Jewish father, Gayle has published two historical romances with black female protagonists: *Sunshine and Shadows* (1995) and *Moonrise* (1996). Gayle says she believes that woman's strength comes from her weakness, but her protagonists appear weak only in their vulnerability in love. Gayle was asked by her editor to tone down the strength of her protagonist Clara Winslow, because the editor saw Clara as a superwoman in her interaction with the Ute. The Native American and black exchange in *Sunshine and Shadows* grows out of her own biracial connections with ethnic groups in the East and with her interest in the interconnection between whites, blacks, and Native Americans in the expanding West. "African Americans have had so much to do with the settlement of the West," Gayle says. "And blacks and Native Americans supported and helped white settlers to survive." Gayle locates blacks and Native Americans in an historical bonding that eschews the stereotyping of the two races in white Hollywood films (Gayle telephone interview with Dandridge).

4. Hudson-Weems refers to the African American woman activist as an "Africana womanist" and identifies eighteen characteristics of this activist (55–73).

5. Twentieth-century historical romances written by black women extend a tradition pioneered by Frances Harper in *Iola Leroy*, published in 1892.

6. The pre-civil war cases of Jarena Lee and Maria Stewart are legendary. Lee's ordination to preach in the A.M.E. Church was delayed eight years by Bishop Allen, who had founded the church because of the racial injustices he perceived in the white church (Lee 494–514). Stewart publicly alluded to the sexism of men of color: "I am sensible that there are many highly intelligent gentlemen of color in these United States, in the force of whose arguments, doubtless, I shall discover my inferiority; but if they are blest with wit and talent ... why have they not made themselves men of eminence by ... endeavoring to alleviate the woes of their brethren in bondage?" (Loewenberg and Bogin 196).

7. See slave narratives, especially, for the difficulty that black men and women had in establishing a viable romantic relationship.

8. Uintah Valley refers to the site of two Ute reservations in Utah, the Uintah and Ouray. Utah derives its name from the Indian word "Eutaw" or "Yuta" which means "dwellers in the tops of the mountains."

Works Cited

Abrams, M. H. *A Glossary of Literary Terms*. 7th ed. Fort Worth: Harcourt Brace College Publishers, 1999.
Ai, Tan Ling. "Chamber of Pleasures for Book-lovers." *New Straits Times* [Malaysia] 10 Jan. 1998: 11.
Alexander, Hilary. "Ambiguous Message of Passionless Sex." *The Daily Telegraph* 8 Mar. 1993: 6.
Alvarez, Julia. *In the Time of the Butterflies*. New York: Plume, 1994.
Anderson, Rachel. *The Purple Heart Throbs: The Sub-Literature of Love*. London: Hodder and Stoughton, 1974.
Attridge, Derek, Geoff Bennington, and Robert Young, eds. *Post-structuralism and the Question of History*. Cambridge: Cambridge UP, 1987.
Baker, Houston A. Jr., ed. *Three American Literatures*. New York: MLA, 1982.
Bakhtin, Mikhail. *Art and Answerability: Early Philosophical Essays*. Eds. Michael Holquist and Vadim Liapunov. Austin: U of Texas P, 1990.
Barker, Raffaella. *Hens Dancing*. London: Review, 1999.
Barthes, Roland. *S/Z: An Essay*. Trans. Richard Howard. New York: Hill and Wang, 1974.
Bell, Kathleen. "Cross-Dressing in Wartime: Georgette Heyer's *The Corinthian* in its 1940 Context." *War Culture: Social Change and Changing Experience in World War Two*. Eds. Pat Kirkham and David Thoms. London: Lawrence and Wishart, 1995. 151–58.
Bennington, Geoff, and Robert Young. "Introduction: Posing the Question." Attridge, Bennington and Young 1–11.
Benoit, Hubert. *The Many Faces of Love: The Psychology of Emotional and Sexual Life*. Trans. Philip Mairet. New York: Octagon, 1980.
Bergland, Renée L. *The National Uncanny: Indian Ghosts and American Subjects*. Hanover, NH: UP of New England, 2000.
Bernard, Peter. "Good Drama, No Crisis." *The Times* 28 Jan. 1995. Lexis-Nexis Academic. 30 Oct. 1998. <http://web.lexis-nexis.com/universe>.
Biddiss, Michael D. "The Universal Races Congress of 1911." *Race* 13.1 (1971): 37–46.
Biggs, John M. *The Concept of Matrimonial Cruelty*. London: U of London, Athlone Press, 1962.
Billington, Ray Allen. *Westward Expansion: A History of the American Frontier*. 4th ed. New York: Macmillan, 1974.

Works Cited

"Biographical Information for Georgette Heyer." 1999. 2 Aug. 1999 <http://www.barnesandnoble.com>.
Black, Stephen. "Black Men and White Women." *English Review* 29 (1919): 352–57.
Blanchot, Maurice. *The Infinite Conversation*. Trans. Susan Hanson. Minneapolis: U of Minnesota P, 1993.
Blunt, Lady Anne. *A Pilgrimage to Nejd*. London: John Murray, 1881.
Boas, Franz. "Instability of Human Types." Spiller 99–103.
Boone, Joseph Allen. *Tradition Counter Tradition: Love and the Form of Fiction*. Chicago: U of Chicago P, 1987.
Brantlinger, Patrick. *Rule of Darkness: British Literature and Imperialism, 1830–1914*. Ithaca: Cornell UP, 1988.
Burroughs, Edgar Rice. *Tarzan of the Apes*. Chicago: A. C. McClurg, 1914.
Butler, Judith. *Bodies That Matter: On the Discursive Limits of "Sex"*. New York: Routledge, 1993.
Byatt, A. S. "An Honourable Escape: Georgette Heyer." 1969. *Passions of the Mind*. New York: Vintage, 1991. 233–40.
———. *Still Life*. New York: Vintage, 1985.
———. *The Virgin in the Garden*. New York: Vintage, 1978.
Cagidemetrio, Alide. "A Plea for Fictional Histories and Old-Time 'Jewesses.'" *The Invention of Ethnicity*. Ed. Werner Sollors. New York: Oxford UP, 1989. 14–43.
Calderón, Héctor and José Davíd Saldívar, eds. *Criticism in the Borderlands: Studies in Chicano Literature, Culture, and Ideology*. Durham: Duke UP, 1991.
Callaway, Helen. "Purity and Exotica in Legitimating the Empire: Cultural Constructions of Gender, Sexuality and Race." *Legitimacy and the State in Twentieth-Century Africa: Essays in Honour of A. H. M. Kirk-Greene*. Ed. Terence Ranger and Olufemi Vaughan. London: Macmillan, 1993. 31–61.
Chai, Arlene J. *Eating Fire and Drinking Water*. New York: Fawcett, 1996.
Chan, Sucheng. *Asian Americans: An Interpretive History*. Boston: Twayne, 1991.
Chase, Richard. *The American Novel and Its Tradition*. New York: Doubleday Anchor, 1957.
Cline, Catherine. *E. D. Morel 1873–1924: The Strategies of Protest*. Belfast: Blackstaff Press, 1980.
Cohn, Jan. *Romance and the Erotics of Property: Mass-Market Fiction for Women*. Durham: Duke UP, 1988.
Collins, Patricia Hill. *Black Feminist Thought: Knowledge, Consciousness, and the Politics of Empowerment*. New York: Routledge, 1991.
Cooper, James Fenimore. *The Last of the Mohicans; A Narrative of 1757*. 1826. *The Leatherstocking Tales* Vol. 1. New York: Library of America, 1985.
———. *The Pathfinder*. 1840. *The Leatherstocking Tales* Vol. 2. New York: Library of America, 1985.
Cooper, Rand Richards. "Charming Alice: A Unique Voice in American Fiction." *Commonweal* 125.6 (27 Mar. 1998): 10–13.
Creekmur, Corey K., and Alexander Doty, eds. *Out In Culture: Gay, Lesbian, and Queer Essays on Popular Culture*. Durham: Duke UP: 1995.
Danticat, Edwidge. *Breath, Eyes, Memory*. New York: Vintage, 1994.
———. *The Farming of Bones*. New York: Soho, 1998.
———. *Krik? Krak!* New York: Vintage, 1995.

De Besault, Lawrence. *President Trujillo: His Work and the Dominican Republic*. 2nd ed. n.p.: The Washington Publishing Co., 1936.
Decker, Ed. "Beverly Jenkins." *Contemporary Black Biography*. Ed. Mpho L. Mabunde and Shirelle Phelphs. Vol. 14. Detroit: Gale Research, 1997. 138–40.
Dekker, George. *The American Historical Romance*. New York: Cambridge UP, 1987.
De Lauretis, Teresa. *Technologies of Gender*. Bloomington: Indiana UP, 1987.
Derrida, Jacques. *Of Grammatology*. Trans. Gayatri Chakravorty Spivak. Baltimore: Johns Hopkins UP, 1974.
Diederich, Bernard. *Trujillo: The Death of the Goat*. Boston: Little, Brown, 1978.
Diner, Hasia R. "'The Most Irish City in the Union': The Era of the Great Migration, 1844–1877." *The New York Irish*. Ed. Ronald H. Baylor and Timothy J. Meagher. Baltimore: Johns Hopkins UP, 1996. 87–106.
Dixon, jay. *The Romance Fiction of Mills and Boon, 1909–1990*. London: University College London, 1999.
Doane, Mary Ann. "Film and the Masquerade: Theorizing the Female Spectator." Erens 41–57.
Drinnon, Richard. *Facing West: The Metaphysics of Indian Hating*. Minneapolis: U of Minnesota P, 1980.
Dubino, Jeanne. "The Cinderella Complex: Romance Fiction, Patriarchy, and Capitalism." *Journal of Popular Culture* 27 (Winter 1993): 103–18.
DuBois, W. E. B. "The First Universal Races Congress." Sundquist 55–59.
DuPlessis, Rachel Blau. *Writing Beyond the Ending: Narrative Strategies of Twentieth-Century Women Writers*. Bloomington, IN: Indiana UP, 1985.
Dvorkin, Joseph Henry. 16 Nov. 2000, <http://voices.cla.umn.edu/authors/JosephinaNiggli.html>.
Eberly, Barbara Walters. 16 Nov. 2000, <http://www3.wcu.edu/eberly/awa99/conhon/niggli/jniggli.htm>.
Ebert, Teresa L. "The Romance of Patriarchy: Ideology, Subjectivity, and Postmodern Feminist Cultural Theory." *Cultural Critique* 10 (1988): 19–57.
Elam, Diane. *Romancing the Postmodern*. London: Routledge, 1992.
Elliot, Emory, gen. ed. *The Columbia History of the American Novel*. New York: Columbia UP, 1991.
———, gen. ed. *The Columbia Literary History of the United States*. New York: Columbia UP, 1988.
Ellsworth, Elizabeth. "Illicit Pleasures: Feminist Spectators and *Personal Best*." Erens 183–96.
England, Paula. "The Separative Self: Androcentric Bias in Neoclassical Assumptions." *Beyond Economic Man: Feminist Theory and Economics*. Ed. Marianne A. Ferber and Julie A. Nelson. Chicago: U of Chicago P, 1993. 37–53.
Erdrich, Louise. *The Antelope Wife*. New York: Harper, 1998.
———. *Tracks*. New York: Harper, 1988.
Erens, Patricia, ed. *Issues in Feminist Film Criticism*. Bloomington, IN: Indiana UP, 1990.
Fahnestock-Thomas, Mary. *Georgette Heyer: A Critical Retrospective*. Saraland, AL: Prinny World Press, 2001.
Fallon, Eileen. *Words of Love: A Complete Guide to Romance Fiction*. New York: Garland, 1984.
Fenton, Kate. "I've Read Her Books to Ragged Shreds." *The Telegraph* 29 July 2002. 30 July 2002 <http://www.telegraph.co.uk>

Fiedler, Leslie. *Love and Death in the American Novel.* 1966. New York: Anchor, 1992.
Forman, Amanda. *Georgiana, Duchess of Devonshire.* New York: Random House, 1998.
Foucault, Michel. "Nietzsche, Genealogy, History." Trans. Donald Bouchard and Sherry Simon. *Language, Counter-Memory, Practice.* Ed. Donald Bouchard. Ithaca: Cornell UP, 1977. 139–64.
Fraiman, Susan. "Geometries of Race and Gender: Eve Sedgwick, Spike Lee, Charlayne Hunter-Gault." *Feminist Studies* 20.1 (1994): 67–82.
Francis, Donette. "Unsilencing the Past: Edwidge Danticat's *The Farming of Bones.*" *Small Axe* 5 (Mar. 1999): 168–75.
Freeman, Suzanne. "Both Nightmare and Poetry." *Boston Globe* 13 Sep. 1998: C1, 4.
Frye, Northrop. *Anatomy of Criticism: Four Essays.* Princeton: Princeton UP, 1957.
"Future of Syria." *Spectator* 116 (5 Feb. 1916): 180.
Gaines, Jane. "White Privilege and Looking Relations: Race and Gender in Feminist Film Theory." Erens 197–214.
Gates, Henry Louis, Jr. *The Signifying Monkey: A Theory of Afro-American Literary Criticism.* New York: Oxford UP, 1988.
Gaunt, Mary. *Alone in West Africa.* London: T. Werner Laurie; New York: Scribners, 1912.
———. *The Silent Ones.* London: T. Werner Laurie, 1909.
Gaunt, Mary, and John Ridgwell Essex. *The Arm of the Leopard.* London: Grant Richards, 1904.
Gayle. Roberta. *Sunshine and Shadows.* New York: Pinnacle, 1995.
———. Telephone interview with Rita B. Dandridge, 16 Nov. 2000.
Geertz, Clifford. *Peddlers and Princes: Social Development and Economic Change in Two Indonesian Towns.* Chicago: U of Chicago P, 1963.
Gilbert, Sandra M., and Susan Gubar. *The Madwoman in the Attic: The Woman Writer and the Nineteenth-Century Literary Imagination.* New Haven: Yale UP, 1984.
Gillman, Susan. "The Mulatto, Tragic or Triumphant? The Nineteenth-Century American Race Melodrama." Samuels 221–43.
Glass, E. R., and A. Mineo. "Georgette Heyer and the Uses of the Regency." *La Performance del Testo.* Ed Franco Marucci and Adriano Bruttini. Siena: Ticci, 1986. 283–92.
Goring, Rosemary. "Regency Revisited." *The Scotsman* 30 May 1999: 13.
Gregory, Philippa. "The Slave State of Britain." *The Times* 12 Nov. 1994.
Grice, Elizabeth. "Prime Presents of Pillow Talk." *The Daily Telegraph* 14 Feb. 1995: 15.
Gyurko, Lanin A. "Fuentes, Guzmán, and the Mexican Political Novel." *Ibero-Amerikanisches Archiv* 16.4 (Berlin, 1990): 545–610.
Guzmán, Martín Luís. *La sombra del caudillo.* Madrid: Espasa Calpe, 1929.
Hackett, Alice Payne. *70 Years of Best Sellers, 1895–1965.* New York: Bowker, 1967.
Hailstock, Shirley. *Clara's Promise.* New York: Pinnacle, 1995.
———. <http://www.geocities.com/Paris/Bistrp/6812>.
———. Telephone interview with Rita B. Dandridge, 7 Dec. 2000.
Hamilton, Paul. *Historicism.* London: Routledge, 1996.
Hannah, Kristen. *The Enchantment.* New York: Fawcet, 1999.
Harper, Frances. *Iola Leroy, or Shadows Uplifted.* 1892. Rpt. New York: AMS, 1971.
Harris, Janice Hubbard. *Edwardian Stories of Divorce.* New Brunswick: Rutgers UP, 1996.
Heller, Dana. "Housebreaking History: Feminism's Troubled Romance with the Domestic Sphere." *Feminism Beside Itself.* Ed. Diane Elam and Robyn Wiegman. New York: Routledge, 1995. 217–33.

Herrera-Sobek, Maria. "Josephina Niggli: A Border Writer and Precursor of Chicano/a Literature." Niggli xv–xxix.
Heyer, Georgette. *Arabella*. 1949. London: Mandarin, 1997.
———. *Barren Corn*. 1930. Mattituck, NY: Ameron House, 1998.
———. *Bath Tangle*. 1955. London: Pan Books Ltd., 1967.
———. *Frederica*. 1965. New York: Avon Books, 1970.
———. *The Grand Sophy*. 1950. London: Mandarin, 1991.
———. *Helen*. New York: Longmans, Green, and Co., 1928.
———. *Instead of the Thorn*. 1923. Boston: Small, Maynard, and Company, Inc., 1924.
———. *Lady of Quality*. New York: E. P. Dutton, 1972.
———. *Pastel*. 1929. Cutchogue, NY: Buccaneer Books, 1976.
———. *Sylvester, or the Wicked Uncle*. 1957. London: Pan Books Ltd., 1970.
———. *The Talisman Ring*. 1936. London: Pan Books, 1961.
———. *Venetia*. 1958. London: Pan Books Ltd., 1971.
Hicks, Albert C. *Blood in the Streets: the Life and Rule of Trujillo*. New York: Creative Age Press, Inc., 1946.
Hicks, Emily D. *Border Writing: The Multidimensional Text*. Minneapolis: U of Minnesota P, 1991.
Higginbotham, Evelyn. "African American Women's History and the Metalanguage of Race." *Signs: Journal of Women in Culture and Society* 17 (Winter 1992): 251–74.
Hirschman, Albert O. *The Passions and the Interests: Political Arguments for Capitalism before Its Triumph*. Princeton: Princeton UP, 1977.
Hite, Molly. *The Other Side of the Story: Structures and Strategies of Contemporary Feminist Narratives*. Ithaca: Cornell UP, 1989.
Hodge, Jane Aiken. *The Private World of Georgette Heyer*. London: The Bodley Head, 1984.
Hodson, Joel C. *Lawrence of Arabia and American Culture*. Westport, CT: Greenwood Press, 1995.
Hofstadter, Beatrice K. "Popular Culture and the Romantic Heroine." *American Scholar* 30 (1961): 98–116.
Holland, Clive. *My Japanese Wife: A Japanese Idyll*. Westminster: Constable, 1895.
———. *Mousmé: A Story of the West and East*. New York: Frederick A. Stokes, 1901.
Holman, C. Hugh, and William Harmon. *A Handbook to Literature*. 6th ed. New York: Macmillan, 1992.
hooks, bell. "In Our Glory: Photography and Black Life." *Picturing Us: African American Identity and Photography*. Ed. Deborah Willis. New York: New Press, 1994. 42–53.
Houlihan, Mary. "A Novel Idea: Torrid Romances Take to the Stage." *Chicago Sun-Times* 9 June 2000: 13.
Howard, Philip. "Philip Howard Column." *The Times* 27 Feb. 1998. *Lexis-Nexis Academic*. 29 Oct. 1998. <http://web.lexis-nexis.com/universe>.
Hudson-Weems, Clenora. *Africana Womanism: Reclaiming Ourselves*. Troy, MI: Bedford, 1993.
Hughes, Helen. *The Historical Romance*. London: Routledge, 1993.
Hull, E. M. *Camping in the Sahara*. New York: Dodd, Mead, 1927.
———. *The Sheik*. 1919. Boston: Small, Maynard, 1921.
———. *The Sons of the Sheik*. New York: A. L. Burt, 1925.
Hurtubise, Josef. "A Consideration of Her Period Influences." 1998. 11 Feb. 1999, <http://www.geocities.com/Paris/LeftBank/9278/georgetteheyer.html>.

Irigaray, Luce. *This Sex Which Is Not One*. Trans. Catharine Porter with Carolyn Burke. 1977. Ithaca: Cornell UP, 1985.
Jackson, Stevi. "Women and Heterosexual Love: Complicity, Resistance and Change." Pearce and Stacey 49–62.
Jameson, Fredric. *The Political Unconscious: Narrative as a Socially Symbolic Act*. Ithaca: Cornell UP, 1981.
———. "Reification and Utopia in Mass Culture." *Social Text* 1 (1979): 130–48.
Jardine, Cassandra. "Georgette Heyer Made Me a Good Judge of Character." *The Daily Telegraph* 19 Dec. 1996: 18.
Jenkins, Beverly. *Indigo*. New York: Avon, 1996.
Jennings, Ann L. "Public or Private? Institutional Economics and Feminism." *Beyond Economic Man: Feminist Theory and Economics*. Ed. Marianne A. Ferber and Julie A. Nelson. Chicago: U of Chicago P, 1993. 111–30.
Johnston, Sir Harry H. "Race Problems in the New Africa." *Foreign Affairs* 2 (1924): 598–612.
———. "The World-Position of the Negro and Negroid." Spiller 328–36.
Jones, Jacquelyn. *Labor of Love, Labor of Sorrow: Black Women, Work, and the Family from Slavery to the Present*. New York: Basic, 1985.
Joy, Dara. *Mine to Take*. New York: Leisure Books, 1999.
Juhasz, Suzanne. *Reading from the Heart: Women, Literature, and the Search For True Love*. New York: Viking, 1994.
Kaplan, Amy. "Left Alone with America: The Absence of Empire in the Study of American Culture." Pease and Kaplan 3–21.
Kaplan, E. Ann. *Women and Film: Both Sides of the Camera*. New York: Methuen, 1983.
Kingsolver, Barbara. *The Poisonwood Bible*. New York: Harper, 1998.
Krentz, Jayne Ann, ed. *Dangerous Men and Adventurous Women: Romance Writers on the Appeal of the Romance*. Philadelphia: U of Pennsylvania P, 1992.
Krentz, Jayne Ann. "Trying to Tame the Romance: Critics and Correctness." Krentz 107–14.
Kuiper, Edith, and Jolande Sap, eds. *Out of the Margin: Feminist Perspectives on Economics*. London: Routledge, 1995.
LaCapra, Dominick. *History & Criticism*. Ithaca: Cornell UP, 1985.
Langbauer, Laurie. *Women and Romance: The Consolations of Gender in the English Novel*. Ithaca: Cornell UP, 1990.
Lawrence, D. H. *Studies in Classic American Literature*. 1923. New York: Penguin, 1977.
LeClair, Tom. "Charming Billy." *The Nation* 23 Nov. 1998: 27.
Lee, Jarena. *The Life and Religious Experiences of Jarena Lee: A Colored Lady Giving an Account of Her Call to Preach the Gospel. Early Negro Writing 1760–1837*. Ed. Dorothy Porter. Boston: Beacon, 1971. 494–514.
Lemert, Charles and Esme Bhan, eds. *The Voice of Anna Julia Cooper, Including "A Voice from the South" and Other Important Essays, Papers, and Letters*. New York: Rowman and Littlefield, 1998.
Lévi-Strauss, Claude. *The Elementary Structures of Kinship*. Trans. James Harle Bell, John Richard Von Sturmer, and Rodney Needham. Ed. Rodney Needham. Boston: Beacon, 1969.
Ling, Amy. *Between Worlds: Women Writers of Chinese Ancestry*. New York: Pergamon Press, 1990.
———. "Creating One's Self: The Eaton Sisters." *Reading the Literatures of Asian America*. Eds. Shirley Geok-lin Lim and Amy Ling. Philadelphia: Temple UP, 1992. 305–18.

Ling, Amy, and Annette White-Parks. "Introduction." *Mrs. Spring Fragrance and Other Writings*. Eds. Amy Ling and Annette White-Parks. Urbana: U of Illinois P, 1995. 1–8.
Linz, Cathie. "Setting the Stage: Facts and Figures." Krentz 11–14.
Loewenberg, Bert and Ruth Bogin. *Black Women in Nineteenth-Century American Life: Their Words, Their Thoughts, Their Feelings*. University Park: Pennsylvania State UP, 1976.
Long, John Luther. "Madame Butterfly." *Madame Butterfly*. New York: Century, 1898. 1–86.
———. *Miss Cherry Blossom of Tokyo*. 1895. Philadelphia: Lippincott, 1905.
Loti, Pierre. *Madame Chrysanthème*. 1887. Paris: Levy, 1893.
Lowe, Lisa. *Critical Terrains: French and British Orientalisms*. Ithaca: Cornell UP, 1991.
Lugard, Frederick D. "The White Man's Task in Tropical Africa." *Foreign Affairs* 5 (Oct. 1926): 57–68.
Macpherson, C. B. *The Political Theory of Possessive Individualism: Hobbes to Locke*. Oxford: Oxford UP, 1962.
Mandler, Peter. "Liberty and the Pursuit of Love." *The Times* 21 Apr. 1994. *Lexis-Nexis Academic*. 30 Oct. 1998. <http://web.lexis-nexis.com/universe>.
Mansfield, Elizabeth. "Why I Am Not Jane Austen: An Overview of Today's Romantic Fiction and How It Got That Way." 29 July 1999. <http://www.elizabethmansfield.com>.
Marchetti, Gina. *Romance and the "Yellow Peril": Race, Sex, and Discursive Strategies in Hollywood Fiction*. Berkeley: U of California P, 1994.
Marlowe, John. *Arab Nationalism and British Imperialism: A Study in Power Politics*. New York: Praeger, 1961.
Massé, Michelle A. *In the Name of Love: Women, Masochism, and the Gothic*. Ithaca: Cornell UP, 1992.
Matsukawa, Yoko. "Cross-Dressing and Cross-Naming: Decoding Onoto Watanna." *Tricksterism in Turn-of-the-Century American Literature: A Multicultural Perspective*. Eds. Elizabeth Ammons and Annette White-Parks. Hanover, NH: UP of New England, 1994. 106–25.
McCaffrey, Lawrence J. *The Irish Catholic Diaspora in America*. Washington, DC: The Catholic U of America P, 1997.
McDermott, Alice. *At Weddings and Wakes*. New York: Dell, 1992.
———. *Charming Billy*. New York: Dell, 1998.
Melman, Billie. *Women and the Popular Imagination in the Twenties: Flappers and Nymphs*. New York: St. Martin's, 1988.
Miller, Kerby, and Paul Wagner. *Out of Ireland: The Story of Irish Immigration to America*. Niwot, CO: Roberts Rinehart, 1997.
Modleski, Tania. "Hitchcock, Feminism, and the Patriarchal Unconscious." Erens 58–74.
———. *Loving with a Vengeance: Mass-produced Fantasies for Women*. Hamden, CT: Archon, 1982.
———. *Old Wives' Tales and Other Women's Stories*. New York: New York UP, 1998.
Morgan, Lewis Henry. *The Indian Journals, 1859–62*. Ed. Leslie A. White. Ann Arbor: U of Michigan P, 1959.
Morris, Robert C. *Reading, Riting and Reconstruction: The Education of Freedmen in the South, 1861–1870*. Chicago: U of Chicago P, 1981.
Morrison, Toni. *Beloved*. New York: Knopf, 1987.
———. *Paradise*. New York: Knopf, 1998.
Mulvey, Laura. "Visual Pleasure and Narrative Cinema." Erens 28–40.

Mussell, Kay. *Fantasy and Reconciliation: Contemporary Formulas of Women's Romantic Fiction*. Westport, CT: Greenwood Press, 1984.
———. "Where's Love Gone?" *Paradoxa* 3 (1997): 3–14.
Myers, Charles S. "On the Permanence of Racial Mental Differences." Spiller 73–79.
Newman, Karen. "Directing Traffic: Subjects, Objects, and the Politics of Exchange." *Differences: A Journal of Feminist Cultural Studies* 2.2 (1990): 41–54.
Niggli, Josephina. *Mexican Village*. Albuqueque: U of New Mexico P, [1945] 1994.
O'Brien, R. Barry. "Agatha Christie Continues to Top Best-read List." *The Daily Telegraph* 5 Jan. 1990: 6.
O'Connor, Louise. Letter to the Editor. "Orange Heroines Are Really Lemons." *Sunday Telegraph* 30 Apr. 2000. *Lexis-Nexis Academic*. 30 May 2000. <http://web.lexis-nexis.com/universe>.
Oishi, Eve. "Introduction, 1999." *Miss Numè of Japan: A Japanese-American Romance*. By Onoto Watanna. Baltimore: Johns Hopkins UP, 1999. xi–xxxiii.
Olsen, Tillie. "I Stand Here Ironing." *Tell Me a Riddle*. New York: Delta, 1961. 1–12.
Ormsby-Gore, W. "The Economic Development of Tropical Africa and Its Effect on the Native Population." *Geographical Journal* 68 (Sep. 1926): 240–53.
Paredes, Raymund A. "The Evolution of Chicano Literature." *MELUS* 5 (1978): 71–110.
———. "The Evolution of Chicano Literature." Baker 33–79.
———. "Mexican American Literature." Elliot 800–810.
Parham, Thomas A., et al. *The Psychology of Blacks: An African-Centered Perspective*. Saddle River, NJ: Prentice Hall, 1999.
Parker, Andrew, et al. *Nationalisms and Sexualities*. New York: Routledge, 1992.
Pearce, Lynne, and Gina Wisker, eds. *Fatal Attractions: Re-scripting Romance in Contemporary Literature and Film*. London: Pluto Press, 1998.
———. "Rescripting Romance: An Introduction." Pearce and Wisker 1–19.
Pearce, Lynne, and Jackie Stacey, eds. *Romance Revisited*. New York: New York UP, 1995.
Pease, Donald E. and Amy Kaplan, eds. *Cultures of U.S. Imperialism*. Durham: Duke UP, 1993.
Pocock, J. G. A. *Virtue: Commerce, and History: Essays on Political Thought and History, Chiefly in the Eighteenth Century*. Cambridge: Cambridge UP, 1985.
Pratt, Mary Louise. *Imperial Eyes: Travel Writing and Transculturation*. New York: Routledge, 1992.
Quarles, Benjamin. *Black Abolitionists*. New York: Oxford UP, 1969.
Rabine, Leslie W. *Reading the Romantic Heroine: Text, History, Ideology*. Ann Arbor: U of Michigan P, 1985.
Radway, Janice. *Reading the Romance: Women, Patriarchy, and Popular Literature*. Chapel Hill: U of North Carolina P, 1984; rpt. 1991.
———. "Romance and the Work of Fantasy." *Feminism and Cultural Studies*. Ed. Morag Shiach. New York: Oxford UP, 1999. 395–415.
———. "The Utopian Impulse in Popular Literature: Gothic Romances and 'Feminist' Protest." *American Quarterly* 33 (1981): 140–62.
Raine, Harmony. *The Georgette Heyer Compendium*. Cutchogue, NY: Buccaneer Books, Inc., 1983.
Raub, Patricia. "Issues of Passion and Power in E. M. Hull's *The Sheik*." *Women's Studies* 21 (1992): 119–28
Rev. of *The Sheik* by E. M. Hull. *Literary Review* 5 Mar. 1921: 12.

Rev. of *The Sheik* by E. M. Hull. *New York Times Book Review* 1 May 1921: 24–25.
Reynolds, Gillian. "The Arts: Air Turns Pink with Romance." *The Daily Telegraph* 14 Feb. 1995: 17.
Rich, Paul B. "'The Baptism of a New Era': The 1911 Universal Races Congress and the Liberal Ideology of Race." *Ethnic and Racial Studies* 7 (1984): 534–50.
———. *Race and Empire in British Politics*. Cambridge: Cambridge UP, 1986.
Richardson, Samuel. *Pamela Or Virtue Rewarded*. New York: Norton, 1958.
Robards, Karen. *Nobody's Angel*. New York: Dell, 1992.
Romantic Times Website. <http://www.romantictimes.com>.
Romero, Lora. "Vanishing Americans: Gender, Empire, and New Historicism." *American Literature* 63: 385–404.
Roof, Judith. *Come as You Are: Sexuality and Narrative*. New York: Columbia UP, 1996.
Rubin, Gayle. "The Traffic in Women: Towards a Political Economy of Sex." *Toward an Anthropology of Women*. Ed. Rayna R. Reiter. New York: Monthly Review P, 1975.
Said, Edward W. *Orientalism*. 1978. London: Penguin, 1991.
Saks, Eva. "Representing Miscegenation Law." *Raritan* 8.2 (1988): 36–69.
Saldívar, José David. *Border Matters: Remapping American Cultural Studies*. Berkeley: U of California P, 1997.
Samuels, Shirley, ed. *The Culture of Sentiment: Race, Gender, and Sentimentality in Nineteenth-Century America*. New York: Oxford UP, 1992.
Saunders, Kate. "Introduction." *The Sheik*. By E.M. Hull. London: Virago, 1996. v–xi.
Schleifer, Ronald. *Modernism and Time: The Logic of Abundance in Literature, Science, and Culture, 1880–1930*. New York: Cambridge UP, 2000.
Sedgwick, Eve Kosofsky. *Between Men: English Literature and Male Homosocial Desire*. New York: Columbia UP, 1985.
Sharpe, Jenny. *Allegories of Empire: The Figure of Woman in the Colonial Text*. Minneapolis: U of Minnesota P, 1993.
Shea, Renee H. "Traveling Worlds with Edwidge Danticat." *Poets & Writers Magazine* Jan./Feb. 1997: 42–51.
The Sheik. Dir. George Melford. Perf. Rudolph Valentino, Agnes Ayres. Paramount, 1921.
Shulman, Irving. *Valentino*. New York: Trident, 1967.
Singh, Amritjit, Joseph T. Skerrett, Jr., and Robert E. Hogan, eds. *Memory, Narrative, and Identity: New Essays in Ethnic American Literatures*. Boston: Northeastern UP, 1994.
Slotkin, Richard. *The Fatal Environment: The Myth of the Frontier in the Age of Industrialization, 1800–1890*. New York: Harper Collins, 1985.
Smith, Barbara. "Towards a Black Feminist Criticism." *Conditions Two* (1970): 24–44.
Smith, Shawn Michelle. *American Archives: Gender, Race, and Class in Visual Culture*. Princeton: Princeton UP, 1999.
Snitow, Ann Barr. "Mass Market Romance: Pornography for Women is Different." *Radical History Review* 20 (1979): 141–61.
Sollors, Werner. *Beyond Ethnicity: Consent and Descent in American Culture*. New York: Oxford UP, 1986.
Sommer, Doris. *Foundational Fictions: The National Romances of Latin America*. Berkeley: U of California P, 1991.
Spiller, G., ed. *Papers on Inter-Racial Problems*. Introd. Hollis R. Lynch. New York: Arno Press and *The New York Times*, 1969. Rpt. of *Papers on Inter-Racial Problems Communicated to*

the First Universal Races Congress Held at the University of London July 26–29, 1911. London and Boston, 1911.

Sterling, Dorothy, ed. *We Are Your Sisters: Black Women in the Nineteenth Century.* New York: W.W. Norton, 1984.

Stewart, Maria W. *Maria W. Stewart: America's First Black Political Writer.* Ed. Marilyn Richardson. Bloomington: Indiana UP, 1987.

Stoler, Ann L. "Making Empire Respectable: The Politics of Race and Sexual Morality in 20th-century Colonial Cultures." *American Ethnologist* 16 (1989): 634–60.

Stone, Les. "Josefina (Maria) Niggli, 1910–1983." *Contemporary Authors.* New Revisions Series. Vol. 32. Gale Group, Literary Index. 1991.

Strobel, Margaret. *European Women and the Second British Empire.* Bloomington: Indiana UP, 1991.

Sundquist, Eric J., ed. *The Oxford W. E. B. Du Bois Reader.* New York: Oxford UP, 1996.

Takaki, Ronald T. *Iron Cages: Race and Culture in Nineteenth-Century America.* New York: Knopf, 1979.

Tatum, Charles M. *Chicano Literature.* Boston: Twayne, 1982.

Thomson, James C, Jr., Peter W. Stanley, and John Curtis Perry. *Sentimental Imperialists: The American Experience in East Asia.* New York: Harper & Row, 1981.

Thurston, Carol. *The Romance Revolution: Erotic Novels for Women and the Quest for a New Sexual Identity.* Urbana: U of Illinois P, 1987.

Tompkins, Jane. *Sensational Designs: The Cultural Work of American Fiction, 1790–1860.* New York: Oxford UP, 1985.

Torgovnick, Marianna. *Gone Primitive: Savage Intellects, Modern Lives.* Chicago: U of Chicago P, 1990.

Upchurch, Michael. "No Room for the Living." *New York Times Book Review* 27 Sep. 1998: 13.

Vega, Bernardo. *Trujillo y Haití: Volumen I (1930–1937).* Santo Domingo: Fundación Cultural Dominicana, 1988.

Wang, Jennie. *Novelistic Love in the Platonic Tradition: Fielding, Faulkner and the Postmodernists.* Lanham, MD: Rowman & Littlefield, 1997.

Watanna, Onoto. *Miss Numè of Japan: A Japanese-American Romance.* Chicago: Rand, McNally, 1899. Introd. Eve Oishi. Baltimore: Johns Hopkins UP, 1999.

———. *Me: A Book of Remembrance.* New York: Century, 1915. Afterword by Linda Trinh Moser. Jackson: UP of Mississippi, 1997.

Watt, Ian. *The Rise of the Novel: Studies in Defoe, Richardson and Fielding.* Berkeley: U of California P, 1957.

Webb, Sidney and Beatrice. "What Is Socialism? XVII.—The Guardianship of the Non-Adult Races." *New Statesman* 1 (2 Aug. 1913): 525–26.

White, Hayden. *Metahistory: The Historical Imagination in Nineteenth-Century Europe.* Baltimore: Johns Hopkins UP, 1973.

White, Richard. *The Middle Ground: Indians, Empires, and Republics in the Great Lakes Region, 1650–1815.* Cambridge, UK: Cambridge UP, 1991.

White-Parks, Annette. "'We Wear the Mask': Sui Sin Far as One Example of Trickster Authorship." In *Tricksterism in Turn-of-the-Century American Literature: A Multicultural Perspective.* Eds. Elizabeth Ammons and Annette White-Parks. Hannover: UP of New England, 1994. 1–20.

Works Cited

Wilkins, W. H. *The Romance of Isabel Lady Burton: The Story of Her Life, told in part by herself and in part by W. H. Wilkins.* Vol. 2. London: Hutchinson & Co., 1897.

Wilkinson, Endymion. *Japan Versus the West: Image and Reality.* London: Penguin, 1990.

Williams, Raymond. *The Long Revolution.* New York: Columbia UP, 1961.

Wood, Ellen Meiksins. *Democracy against Capitalism: Reviewing Historical Materialism.* Cambridge: Cambridge UP, 1995.

Woodiwiss, Kathleen E. *The Flame and the Flower.* New York: Avon Books, 1972.

Woolf, Leonard. *Empire and Commerce in Africa: A Study in Economic Imperialism.* London: Labour Research Department and Allen and Unwin, 1919.

Wyatt, Jean. *Reconstructing Desire: The Role of the Unconscious in Women's Reading and Writing.* Chapel Hill: U of North Carolina P, 1990.

Yamamoto, Traise. *Masking Selves, Making Subjects: Japanese American Women, Identity, and the Body.* Berkeley: U of California P, 1999.

Young, Robert J. C. *Colonial Desire: Hybridity in Theory, Culture and Race.* London: Routledge, 1995.

About the Contributors

SUSAN L. BLAKE is Professor of English at Lafayette College, where she teaches American and African literature and popular literary genres. She is the author of a travel narrative, *Letters from Togo*, and essays on African American literature, contemporary writers, and travel writing that have appeared in journals and collections including *African American Review*, *CLA Journal*, *PMLA*, *Research in African Literatures*, and Scribner's *American Writers*.

STEPHANIE BURLEY is completing her doctorate at the University of Maryland; she earned an MA in Women's Studies at Ohio State University. She has co-edited a forthcoming volume of Helen Maria Williams's letters, and her article on the racial politics of category romance appeared in *Paradoxa*. She is completing a dissertation on the racial politics of popular romance.

RITA B. DANDRIDGE is Professor of English and Foreign Languages at Norfolk State University, where she teaches courses in women's studies and African American literature. Her articles on African American women writers have appeared in *CLA Journal*, *The Oxford Companion to African American Literature*, *MELUS*, and *African American Review*. Her published books are *Ann Allen Shockley: An Annotated Primary and Secondary Bibliography* (1987) and *Black Women's Blues: A Literary Anthology 1934–1988* (1992). She is currently working on an essay titled "Expanding the African American Literary Canon: A Case for African American Historical Romances."

JANET DEAN is Assistant Professor of English at the University of South Dakota, where she teaches courses in American literature and American studies. Her essays on the frontier and Western American literature have appeared in *Arizona Quarterly*, *Modern Fiction Studies*, the anthology *Scorned Literature*, and several reference works. She is currently completing a book titled *Mediating Women: Gender and the Frontier in the American Imagination*.

CHARLES H. HINNANT is Professor of English at the University of Missouri-Columbia. He teaches courses in eighteenth-century literature and contemporary critical theory. His most recent books include *The Poetry of Anne Finch: An Essay in Interpretation* (1994) and *The Anne Finch Wellesley Manuscript Poems*, co-edited with Barbara McGovern (1998).

Contributors

RITA KERESZTESI is Assistant Professor of English at the University of Oklahoma. Her research and teaching focus on the areas of modernism and postmodernity, cultural studies, theory, and twentieth-century American ethnic and minority literatures. Her manuscript in progress, *Strangers at Home: Ethnic Modernism between the World Wars*, examines the impact of American ethnic and minority writers on the discourse of modernist studies. She has published a translation of an essay by György Lukács, in *The Yale Journal of Criticism*, and an article on Mourning Dove in the collection, *Literature and Racial Ambiguity*.

HUINING OUYANG is Assistant Professor of English at Edgewood College, where she teaches multiethnic and immigrant literatures, literary criticism, and college writing. The essay that appears here is part of a longer project on Watanna's romance novels. She has published an article on tricksterism in Watanna and Sui Sin Far in *Alternative Rhetorics: Challenges to the Rhetorical Tradition*.

MARY PANICCIA CARDEN is Assistant Professor of English at Edinboro University of Pennsylvania, where she teaches courses in American literature and ethnic literatures. Her articles on Toni Morrison, Willa Cather, Jane Smiley, Zitkala-Sa, and Ann Petry have appeared in *Twentieth-Century Literature, Modern Fiction Studies, Frontiers: A Journal of Women's Studies, Prose Studies*, and *Journal of Contemporary Thought*. She is currently at work on a manuscript entitled *Sons and Daughters of Self-Made Men*.

SUSAN STREHLE is Professor of English at the State University of New York at Binghamton and was for several years Dean of the Graduate School at Binghamton. She published *Fiction in the Quantum Universe*, a study of representational strategies in contemporary fiction and their relations to the new physics; she has also published essays on contemporary fiction in *Critique, Modern Fiction Studies, Contemporary Literature, The Journal of Narrative Technique*, and *The Review of Contemporary Fiction*, among other places. Her current work focuses on revisions of home in contemporary women's fiction.

KARIN E. WESTMAN is an Assistant Professor of English at Kansas State University. Her research and teaching interests include modernism, contemporary British literature and culture, and women's literature. She has published essays on Virginia Woolf, Pat Barker, A. S. Byatt, and J. K. Rowling, as well as *Pat Barker's Regeneration: A Reader's Guide* (2001). She is currently completing a book-length study on contemporary British women writers and realism.

Index

Abrams, M. H., xiii, xiv
Alexander, Hilary, 168
Alvarez, Julia, 43, 205 n
Anderson, Rachel, 68
Anti-romance: in Danticat, 26, 27, 35–37, 40; as discourse, 5; in Heyer, 180; in McDermott, 7–11, 13–23; in popular romance, 141
Austen, Jane, 166, 167, 168, 169, 209 n, 210 n

Bakhtin, Mikhail, 208 n
Bannon, Ann, 130
Barthes, Roland, xxii, 147, 163
Belasco, David, 87, 96, 207 n
Bell, Kathleen, 210 n
Bennington, Geoff, and Robert Young, xxiii
Benoit, Hubert, 200
Bergland, Renée, 205 n
Bernard, Peter, 210 n
Beverley, Jo, 132
Biddiss, Michael, 71
Biggs, John, 81
Billington, Ray Allen, 197
Black, Stephen, 73, 85
Blanchot, Maurice, 125
Blunt, Lady Anne, 74, 206 n
Boas, Franz, 72
Boone, Joseph Allen, xx, 4
Brantlinger, Patrick, 206 n

Burton, Lady Isabel, 74–75, 77
Burton, Richard, 74, 206 n
Butler, Judith, 204 n
Byatt, A. S., 210 n, 211 n

Cagidemetrio, Alide, 205 n
Calderón, Héctor, and José Saldívar, 121
Callaway, Helen, 206 n
Cartland, Barbara, 68
Chai, Arlene, 43
Chan, Sucheng, 207 n
Chase, Richard, xiv
Christie, Agatha, 166
Cline, Catherine, 73
Cohn, Jan, xiv, xx, 157, 203 n, 209 n
Collins, Patricia, 186
Colonialism: and America, 154; and Asia, 89–90, 105, 207 n; and hybridity, 119, 121; and Ireland, 124; and race, 71–73; and Spain, 113; and U.S. imperialism, 109–11, 114, 116
Cooper, Anna Julia, 193
Cooper, James Fenimore, xxviii–xxix, 45–66; *Last of the Mohicans, The*, 45–66; *Pathfinder, The*, 54
Cooper, Rand Richards, 204 n
Coulter, Catharine, 132
Creekmur, Corey, and Alexander Doty, 208 n

Danticat, Edwidge, xxvii, 24–44; *Breath, Eyes, Memory*, 25, 34; *Farming of Bones, The*, xxvii–xxviii, 24–44; *Krik? Krak!*, 25; "Nineteen Thirty-Seven," 25
De Besault, Lawrence, 29, 30
Dekker, George, 185
De Lauretis, Teresa, 204 n
Derrida, Jacques, xxii, xxiii
Desire. *See* Sexuality
Diederich, Bernard, 205 n
Diner, Hasia, 7, 204 n
Divorce, 70; and wife-abuse, 78–83
Dixon, Jay, 210 n, 211 n
Doane, Mary Ann, 53
Drinnon, Richard, 50
Dubino, Jeanne, 209 n
DuBois, W. E. B., 70–71
DuPlessis, Rachel Blau, xi, xviii–xix, 3–4, 23, 33, 34, 35, 86, 105–06, 116, 119, 125, 126, 204 n
Dvorkin, Joseph, 207 n

Eberly, Barbara, 207 n
Ebert, Teresa, 209 n
Elam, Diane, xxi, 29
Ellsworth, Elizabeth, 53
Endings, happy, xxi, 3–4; in Danticat, 31; in Heyer, 210–11 n; in McDermott, 5, 7, 10, 11, 23; in Woodiwiss, 156. *See also* Romance plot, conventional; Marriage
England, Paula, 149
Erdrich, Louise, 43

Fahnestock-Thomas, Mary, 210 n
Failed romance. *See* Anti-romance
Fallon, Eileen, xvi, 203 n
Feiner, Susan, 149
Fenton, Kate, 210 n
Fiedler, Leslie, 58
Forman, Amanda, 211 n
Foucault, Michel, xxii, 28, 29. *See also* History, genealogy and

Fraiman, Susan, 205 n
Francis, Donette, 31
Freeman, Suzanne, 26
Frye, Northrop, xiii

Gates, Henry Louis, Jr., 97, 207 n
Gaunt, Mary, 72, 84
Gayle, Roberta, xxxiii, 185, 187, 189, 196–201, 212 n
Geertz, Clifford, 155, 209 n
Gilbert, Sandra, and Susan Gubar, xvii, xxiv
Gillman, Susan, 116, 119, 207 n
Glass, E. R., and A. Mineo, 168, 210–11 n
Goring, Rosemary, 165
Gregory, Philippa, 168
Guzmán, Martín Luís, 111–12, 122, 207 n
Gyurko, Lanin, 112

Hackett, Alice Payne, 67
Hailstock, Shirley, xxxiii, 185, 187, 188, 189, 192–96, 201, 211 n
Hamilton, Paul, xxiii–xxiv
Hannah, Kristen, 143–45
Harper, Frances, 212 n
Harris, Janice Hubbard, 81
Hawthorne, Nathaniel, xiv
Heller, Dana, xii
Herrera-Sobek, Maria, 207 n
Heyer, Georgette, xxxi–xxxii, 165–84; *Barren Corn*, 180; *Bath Tangle*, 171, 176–79, 182; *Frederica*, 171, 173–74, 176; *Grand Sophy, The*, 171, 173, 174–76; *Helen*, 166, 180, 182–83; *Infamous Army, An*, 167; *Instead of the Thorn*, 180–81; *Lady of Quality*, 171, 176, 179–80; *Pastel*, 180, 181–82, 183; *Powder and Patch*, 166; *Regency Buck*, 169; *Sylvester*, 171–73; *Talisman Ring, The*, 169–70, 210 n; *Venetia*, 211 n
Hicks, Albert, 205 n
Hicks, Emily, 122
Higginbotham, Evelyn, 190
Hirschman, Albert, 161

Index

Historical romance: African American women writers and, 185–201; Danticat and, 27; and gender-crossing, xxxi–xxxiii; Heyer and, 167, 183; as neglected genre, 165; Woodiwiss as, 156

History: activism and, 185, 189, 198, 201; gender and, 30–31; genealogy and, 28–30, 117, 123; narrative and, xxiii, 24–26, 43, 109, 111–12, 116; postmodernism and, xxii–xxv, 28–30, 44 (*see also* Romance, postmodernism and); romance and, xxiv–xxvi, 26, 31–32, 109, 118, 188. *See also* Romance, history and

Hite, Molly, 28
Hodge, Jane, 210 n
Hodson, Joel, 206 n
Hofstadter, Beatrice, 68
Holland, Clive, 87, 88, 90, 93, 207 n
Holman, C. Hugh, and William Harmon, xiii
hooks, bell, 52
Houlihan, Mary, 210 n
Hudson-Weems, Clenora, 187, 212 n
Hughes, Helen, 168
Hull, E. M., xxviii, xxix, 67–85, 206 n; *Camping in the Sahara*, 206 n; *Sheik, The*, 67–85, 206 n
Hurtubise, Josef, 168
Hybridity: of genre in borderlands romance, 109, 124; in Hull, xxviii; in Niggli, xxx, 116, 119, 121

Immigration, and history: in Danticat, 30; in McDermott, xxvii, 5–7, 11–15
Irigaray, Luce, 50, 51

Jackson, Andrew, 49–50, 51, 63
Jackson, Stevi, xvi–xvii, xviii
Jameson, Fredric, xx–xxi, xxiii, 70, 79, 113, 115–16, 121, 147, 207 n
Jardine, Cassandra, 210 n
Jenkins, Beverly, xxxiii, 185, 186, 188–92, 201, 211 n

Jennings, Ann, 149
Johnson, Jack, 73
Johnston, Sir Harry, 73, 74, 77
Jones, Jacqueline, 196
Joy, Dara, 145–46
Juhasz, Suzanne, 133–35, 203 n, 208 n

Kaplan, Amy, 121
Kaplan, E. Ann, 53
Kingsolver, Barbara, 43
Kohake, Rosanne, 132
Krentz, Jayne Ann, xvii, 132, 149, 203 n, 211 n

LaCapra, Dominick, xxiii
Langbauer, Laurie, xx–xxi
Lawrence, D. H., 66
Lawrence, T. E., 70, 74, 206 n
LeClair, Tom, 16
Lee, Jarena, 212 n
Leger, George, 24
Lévi-Strauss, Claude, 46, 47, 48, 50
Ling, Amy, 207 n; and Annette White-Parks, 106
Linz, Cathie, xvi
Long, John Luther, 87, 88, 90, 93, 95–96, 103, 207 n
Loti, Pierre, 87, 88, 90, 93, 207 n
Lowe, Lisa, 106
Lugard, Frederick, 71

Mandler, Peter, 168
Maney, Mabel, 130
Mansfield, Elizabeth, 166
Marchetti, Gina, 90, 95
Marlowe, John, 206 n
Marriage: in African American romance, xxxiii; in Danticat, 25, 34, 36; in DuPlessis, xii, xviii, 105, 116; in exotic romance, 90, 95; in Gayle, 198; and the gaze, 52; in Hailstock, 193, 195; in Heyer, 167, 171, 176, 177, 180, 181, 183; in Hull, 70, 76, 80–81; in Jenkins, 192; in Lévi-Strauss, 46–47;

in McDermott, 11, 15, 17–19; as metaphor, 4, 6; in Niggli, 117–18, 126; in Rubin, 49; in Sommer, 120; in Watanna, 102, 103–04; in Woodiwiss, 153, 155–56, 157, 158. *See also* Endings, happy; Romance plot, conventional

Masculinity: and authority in Heyer, 166, 173, 174, 175, 176, 177, 180; in Danticat, 33–34; in exotic romance, 87; in McDermott, 13–14, 16; in Niggli, 112; in popular romance, 146; and self-sufficiency, 148, 149, 159, 162; in Woodiwiss, 153

Massé, Michelle, 28, 205 n

Matsukawa, Yoko, 207 n

McCaffrey, Lawrence, 7, 204 n

McDermott, Alice, xxvii, 3–23; *At Weddings and Wakes*, xxvii, 5, 7, 8–11, 12, 13, 23; *Charming Billy*, xxvii, 5, 7, 11–23

Melman, Billie, 68, 206 n

Miller, Isabel, 135

Miller, Kerby, and Paul Wagner, 7

Mirabal sisters, 31, 43, 205 n

Miscegenation: in Cooper, 58–59, 65–66; and discourse of race, 72–73, 74–75; and excess, xxviii; and the frontier, 49–50, 51; in Hull, 69–70, 76, 83, 206 n; in Lévi-Strauss, 47; in Niggli, 109–26; and romance, 84–85; in Watanna, 94, 98, 103. *See also* Hybridity; Orientalism; Race

Modleski, Tania, xix–xx, xxxi, 28, 53, 127–28, 144, 203 n, 208 n

Morel, E. D., 73

Morgan, Lewis Henry, 49, 51

Morris, Robert, 193

Morrison, Toni, 41, 43

Mulvey, Laura, 52, 53

Mussell, Kay, 203 n, 209 n

Myers, Charles, 72

Naked Came the Ladies, 138–40

Naked Ladies, 138–40

Niggli, Josephina, xxx, 107–26; *Mexican Village*, 108–26

O'Brien, R. Barry, 210 n

Oishi, Eve, 207 n

Olsen, Tillie, 39, 205 n

Orientalism: and Arabs, 74; in exotic romance, 88–89, 105–06; in Hull, 69–70; in Watanna, xxix, 86–87, 91–93, 95–96, 106

Ormsby-Gore, W., 71

Paradoxa: Studies in World Literary Genres, 208 n

Paredes, Raymund, 108–09, 207 n

Parham, Thomas, 187

Parker, Andrew, et al., 207 n

Patriarchy: black, in African American women's romance, 187–88, 191; in Cooper, 59–60, 66; critiqued in romance, xvi–xx, xxix, 32–34, 42–44, 84–85, 92, 95, 99–103, 111–12, 127–28, 131–32, 185, 196, 203 n; in Danticat, 40–41; in Gayle, 199; in Hailstock, 194–95; in Heyer, 166, 177, 179; in McDermott, 13–14; in Mexican political novel, 109; in romance and history, 27; in Watanna, 87, 90, 103–04; women in, 69, 78–83, 171, 181; in Woodiwiss, 150, 153–54

Pearce, Lynne: and Gina Wisker, 33, 203 n, 208 n; and Jackie Stacey, 203 n

Pocock, J. G. A., 209 n

Postmodernism. *See* History, postmodernism and; Romance, postmodernism and

Pratt, Mary Louise, 121

Quarles, Benjamin, 188

Queer theory, xxx–xxxi, 129–30, 135, 143–46, 208 n

Rabine, Leslie, xxiv, 4, 203 n, 209 n

Race: in African American women's romances, 185–201; in Cooper, 45–66, 205–06 n; in exotic romance, 90; genocide and, xxxiii, 25–26, 30–32; in Gillman, 116; in Hull, 69–85; in Niggli, 119, 124; in romance, xxvii–xxix, 86–87; in Watanna,

98, 100–03, 105. *See also* Miscegenation; Orientalism
Radway, Janice, xix, xxxi, 32, 34, 84, 94–95, 128, 132, 133, 136–37, 141, 147–48, 203 n, 208 n, 209 n
Raine, Harmony, 167
Raub, Patricia, 68–69
Read, Opie, 92
Reynolds, Gillian, 210 n
Rich, Paul, 72, 73, 206 n
Richardson, Samuel, xv, xvi
Robards, Karen, 132, 142–43, 145
Romance: borderlands, xxx, 109–26 (*see also* Hybridity); capitalism transformed in, 147–64; contradiction in, xii, xviii, xix–xx, 27, 32–36, 43, 90, 106, 158, 203 n; desert, 68; empowerment and, xvii–xviii, 28, 42–43, 165–80, 183–84, 186, 187, 195–96, 200–01, 208 n, 209 n; as epistemology, 5, 6, 8, 22–23; exotic, xxix, 86–93, 104–06, 115, 207 n (*see also* Orientalism); family, xxvi, 22–23, 33, 36, 117, 118, 119, 120, 135, 136; feminism and, xvi–xix, 127, 208–09 n; gender and, xxxi–xxxiii, 27–28, 32–34, 43–44, 209 n; history and, xx–xxi, xxvii, xxx, xxxiii, 4–6, 11–13, 20–23, 42–44, 116–17, 120, 165–66 (*see also* History, romance and); as metaphor, 4–7, 13; national identity and, 5–7, 12–13, 43; novel and, xiv–xv; popular, xii, xvii, xix, xx, xxii, xxvi, xxxi–xxxii, 67–85, 127–46, 147–64, 165–84, 185–201, 208 n; postmodernism and, xx–xxii (*see also* History, postmodernism and)
Romance plot, conventional, 3, 4, 20, 25–27, 33, 36–37, 43, 86, 90, 92, 94–95, 100, 106, 129, 132, 155, 204 n, 209 n. *See also* Endings, happy; Marriage
Romantic Times, 132, 136, 138–39, 145, 208 n, 209 n
Romero, Lora, 205 n
Roof, Judith, 4, 204 n
Rubin, Gayle, xxviii, 46, 47, 48–49, 50, 51

Said, Edward, 74, 88. *See also* Orientalism
Saks, Eva, 59
Saunders, Kate, 68
Sayers, Dorothy, 166
Schleifer, Ronald, 208 n
Sedgwick, Eve Kosofsky, xxx, xxxi, 129, 131–32, 141–42, 205 n. *See also* Queer theory; Sexuality
Sexuality: and *doux* commerce in Woodiwiss, 162–63; in Gayle, 198, 200; in Hailstock, 195; homoerotic, 127–46; in Hull, 80; interracial, 94; in Jenkins, 191–92; and male desire in Heyer, 166, 177–79, 181, 182; male predatory, 151–53; in 1910s, 68; promiscuity in Woodiwiss, 159; in Radway, 209 n; in romance, xxx–xxxi, 50, 62; in Sommer, 119–20; in Watanna, 96–101
Sharpe, Jenny, 206 n
Shea, Renee, 24, 31
Shulman, Irving, 206 n
Simms, William Gilmore, xiv
Slotkin, Richard, 53, 54, 205 n
Smith, Barbara, 186
Smith, Jill, 132
Smith, Shawn Michelle, 52, 205 n
Snitow, Ann Barr, 203 n, 208 n
Sollors, Werner, 5–6
Sombrero, 207 n
Sommer, Doris, 119–20
Spencer, LaVyrle, 132–33
Spiller, Gustav, 72, 84
Sterling, Dorothy, 193
Stewart, Maria, 186, 198, 212 n
Stoler, Ann, 89, 207 n
Stone, Les, 207 n
Strobel, Margaret, 206 n
Sui Sin Far, 91

Takaki, Ronald, 207 n
Tatum, Charles, 207 n
Thomson, James, Peter Stanley, and John Curtis Perry, 89, 207 n

Thurston, Carol, xxxi, 68, 132, 203 n, 209 n
Tompkins, Jane, 58, 205–06 n
Torgovnick, Marianna, 84, 85
Tricksterism, 91–106, 207 n
Trujillo, Generalissimo, 26–27, 29–31, 39, 43, 205 n

Upchurch, Michael, 26

Valentino, Rudolph, 68, 206 n
Vega, Bernardo, 29–30, 204 n
Vincent, Sténio, 24, 204 n

Wang, Jennie, xxii
Watanna, Onoto, xxviii, xxix, 86–106
Watt, Ian, xiii–xv, xx–xxi
Webb, Sidney and Beatrice, 71
White, Hayden, xxii–xxiii

White, Richard, 205 n
White-Parks, Annette, 91
Wilkins, W. H., 75
Wilkinson, Endymion, 207 n
Williams, Raymond, 207 n
Women: agency and, 48, 53, 59–61, 64, 66, 149–50, 166, 170, 176, 183, 185–86; constructions of, 27–28, 37, 44, 88–90, 98, 159–60, 179; maternity and, 62; traffic in, 46–53, 62–64, 205 n
Wood, Ellen Meiksins, 150
Woodiwiss, Kathleen, xvi, xxxi–xxxii, 132–33, 147–64
Woolf, Leonard, 71
Wyatt, Jean, 203 n

Yamamoto, Traise, 88
Young, Robert, 207 n

www.ingramcontent.com/pod-product-compliance
Lightning Source LLC
Chambersburg PA
CBHW030339240426
43661CB00052B/1688